UNIVERSITY COLLEGE BIRMINGHAM
COLLEGE LIBRARY, SUMMER ROW
BIRMINGHAM. B3 1JB
Tel: (0121) 243 0055

DATE OF RETURN		

Please remember to return on time or pay the fine

INDIA ON THE MOVE

INDIA ON THE MOVE

LEA M. SURIT
EDITOR

Nova Science Publishers, Inc.
New York

For permission to use material from this book please contact us:
Telephone 631-231-7269; Fax 631-231-8175
Web Site: http://www.novapublishers.com

NOTICE TO THE READER
The Publisher has taken reasonable care in the preparation of this book, but makes no expressed or implied warranty of any kind and assumes no responsibility for any errors or omissions. No liability is assumed for incidental or consequential damages in connection with or arising out of information contained in this book. The Publisher shall not be liable for any special, consequential, or exemplary damages resulting, in whole or in part, from the readers' use of, or reliance upon, this material.

Independent verification should be sought for any data, advice or recommendations contained in this book. In addition, no responsibility is assumed by the publisher for any injury and/or damage to persons or property arising from any methods, products, instructions, ideas or otherwise contained in this publication.

This publication is designed to provide accurate and authoritative information with regard to the subject matter covered herein. It is sold with the clear understanding that the Publisher is not engaged in rendering legal or any other professional services. If legal or any other expert assistance is required, the services of a competent person should be sought. FROM A DECLARATION OF PARTICIPANTS JOINTLY ADOPTED BY A COMMITTEE OF THE AMERICAN BAR ASSOCIATION AND A COMMITTEE OF PUBLISHERS.

LIBRARY OF CONGRESS CATALOGING-IN-PUBLICATION DATA

India on the move / Lea M. Surit (editor).
    p. cm.
  Includes index.
  ISBN-13: 978-1-60021-813-2 (hardcover)
  ISBN-10: 1-60021-813-X (hardcover)
  1. Nuclear weapons--India. 2. India--Economic policy--21st century. 3. India--Foreign relations.
I. Surit, Lea M.
U264.5.I4I634 2008
355.02'170954--dc22
                         2007029798

Published by Nova Science Publishers, Inc. ✦ New York

CONTENTS

PREFACE

Very few countries in the world can be considered economically on the move forward but India, as well as China, is one of them. This new book presents a country profile, several issue papers including those dealing with nuclear issues and a chronology of recent events.

Chapter 1 is a country profile of India.

Chapter 2 - Long considered a "strategic backwater"from Washington's perspective, South Asia has emerged in the 21st century as increasingly vital to core U.S. foreign policy interests. India, the region's dominant actor with more than one billion citizens, is now recognized as a nascent major power and "natural partner" of the United States, one that many analysts view as a potential counterweight to China's growing clout. Washington and New Delhi have since 2004 been pursuing a "strategic partnership" based on shared values such as democracy, multi-culturalism, and rule of law. Numerous economic, security, and global initiatives, including plans for "full civilian nuclear energy cooperation," are underway. This latter initiative, launched by President Bush in July 2005 and provisionally endorsed by the 109th Congress in late 2006 (P.L. 109-401), reverses three decades of U.S. nonproliferation policy. It would require, among other steps, conclusion of a peaceful nuclear agreement between the United States and India, which would itself enter into force only after a Joint Resolution of Approval by Congress. Also in 2005, the United States and India signed a ten-year defense framework agreement that calls for expanding bilateral security cooperation. Since 2002, the two countries have engaged in numerous and unprecedented combined military exercises. The issue of major U.S. arms sales to India may come before the 110th Congress. The influence of a growing and relatively wealthy Indian-American community of more than two million is reflected in Congress's largest country-specific caucus.

Further U.S. interest in South Asia focuses on ongoing tensions between India and Pakistan, a problem rooted in unfinished business from the 1947 Partition, competing claims to the Kashmir region, and, in more recent years, "cross-border terrorism" in both Kashmir and major Indian cities. In the interests of regional stability, the United States strongly encourages an ongoing India-Pakistan peace initiative and remains concerned about the potential for conflict over Kashmiri sovereignty to cause open hostilities between these two nuclear-armed countries. The United States seeks to curtail the proliferation of nuclear weapons and ballistic missiles in South Asia. Both India and Pakistan have resisted external pressure to sign the major nonproliferation treaties. In 1998, the two countries conducted nuclear tests that evoked international condemnation. Proliferation-related restrictions on U.S.

aid were triggered, then later lifted through congressional-executive cooperation from 1998 to 2000. Remaining sanctions on India (and Pakistan) were removed in October 2001.

India is in the midst of major and rapid economic expansion. Many U.S. business interests view India as a lucrative market and candidate for foreign investment. The United States supports India's efforts to transform its once quasi-socialist economy through fiscal reform and market opening. Since 1991, India has taken steps in this direction, with coalition governments keeping the country on a general path of reform. Yet there is U.S. concern that such movement remains slow and inconsistent. Congress also continues to have concerns about abuses of human rights, including caste- and gender-based discrimination, and religious freedoms in India. Moreover, the spread of HIV/AIDS in India has attracted congressional attention as a serious development.

Chapter 3 - On July 18, 2005, President Bush announced he would "work to achieve full civil nuclear energy cooperation with India" and would "also seek agreement from Congress to adjust U.S. laws and policies," in the context of a broader, global partnership with India to promote stability, democracy, prosperity and peace. Administration officials have promoted nuclear cooperation with India as a way to reduce India's carbon dioxide emissions and its dependence on oil, bring India into the "nonproliferation mainstream" and create jobs for U.S. industry.

India, which has not signed the Nuclear Nonproliferation Treaty (NPT) and does not have International Atomic Energy Agency safeguards on all nuclear material in peaceful nuclear activities, exploded a "peaceful" nuclear device in 1974, convincing the world of the need for greater restrictions on nuclear trade. The United States created the Nuclear Suppliers Group (NSG) as a direct response to India's test, halted nuclear exports to India a few years later, and worked to convince other states to do the same. India tested nuclear weapons again in 1998.

Nonproliferation experts have argued that the potential costs of nuclear cooperation with India to U.S. and global nonproliferation policy may far exceed the benefits. At a time when the United States has called for all states to strengthen their domestic export control laws and for tighter multilateral controls, U.S. nuclear cooperation with India would require loosening its own nuclear export legislation, as well as creating a NSG exception. This is at odds with nearly three decades of U.S. nonproliferation policy and practice. Some believe the proposed agreement undercuts the basic bargain of the NPT, could undermine hard-won restrictions on nuclear supply, and could prompt some suppliers, like China, to justify supplying other states outside the NPT regime, like Pakistan. Others contend that allowing India access to the international uranium market will free up its domestic uranium sources to make more nuclear weapons.

U.S. nuclear cooperation is governed by the Atomic Energy Act (AEA). The Administration proposed legislation in 2006 that, in addition to providing waivers of relevant provisions of the AEA (Sections 123 a. (2), 128, and 129), would have allowed an agreement to enter into force without a vote from Congress, as though it conformed to AEA requirements. In late July, the House passed H.R. 5682, which provided the necessary waivers but retained the prerogative of Congress to vote on the actual cooperation agreement later. The Senate passed its version of H.R. 5682 on November 16, 2006, and on December 7, the House approved the conference report. The Senate approved the conference report by unanimous consent early on December 9, and President Bush signed the bill into law (P.L. 109-401) on December 18. The law requires that the following, among other things, must occur before nuclear cooperation can proceed: submission of a finalized text of a cooperation agreement to Congress, approval of an IAEA safeguards agreement by the IAEA Board of Governors, consensus agreement within the NSG to make an exception for India, and passage of a joint resolution of approval of the agreement by the Congress. Chapter 4 - In March 2006, the Bush Administration proposed legislation to create an exception for India from certain provisions of the Atomic Energy Act to facilitate a future nuclear cooperation agreement. After hearings in April and May, the House International Relations Committee and the Senate Foreign Relations Committee considered bills in late June 2006 to provide an exception for India to certain provisions of the Atomic Energy Act related to a peaceful nuclear cooperation agreement. On July 26, 2006, the House passed its version of the legislation, H.R. 5682, by a vote of 359 to 68. On November 16, 2006, the Senate incorporated the text of S. 3709, as amended, into H.R. 5682 and passed that bill by a vote of 85 to 12. The Senate insisted on its amendment, and a conference committee produced a conference report on December 7, 2006. The House agreed to the conference report (H.Rept. 109-721) on December 8 in a 330-59 vote; the Senate agreed by unanimous consent to the conference report on December 9. The President signed the bill into law (P.L. 109-401) on December 18, 2006.

The Senate and House versions of the India bill contained similar provisions, with four differences. The Senate version contained an additional requirement for the President to execute his waiver authority, an amendment introduced by Senator Harkin and adopted by unanimous consent that the President determine that India is "fully and actively participating in U.S. and international efforts to dissuade, sanction and contain Iran for its nuclear program." This provision was watered down into a reporting requirement in the conference report. The Senate version also had two unique sections related to the cooperation agreement, Sections 106 and 107, both of which appear in the conference report. Section 106 (now Section 104 (d) (4)) prohibits exports of equipment, material or technology related for uranium enrichment, spent fuel reprocessing or heavy water production unless conducted in a multinational facility participating in a project approved by the International Atomic Energy Agency (IAEA) or in a facility participating in a bilateral or multilateral project to develop a proliferation-resistant fuel cycle. Section 107 (now Section 104 (d) (5)) would establish a program to monitor that U.S. technology is being used appropriately by Indian recipients. Finally, the Senate version also contained the implementing legislation for the U.S. Additional Protocol in Title II, which was retained in the conference bill.

This report provides a thematic side-by-side comparison of the provisions of the conference report with H.R. 5682 as passed by the House and by the Senate, and compares them with the Administration's initially proposed legislation, H.R. 4974/S. 2429, and the conference report. The report concludes with a list of CRS resources that provide further discussion and more detailed analysis of the issues addressed by the legislation summarized in the table.

Chapter 5 - On July 18, 2005, President Bush and Indian Prime Minister Manmohar Singh announced the creation of a "global partnership," which would include "full" civil nuclear cooperation between the United States and India. This is at odds with nearly three decades of U.S. nonproliferation policy and practice. President Bush promised India he would persuade Congress to amend the pertinent laws to approve the agreement, as well as persuade U.S. allies to create an exception to multilateral Nuclear Suppliers Group (NSG) guidelines for India. India committed to, among other things, separating its civilian nuclear facilities from its military nuclear facilities, declaring civilian facilities to the International Atomic Energy Agency (IAEA) and placing them under IAEA safeguards, and signing an Additional Protocol.

The separation plan announced by Prime Minister Singh and President Bush on March 2, 2006, and further elaborated on May 11, 2006, would place 8 power reactors under inspection, bringing the total up to 14 out of a possible 22 under inspection. Several fuel fabrication and spent fuel storage facilities were declared, as well as 3 heavy water plants that were described as "safeguards-irrelevant." The plan excludes from international inspection 8 indigenous power reactors, enrichment and spent fuel reprocessing facilities (except as currently safeguarded), military production reactors and other military nuclear plants and 3 heavy water plants. Administration officials have defended the separation plan as credible and defensible because it covers more than just a token number of Indian facilities, provides for safeguards in perpetuity, and includes upstream and downstream facilities.

U.S. officials acknowledge the importance of a credible separation plan to ensuring that the United States complies with its Article I obligations under the Nuclear Nonproliferation Treaty (NPT) — to not in any way assist a nuclear weapons program in a non-nuclear weapon state. For almost 30 years, the U.S. legal standard has been that only nuclear safeguards on all nuclear activities in a state provides adequate assurances. The Administration is apparently asking Congress to back a lower level of assurance by proposing that the separation plan take the place of comprehensive safeguards.

Congress is likely to consider this issue as well as others when the Administration eventually submits its cooperation agreement with India for approval by both chambers. P.L. 109-401, signed on December 18, 2006, provides waivers for a nuclear cooperation agreement with India from relevant Atomic Energy Act provisions, and requires detailed information on the separation plan and resultant safeguards.

Chapter 6 - Members of Congress have questioned whether India's cooperation with Iran might affect U.S. and other efforts to prevent Iran from developing nuclear weapons. India's long relationship with Iran and its support of Non-Aligned Movement (NAM) positions on nonproliferation are obstacles to India's taking a hard line on Iran, yet the Bush Administration has asserted that U.S.-India nuclear cooperation would bring India into the "nonproliferation mainstream." India, like most other states, does not support a nuclear weapons option for Iran. However, its views of the Iranian threat and appropriate responses differ significantly from U.S. views. Entities in India and Iran appear to have engaged in very limited nuclear, chemical and missile-related transfers over the years, and some sanctions have been imposed on Indian entities for transfers to Iran, the latest in July 2006.

In congressional hearings on the proposed U.S. nuclear cooperation agreement with India, Members questioned how India's cooperation with Iran might affect U.S. efforts to prevent Iran from developing nuclear weapons. India's long relationship with Iran and its support of Non-Aligned Movement (NAM) positions on nonproliferation are obstacles to India's taking a hard line on Iran, yet the Bush Administration has asserted that U.S.-India nuclear cooperation would bring India into the "nonproliferation mainstream." U.S. law requires recipients of U.S. nuclear cooperation to guarantee the nonproliferation of any U.S. material or equipment transferred. If a recipient state assists, encourages or induces a non-nuclear weapon state to engage in nuclear-weapons related activities, exports must cease. India's nonproliferation record continues to be scrutinized, as India continues to take steps to strengthen its own export controls. Additional measures of Indian support *could include* diplomatic support for negotiations with Iran; support for Bush Administration efforts to restrict enrichment and reprocessing; support for multilateral fuel cycle initiatives, and for the Proliferation Security Initiative.

Chapter 7 - This report provides a reverse chronology of recent events involving India and India-U.S. relations. Sources include, but are not limited to, major newswires, the U.S. Department of State, and Indian news outlets.

In: India on the Move
Editor: Lea M. Surit, pp. 1-31

ISBN: 978-1-60021-813-2
© 2007 Nova Science Publishers, Inc.

Chapter 1

COUNTRY PROFILE:
INDIA DECEMBER 2004 COUNTRY

Formal Name: Republic of India (The official, Sanskrit name for India is Bharat, the name of the legendary king in the *Mahabharata*).

Short Form: India.

Term for Citizen(s): Indian(s).

Capital: New Delhi (formally called the National Capital Territory of Delhi).

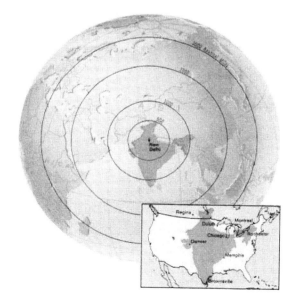

Other Major Cities: India has 35 cities and urban agglomerations with more than 1 million persons. The most populous cities are Mumbai (Bombay) with 16.4 million people, Kolkata (Calcutta, 13.2 million), New Delhi (12.8 million), Chennai (Madras, 6.4 million), Bangalore (5.7 million), Hyderabad (5.5 million), and Ahmadabad (4.5 million).

Date of Independence: Proclaimed August 15, 1947, from Britain.

National Public Holidays: Makar Sakranti (January 14); Republic Day (signing of national constitution, January 26); Id-ul-Juha (movable date); Muharram (Islamic New Year, movable date); Holi (movable date in March); Ramnavami (birthday of Rama, movable date in March or April); Mahavir Jayanti (Birthday of Mahavir, movable date in April); Good Friday (movable date in March or April); Milad un Nabi (birthday of Prophet Muhammad, movable date); Buddha Poornima (birthday of Buddha, movable date in April or May); Independence Day (August 15); Mahatma Gandhi's Birthday (October 2); Dussehra (also known as Vijaya Dashmi, movable set of 10 days in September or October); Deepawali (also known as Diwali, movable set of five days in October or November); Id-ul-Fitr (end of Ramadan, movable date); Guru Nanak Jayanti (Birthday of Guru Nanak, November 26); Christmas Day (December 25). Many of these holidays are observed only by particular religions or in specific regions. The three holidays that are observed nationwide are Republic Day, Independence Day, and Mahatma Gandhi's Birthday.

Flag: India's national flag has three horizontal bands. The upper band is orange/saffron in color, the lower is green, and the middle is white with a 24-spoke dark blue wheel in its center. The saffron symbolizes courage, sacrifice, and renunciation; the white represents purity and truth; and the green signifies faith and fertility. The wheel is the Dharma Chakra, an ancient Buddhist symbol used by the Indian king Ashoka to represent a "wheel of law."

HISTORICAL BACKGROUND

Early Empires

Whereas human settlement in India dates back to roughly 400,000 to 200,000 B.C., extensive urbanization and trade appear to have begun in the Indus River Valley around 3000 B.C. with the Harappan civilization. From this period until the termination of British colonial rule in 1947, numerous empires ruled various portions of South Asia, often assimilating a rich array of peoples and each adding its own contribution to an increasingly rich tapestry of cultures, ideas, and technologies. Indeed, many of India's current political, cultural, and economic traits have been influenced by historical events and trends, many of which pre-date European contact.

Among the most influential early empires were the Aryans, who migrated from Persia to northwestern India around 2000 B.C. and brought a new pantheon of anthropomorphic gods, an early form of Sanskrit language, a tiered social system essentially based on ethnicity and occupation, and religious texts that are an important part of living Hindu traditions.

From 326 B.C. to around 200 B.C., the Mauryan Empire emerged as India's first imperial power and ruled its areas with a highly centralized and hierarchical administration. For the next few hundred years, North and South India experienced a succession of ruling powers. From 320 A.D. to 550 A.D., most of North India was ruled by the Gupta Empire, which in contrast to the Mauryan Empire maintained a decentralized form of government, using numerous regional and local officials to govern vast territories with an array of local political, economic, and social arrangements. As under the Aryans, Gupta authority was religiously legitimized, and it was in this period called the Classical Age that the multiple components of Hindu culture became crystallized into a more unified system of thought.

From the disintegration of the Gupta Empire to the mid-thirteenth century, various regional kingdoms emerged, and conflicts among them often led to their defeat but rarely to their total annihilation. As a result, no highly centralized government emerged in South India, and South Indian villages and districts enjoyed much greater local autonomy than those in North India. During this period, South India engaged in flourishing trade with Arabs and Southeast Asia, which facilitated the diffusion of Indian mathematical concepts to the Middle East and Indian art, literature, and social customs to Southeast Asia.

Islamic influence in South Asia emerged around 711 as Arabs conquered part of Sindh (now in Pakistan), and by the tenth century Punjab came under the control of Turkic ruler Mahmud of Ghazni. By the thirteenth century, much of India had been periodically conquered, but rarely held for long, by a steady succession of Turkic rulers collectively referred to as the Delhi Sultanate or Mughal emperors. The most prominent Mughal ruler was the astute and religiously tolerant Akbar, who ruled from 1556 to 1605. Akbar oversaw substantial political and geographic consolidation by using locally established warriors and powerful *zamindar* landlords to control local populations and collect revenues. But over time, the administrative capacities of later Mughal rulers suffered from bloated and excessively corrupt bureaucracies and huge, unwieldy armies.

European Influence

European economic competition in India began soon after the Portuguese arrived in 1498, and by the early 1600s it was manifested in the establishment of commercial companies, such as England's East India Company, that attempted to capture the spice trade. In order to gain competitive advantages over each other, European powers also engaged in commercial and administrative alignments with Mughal power holders. By the late eighteenth century, the British had defeated French and Mughal forces to become the preeminent military and economic power in India.

The British used Indian assistance in various commercial and military matters, which enabled upward mobility for some Indians. The British also adopted numerous local economic and political arrangements that were established by the Mughals, and this practice maintained and exacerbated various forms of social stratification. A major turning point in the colonial occupation occurred with the Indian-led Sepoy Rebellion of 1857 to 1858, which seriously threatened British rule and led to a marked shift in colonial attitudes and practices. Although the British made some legal and administrative adjustments to placate Indians, colonial attitudes toward Indians shifted from cultural engagement—albeit to change Indians with Western ideas and technology—to insularity and xenophobia.

Independence Movement

By the 1920s, various Indian groups became active in attempting to end colonial rule, and the Indian National Congress Party, which had been established in 1885, eventually became the most prominent. Led by Mohandas Gandhi and Jawaharlal Nehru, the Congress Party promoted non-violence and self-sufficiency and thus garnered respect and support among both Indians and some British. But the Congress Party generally failed to attract Muslims, who often felt culturally and physically threatened by Hindus, and in 1906 the All-India Muslim League was established. The British periodically jailed Congress Party leaders for their social movement activities, but among the increasingly restive Indian population the British found Congress to be an easier group with which to negotiate than more militant Indian groups. Rising civil disobedience and World War II eventually rendered India too costly and difficult to administer, and the British granted independence in 1947.

Independence

In some ways, the victory was bittersweet, as the country emerged with numerous political, social, and economic difficulties. On Independence Day (August 15, 1947), the country was partitioned into India and Pakistan, which led to massive migration of Hindus and Muslims and substantial communal conflict. Furthermore, the British had left India with a rudimentary industrial and scientific base; tremendous poverty; a large and growing population; social cleavages along caste and economic lines; and contentious territorial boundaries that have led to armed conflicts with Pakistan (1947 to 1949, 1965, 1971), China (1962), and numerous insurgent groups.

In spite of such difficulties, the nation can count a number of successes. With the exception of martial law from 1975 to 1977, India has maintained a democratic political system. Building on the British-established education system, India developed an educational infrastructure that has trained one of the world's largest scientific and technical populations. Using Green Revolution agricultural technologies, the country has become self-sufficient in food production. Moreover, a combination of socialist planning and free enterprise from the 1950s to the 1970s led to substantial industrialization with the goal of making India economically self-sufficient.

In the 1980s and 1990s, socialist economic planning and import substitution industries were slowly replaced by liberalization measures, a large middle class emerged, information technology developed into an important economic sector, and at times economic growth has been impressive. India has also become somewhat influential in international political and economic matters and appears set to continue those trends.

Numerous problems remain, however, such as substantial poverty, large income gaps between wealthy and poor, a large mass of people who lack the skills to participate in the new economy, and numerous insurgencies that threaten the nation's territorial integrity. Some social issues remain unresolved, and the rise of Hindu nationalism has become a particularly contentious topic in both Indian society and politics. Indeed, the Bharatiya Janata Party (BJP) led by Prime Minister Atal Bihari Vajpayee was in power from 1998 to 2004, and the BJP is often associated with Hindu nationalism. Furthermore, some observers believe the nation is facing difficulties in the political capacity to address these problems. Intense multiparty political competition over numerous economic and social issues has resulted in often-fragile coalitions of political parties, and no single political party has held a parliamentary majority since 1989. The government changed nine times from December 1989 to the elections in May 2004 in which the Indian National Congress returned to power under Prime Minister Manmohan Singh. Thus, increasing pluralism of political parties, growing diversity in interest-group representation, and substantial ideological divisions among parties are significant obstacles in policy implementation.

GEOGRAPHY

Location

India occupies much of the South Asian subcontinent, and the Indian mainland stretches eastward from Pakistan in the west to Bangladesh and Burma in the east. On the north, India borders China, Nepal, and Bhutan. The Indian Ocean to the south, the Arabian Sea to the west, and the Bay of Bengal to the east form the country's coastline. Noncontiguous to the mainland are the Lakshadweep Islands in the Arabian Sea and the Andaman and Nicobar Islands located 1,300 kilometers from the mainland in the Bay of Bengal.

Size

The country's exact size is subject to debate because some borders are disputed. The Indian government lists the total area as 3,287,260 square kilometers and the total land area as 3,060,500 square kilometers; the United Nations lists the total area as 3,287,263 square kilometers and total land area as 2,973,190 square kilometers. In either case, India is the seventh largest country in the world and about one-third the size of the United States.

Land Boundaries

Land boundaries total 15,200 kilometers. India shares common borders with Pakistan (3,325 kilometers; the Jammu and Kashmir border is 1,085 kilometers), China (line of actual control is 3,439 kilometers), Bhutan (605 kilometers), Nepal (1,690 kilometers), Burma (1,452 kilometers), and Bangladesh (4,339 kilometers). Although India and Sri Lanka do not share a land boundary, the narrowest distance between the two countries is only 64 kilometers across the Palk Strait.

Disputed Territory

Most of Jammu and Kashmir is contested with Pakistan, and the Aksai Chin area of Jammu and Kashmir is disputed with China, as is the border of Arunachal Pradesh state in northeast India. Nepal claims a 75-square-kilometer-area called Kalapani. Possession of recently emerged New Moore Island (South Talpatty) in the Bay of Bengal has been disputed by Bangladesh, and much of the border with Bangladesh is not demarcated.

Length of Coastline

India's total coastline is 7,516 kilometers in length, which comprises 5,422 kilometers for the mainland, 132 kilometers for the Lakshadweep Islands, and 1,962 kilometers for the Andaman and Nicobar Islands.

Maritime Claims

Under the 1982 United Nations Convention on the Law of the Sea, India has a 200-nautical-mile exclusive economic zone, a 12-nautical-mile territorial sea, a 24-nautical-mile contiguous zone, and a legal continental shelf extending to a depth of 2,500 meters or to the end of the continental margin.

Topography

There are three main geological regions: the Indo-Gangetic Plain and the Himalayas—collectively known as North India—and the Peninsula, or South India. These and other portions of India can be classified into diverse physiological regions that include highlands, plains, deserts, and river valleys. The country's lowest elevation is zero meters at the Indian Ocean, and the highest is 8,598 meters at Kanchenjunga, which is the third highest mountain in the world and located in the Himalayas.

Principal Rivers

India's longest rivers are the Brahmaputra and Indus, which are both 2,896 kilometers long, although neither is entirely within India. Other major rivers are the Ganga (Ganges, 2,525 kilometers), Godavari (1,465), Kaveri (Cauvery, 800), Krishna (1,401), Mahanandi (851), Narmada (1,312), and Yamuna (1,370).

Climate

Climate in India varies significantly from the permanently snow-capped Himalayas in the north to the tropics in the south. The country has four seasons. December to February is relatively dry and cool, March to May is dry and hot, from June to September predominating southwest maritime winds bring monsoon rains to most of the country, and in October and November there are retreating dry monsoons originating from the northeast. Average temperatures range from 12.5° C to 30° C in the northwest, 17.5° C to 30° C in the north and northeast, and 22.5° C to 30° C in the south. Average annual rainfall is around 1,000 to 1,500 millimeters for much of the country, but can be quite low in some parts of the northwest (150 to 300 millimeters annually) and very high in the northeast and along the west coast (1,500 to 2,500 millimeters annually).

Natural Resources

Commercially important natural resources include arable land, bauxite, chromite, coal (fourth-largest reserves in the world), diamonds, iron ore, limestone, manganese, mica, natural gas, petroleum, and titanium ore.

Land Use

In 2000 the total arable land and land planted under permanent crops combined was 1,697,000 square kilometers, and total irrigated land was 548,000 square kilometers. The total of non-arable land and land not under permanent crops was 1,276,190 square kilometers.

Environmental Factors

India is vulnerable to various natural hazards, particularly cyclones and annual monsoon floods, and various combinations of poverty, population growth, increasing individual consumption, industrialization, infrastructural development, poor agricultural practices, and resource maldistribution have led to substantial human transformation of India's natural environment. An estimated 60 percent of cultivated land suffers from soil erosion, waterlogging, and salinity. It is also estimated that between 4.7 and 12 billion tons of topsoil are lost annually from soil erosion. From 1947 to 2002, average annual per capita water availability declined by almost 70 percent to 1,822 cubic meters, and overexploitation of groundwater is problematic in the states of Haryana, Punjab, and Uttar Pradesh. Forest area covers 19.4 percent of India's geographic area (63.7 million hectares). Nearly half of the country's forest cover is found in the state of Madhya Pradesh (20.7 percent) and the seven states of the northeast (25.7 percent); the latter is experiencing net forest loss. Forest cover is declining because of harvesting for fuel wood and the expansion of agricultural land. These trends, combined with increasing industrial and motor vehicle pollution output, have led to atmospheric temperature increases, shifting precipitation patterns, and declining intervals of drought recurrence in many areas. The Indian Agricultural Research Institute has estimated that a 3° C rise in temperature will result in a 15 to 20 percent loss in annual wheat yields. These are substantial problems for a nation with such a large population depending on the productivity of primary resources and whose economic growth relies heavily on industrial growth.

Civil conflicts involving natural resources—most notably forests and arable land—have occurred in eastern and northeastern states. By contrast, water resources have not been linked to either domestic or international violent conflict as was previously anticipated by some observers. Possible exceptions include some communal violence related to distribution of water from the Kaveri River and political tensions surrounding actual and potential population displacements by dam projects, particularly on the Narmada River.

Time Zones

All of India is under a single time zone, which is Greenwich Mean Time plus 5.5 hours.

SOCIETY

Population

The 2004 estimate of India's total population was 1,065,070,607. According to the 2001 Indian census, the total population was 1,028,610,328, a 21.3 percent increase from 1991 and 2 percent average growth rate from 1975 to 2001. India has nearly 17 percent of the world's population, second only to China. About 72 percent of the population resided in rural areas in 2001, yet the country has a population density of 324 persons per square kilometer. Major states have more than 400 persons per square kilometer, but population densities are around 150 persons or fewer per square kilometer in some border states and insular territories.

Demography

In 2001 India's birthrate was 25.4 per 1,000 population, its death rate was 8.4 per 1,000, and its infant mortality rate was 66 per 1,000 live births. In 1995 to 1997, India's total fertility rate was 3.4 children per woman (4.5 in 1980–82). According to the 2001 Indian census, 35.3 percent of the population was under 14 years of age, 59.9 percent between 15 and 64, and 4.8 percent 65 and older (the 2004 estimates are, respectively, 31.7 percent, 63.5 percent, and 4.8 percent); the sex ratio was 933 females per 1,000 males. In 2004 India's median age was estimated to be 24.4. From 1992 to 1996, overall life expectancy at birth was 60.7 years (60.1 years for males and 61.4 years for females) and was estimated to be 64 years in 2004 (63.3 for males and 64.8 for females).

Ethnic Groups

The exact number of ethnic groups depends on source and method of counting, and scholars estimate that only the continent of Africa exceeds the linguistic, cultural, and genetic diversity of India. Seventy-two percent of the population is Indo-Aryan, 25 percent Dravidian, and 3 percent Mongoloid and other. Each of these groups can be further subdivided into various—and changing—combinations of language, religion, and, very often, caste. The Hindu caste system is technically illegal but widely practiced (generally more in rural areas) and comprises four major categories (*varnas*) that are found India-wide but are often subdivided into hundreds of sub-categories (*jatis*), many of which are often found only in specific areas. Similar hereditary and occupational social hierarchies exist within Sikh and Muslim communities but are generally far less pervasive and institutionalized. About 16 percent of the total population is "untouchable" (Scheduled Castes is the more formal, legal term; *Dalit* is the term preferred by "untouchables" and roughly translates to downtrodden); around 8 percent of the population belongs to one of 461 indigenous groups (often called Scheduled Tribes for legal purposes, although the term *adivasi* is commonly used).

Languages

The total number of languages and dialects varies by source and counting method, and many Indians speak more than one language. The Indian census lists 114 languages (22 of which are spoken by one million or more persons) that are further categorized into 216 dialects or "mother tongues" spoken by 10,000 or more speakers. An estimated 850 languages are in daily use, and the Indian Government claims there are more than 1,600 dialects.

Hindi is the official language and the most commonly spoken, but not all dialects are mutually comprehensible. English also has official status and is widely used in business and politics, although knowledge of English varies widely from fluency to knowledge of just a few words. The teaching of Hindi and English is compulsory in most states and union territories. Twenty-two languages are legally recognized by the constitution for various political, educational, and other purposes: Assamese, Bengali, Bodo, Dogri, Gujarati, Hindi, Kannada, Kashmiri, Konkani, Maithali, Malayalam, Manipuri, Marathi, Nepali, Oriya, Punjabi, Sanskrit, Santhali, Sindhi, Tamil, Telugu, and Urdu. Numerous other languages are recognized by individual states but not officially recognized by the central government, and linguistic issues related to education, employment, and politics are sometimes politically contentious. Indeed, some state borders are based on linguistic lines. The most commonly spoken languages are Hindi (40.2 percent of the population), Bengali (8.3 percent), Telugu (7.9 percent), Marathi (7.5 percent), and Tamil (6.3 percent).

Religion

Approximately 80.5 percent of the population is Hindu, 13.4 percent Muslim, 2.3 percent Christian, 1.9 percent Sikh, 0.8 percent Buddhist, and 0.4 percent Jain; another 0.6 percent belongs to other faiths, such as Zoroastrianism and numerous religions associated with Scheduled Tribes. These percentages have changed little since the 1961 census. In spite of Hinduism's inherent pantheism, adherents often focus much of their devotion on a specific deity—such as Vaishnivites (those primarily devoted to Vishnu and related deities) and Shaivites (Shiva and related deities)—but these denominations rarely have notable social, economic, or political consequences. The Indian constitution confers religious freedom for individuals and prohibits religious discrimination, but in spite of this, there have been enduring tensions—and occasional conflict—among religious communities, most notably between Hindus and Muslims.

Education and Literacy

In 2000 the adult literacy rate (percent aged 15 or older) was 58.5 percent (72.3 percent for males, 44.4 percent for females). These figures have all nearly doubled since 1961 and are higher than in most other South Asian nations, but they are still far lower than in most East Asian nations. In 2001 the combined primary, secondary, and tertiary enrollment ratio was 55 percent of the population of official school age for the three levels. Total government expenditures on education in 2001 were Rs841.8 billion (US$17.3 billion), which was 13.2 percent of all government expenditures and 4 percent of gross domestic product (GDP). Since the 1950s, government expenditures on education have increased steadily, as have the number of educational institutions from the primary to the university level.

In most states and union territories, primary school covers grade levels (called "standards") 1 to 8 and secondary education, standards 9 and 10; all states have senior secondary education for standards 11 and 12. As of 1997, most states and union territories had no compulsory level of education. Twelve states and union territories legally require completion of either the fifth- or eighth-grade level, yet drop-out rates are high even in compulsory stages. The majority of states and union territories have free education up to the seventh-grade level, and the majority of primary schools are government funded and managed. However, less than half of secondary schools are government funded and managed.

Indeed, 34 percent of secondary institutions are government funded but privately managed, and 25 percent are privately managed without government funding.

Health

National health indicators are generally lower than in many developing countries but have shown dramatic improvement nationwide, although there are variations among states in India. India's 2002 Human Development Index (HDI is a measure of income, education, and health developed by the United Nations) of 0.595 was an improvement over its 1975 HDI of 0.411, but India ranked 127th in the world out of 177 countries (the 2002 world average HDI was 0.729). An estimated 21 percent of the total population is malnourished, and common diseases include malaria, filariasis, leprosy, cholera, pneumonic plague, tuberculosis, trachoma, goiter, and diarrheal diseases. According to government estimates, about 0.5 percent of the population (about 5.1 million) was infected by the human immunodeficiency virus (HIV) in 2003. In November 2004, the head of the United Nations Acquired Immune Deficiency Syndrome program (UNAIDS) claimed that India, along with China and Russia, is on the "tipping point" of having small, localized AIDS epidemics become major ones that could detrimentally affect the world's capacity to prevent and treat the disease.

The above facts and figures are associated with substantial poverty and relatively low government health expenditures. In 2001 public health expenditures were 3.1 percent of total general government expenditures but only 17.9 percent of total health expenditures. By contrast, private expenditures were 82.1 percent of total health expenditures, all of which was out-of-pocket expense. Furthermore, total health expenditures per capita represented 5.1 percent of gross domestic product (GDP) in 2001, but public health expenditures were only 0.9 percent of GDP, and private health expenditures were 4.2 percent of GDP. The population's health is also a function of the relatively low number of health personnel and low level of infrastructure, which are on a par with many countries in Sub-Saharan Africa. In 1991 public and private primary health centers included more than 14,000 hospitals, 28,000 dispensaries, and 838,000 beds. In 1998 there were 52.2 medical practitioners per 100,000 persons, and in 1994 there were 69 hospital beds per 100,000 persons. In 1992 India had 48 physicians and 45 nurses per 100,000 persons.

Welfare

Generally, central (union) government welfare expenditures are a substantial portion of the official budget, and state and local governments play important roles in developing and implementing welfare policies. In 2000 union government expenditures on social services (includes education, health, family welfare, women and child development, and social justice and empowerment), rural development, and basic minimum services were approximately US$7.7 billion (Rs361.7 billion), which was 11.1 percent of total government expenditures and 1.7 percent of gross domestic product (GDP). Furthermore, the union and state governments maintain a plethora of reserved seats in various political and education institutions for lower castes, indigenous persons, and others based on their percentage of the population. Finally, various innovative development programs have been developed—often at state or local levels—for social development and the empowerment of women and lower castes, and the state of Kerala is internationally known for its noteworthy success in public welfare.

ECONOMY

Overview

From 1947 to the late 1970s, the economy was characterized by central government planning and import substitution industries, and economic production was transformed from primarily agriculture, forestry, fishing, and textile manufacturing to various heavy industries, transportation, and telecommunications. Agriculture still employs nearly 60 percent of the population, but accounts for only 22.6 percent of gross domestic product (GDP). By the 1980s and 1990s, private-sector initiatives noticeably increased, and information technology emerged in importance but has proven vulnerable to changes in foreign demand, out-migration of information technology labor, and a weak but growing domestic market for information technology goods and services.

In the 1980s, government liberalization measures—such as privatization of government industries and reduced tariffs on imported capital goods—have been credited for 1990s economic growth rates of around 4 to 7 percent annually, nearly double the 3 percent growth rates that characterized the previous 40 years. Furthermore, foreign direct investment has increased to an annual range of US$3 billion to US$5 billion, but is seen as hampered by corruption and bureaucratic inefficiency and remains well behind foreign direct investment in neighboring China. Furthermore, India accounts for less than 1 percent of world trade in spite of having 18 percent of the world's population, and the informal economy accounts for 23.1 percent of gross national income (the new term for gross national product). A new union government was elected in May 2004 and is under significant pressure to provide greater economic development in rural areas.

Gross Domestic Product (GDP)/Power Purchasing Parity (PPP)

In 2002 GDP was US$496.8 billion (Rs24.2 trillion). Since the early 1990s, GDP has grown 4 to 7 percent annually, which is higher than GDP growth for the European Union, the United States, or the world as a whole. In 2003 PPP per capita was US$2,880.

Government Budget

Government revenues and expenditures have grown substantially since the early 1990s. According to India's Ministry of Finance, in 2002–03 tax and non-tax revenues were US$49.7 billion (Rs2.3 trillion), total expenditures were US$88.9 billion (Rs4.1 trillion), and the fiscal deficit was US$31.1 billion (Rs1.5 trillion). Government expenditures generally have been highest in the energy, transportation, and social service sectors, which receive about two-thirds of total government expenditures. Tax revenues have grown annually around 10 percent or more since the early 1950s, and tax receipts have increased even more substantially since the mid-1990s with accelerated economic growth and improved government revenue collection capacities. For example, total tax revenues were US$20.8 billion for 1994–95 and US$35.2 billion for 2002–03. Fiscal deficits, however, have also increased from US$17.8 billion in 1994–95 to an estimated US$31.1 billion for 2002–03.

Agriculture, Forestry, and Fishing

Since independence, India has changed from a food importer to a food exporter, but agriculture has declined as a percentage of gross domestic product (GDP; from 32.8 percent in 1991 to 22.6 percent in 2001) and total exports (from 18.5 percent to 14.2 percent). Around 46 percent (141 million hectares) of total land is cultivated, and 16 percent is double cropped (49 million hectares), effectively giving India 190 million hectares of cultivated land. Another 4.8 percent (14.7 million hectares) is permanent pastureland or planted in tree crops or groves. Agriculture continues to employ the major, but declining, proportion of workers (from 69.4 percent in 1951 to 58.4 percent in 2001) and agricultural employment varies substantially among states (from 38.9 percent of workers in Punjab to 77.3 percent in Bihar). Most farmers cultivate plots of two hectares or less, and large landholders have only been divested in a few areas. Agricultural output—and the food security of millions—remains susceptible to often-tenuous access to arable land, credit, fertilizers, and irrigation as well as to natural conditions, particularly annual variations in rainfall.

The remarkable growth in agricultural output is largely due to Green Revolution inputs such as high-yield seed varieties and fertilizers. Rice, wheat, pulses, and oilseeds dominate production, but millet, corn, and sorghum are also important crops. The main commercial crops are sugar (India is the world's second largest producer), rice (world's second largest exporter), wheat, cotton, and jute. However, the rate of output for several crops may have peaked, and problems with soil degradation, rural infrastructure, and declining per capita agricultural holdings may prevent the rate of agricultural growth from keeping pace with increasing rates of population growth and per capita food consumption.

In 1991, 2.1 percent of the population was employed in forestry, fishing, livestock, hunting, and related activities. As a percentage of GDP, forestry has declined from 1.5 percent in 1993–94 to 1.1 percent in 2000–01. In the same period, fishing changed little from 1.1 percent to 1.2 percent of GDP.

Mining and Minerals

Since the early 1990s, mining has accounted for around 2 to 3.5 percent of gross domestic product (GDP) and employed less than 1 percent of the labor force. The majority of minerals produced by India are bauxite, copper, iron, lead, mica, rare earths, uranium ore, and zinc.

Industry and Manufacturing

For decades, Indian industries were largely import substitution industries producing textiles, steel and aluminum, fertilizers and petrochemicals, and electronics and motor vehicles. From 1950 to 2000, industrial output increased from 15 to 27 percent of gross domestic product (GDP), but the sector continues to employ only about 10 percent of the workforce. Several industries face problems with power availability, high interest rates, customs delays, and regulatory obstacles. Domestic automobile manufacturing has increased substantially since the end of government licensing of automobile production in 1995, and car sales rose 50 percent by 2000. Import liberalization has also led to lowered sales for domestic industries, such as computer hardware and cement.

Energy

India is the world's sixth largest energy consumer, and the nation faces substantial challenges in meeting both present and expected demands for energy, particularly electric power. India has a growing nuclear power industry and abundant hydroelectric power (particularly in North India), and it is the world's third largest producer of coal (which provides more than half of domestic energy needs). But it is also a growing consumer and importer of petroleum and natural gas, and consumption of these products is expected to increase substantially. The government appears to be addressing petroleum demand by limiting imports and by expanding domestic exploration and production, but several factors provide little optimism that such measures will be sufficient for future demands. The government continues to pursue various reforms in the electricity sector, but it has abandoned full privatization of the state-owned petroleum industry, raising questions about its commitment to reforms in the petroleum sector. Finally, India faces economic competition from China over potential oil and gas resources in the Indian Ocean that both countries need for their economic development.

Services

From 1951 to 2000, business, information technology, banking, communications, hotels, and other services increased from 27 to 48 percent of gross domestic product (GDP), but most of this growth occurred in the 1990s. The percentage of the Indian workforce employed in services was 23.5 percent in 2000. Information technology services have emerged as an important element of the economy, but the information technology sector is believed to be vulnerable to out-migration of information technology professionals, particularly when the global economy is strong.

Banking and Finance

Under 1990s liberalization measures, restrictions on foreign direct investment have been relaxed, and foreign banks have been allowed to have greater shareholding in domestic banks (up to 49 percent), although foreign banks have faced some difficulties in acquiring such stakes. In 2002 government legislation enhanced banks' capacity to act against debtors, a measure that should help banks in their attempts to address the high level of bad debt held by Indian companies.

Tourism

Tourism industry analysts estimate that India is one of the world's fastest growing tourism markets with an annual growth rate of approximately 8.8 percent. Annual tourist inflows range between 2 and 2.5 million, but tourism has proven to be susceptible to issues such as communal conflict between Hindus and Muslims and occasional spikes in tensions between India and Pakistan.

Labor

The total number of persons in the labor force is unknown. According to official figures, from 1981 to 2001 the total number of workers grew more than 50 percent from approximately 245 million to 402 million persons. These figures count only those who are considered to have "engaged in economically productive activity for 183 days or more." The actual number of persons in the labor force is likely to be much higher. From 1983 to 1994, the nation's unemployment rate declined from 8.3 percent to 6 percent and then increased to 7.3 percent by 2000. Unemployment rates have historically been higher in urban areas, but rural and urban unemployment rates became nearly equal by 2000 (7.2 and 7.7 percent, respectively).

Foreign Economic Relations

India's principal export and import trades are with the European Union, the United States, and Japan. Most aid is provided by the Aid-to-India Consortium, consisting of the World Bank Group, Austria, Belgium, Britain, Canada, Denmark, France, Germany, Italy, Japan, the Netherlands, Norway, Sweden, and the United States. Japan is the largest aid granter and lender. India has its own aid programs with Bangladesh, Bhutan, Nepal, and Vietnam.

Imports

Principal imports are petroleum and petroleum products, capital goods, uncut gems, machinery, and fertilizer. Major imports are from the United States, the European Union (particularly Belgium), Singapore, the United Kingdom, and Saudi Arabia. In 2003 imports totaled US$64.5 billion, a substantial increase over 2002 imports of US$54.2 billion.

Exports

Principal exports are textile goods, finished gems and jewelry, engineered goods (including iron and steel), chemicals, and leather and leather goods. Main destinations of exports are the United States, the United Kingdom, China (particularly Hong Kong), Japan, and the European Union (particularly Germany). In 2003 total exports were valued at US$52.5 billion, a substantial increase over 2002 exports of US$47.7 billion.

Trade Balance

India's negative trade balance has grown steadily since the late 1980s. In 2003 exports were US$52.5 billion and imports were US$65.4 billion, resulting in a negative trade balance of US$12.9 billion.

Balance of Payments

Before 2002 India's surpluses in the capital account were offset by deficits in the current account, but since 2002 India has had surpluses in the current and capital accounts, leading to an accumulation of foreign reserves. The current account surplus is a small percentage of gross domestic product (0.5 percent in 2003) and has been the result of non-factor services and private transfers exceeding trade deficits. Growth in foreign direct investment is largely responsible for steady growth in the capital account, and external commercial borrowings and assistance make up most net outflows.

External Debt

India's total external debt has increased from US$83.8 billion in 1991 to US$112.1 billion in 2003, but external debt declined as a percentage of gross domestic product (GDP) in the same time period (from 28.7 to 20.2 percent). Furthermore, in 1991 India was the world's third highest debtor nation, but it had dropped to eighth by 2002.

Foreign Investment

Foreign direct investment in India has increased from about US$97 million in 1991 to US$3.6 billion for 2003, partly because of various liberalization measures, such as reduced tariffs and relaxed restrictions on foreign ownership of domestic industries.

Currency and Exchange Rate

The rupee (Rs) has depreciated steadily against the dollar since the 1970s. The average annual exchange rate for 2003 was US$1=Rs46.59 and US$1=Rs31.29 for 1993. In December 2004, the exchange rate was approximately US$1=Rs44. Since the late 1990s, the rupee has been stable against the euro as a result of the weakening of the U.S. dollar and worldwide shift away from U.S. dollar assets.

Fiscal Year

India's fiscal year runs from April 1 to March 31.

TRANSPORTATION AND TELECOMMUNICATIONS

Overview

India's transportation infrastructure has undergone tremendous change since independence. While traditional, non-mechanized transport means are still quite common (elephants and camels are not an uncommon sight even in large urban areas), roads, railroads, ports, and aviation continue to expand. India now has the world's second largest road network, and its rail network is among the most used in the world for passengers and freight. Furthermore, increasing incomes and government liberalization measures have contributed to tremendous growth in the numbers of automobiles, two- and three-wheeled vehicles, private and public buses, and urban rail networks. However, there are significant, accompanying problems with pollution, increasing traffic density, unauthorized transportation providers, and high numbers of traffic fatalities.

Roads

There were about 3.3 million kilometers of roads by 2002, of which 1.4 million kilometers were surfaced and more than 1 million kilometers were covered with gravel, crushed stone, or earth. More than 150 highways are rated as national highways and carry about 40 percent of road traffic on a total length of 65,569 kilometers. Around 85 percent of all passenger traffic and 70 percent of all freight traffic travel by road. By 2007, highways are expected to expand by 13,146 kilometers, with road projects aimed at linking the country's major cities and spanning the entire country north-south and east-west. Modes of road transport are a mix of traditional and modern means. Urban transit is dominated by motor vehicles, with increasing use of automobiles, minibuses, buses, trucks, and particularly two- and three-wheeled vehicles. However, bullocks, camels, elephants, and other beasts of burden are seen on Indian roads, even in urban areas.

Railroads

All railroads are government-owned and operated by Indian Railways. In 2002 total route length was 63,028 kilometers, and double and multiple tracks resulted in a total track length of 108,706 kilometers. Of the total track length, 86,526 kilometers were 1.676-millimeter gauge, 18,529 kilometers were 1.000-millimeter gauge, and 3,651 kilometers were 0.762- and 0.610-millimeter gauge. About 16,000 kilometers were electrified, mostly 1.676 millimeter gauge. The rail system includes 7,566 locomotives, 37,840 coaches, 222,147 freight wagons, 6,853 stations, and nearly 116,000 bridges. Both passenger and freight carriage continue to expand annually, and the rail system is the fourth most heavily used in the world, both for passengers and freight. For the financial year 2004, Indian Railways carried 557 million freight tons and more than 5 billion passengers. There are some high-speed routes and increasing use of them. Most rolling stock and other components are still domestically produced, but they are increasingly manufactured through commercial agreements with foreign companies. There have been major government investments in modernization since the early 1990s, but Indian Railways has also experienced dwindling government budgetary support and has suffered from the dual role of being both a public utility and a commercial enterprise.

India also has several urban passenger rail systems. Kolkata (Calcutta) has a full metro system, and New Delhi's metro system is operational and expanding. Chennai has a rapid transit system, and there are suburban rail networks in Bangalore, Mumbai (Bombay), and New Delhi. There are plans for metro, light rail, or both in Bangalore, Coimbatore, Hyderabad, Jaipur, Lucknow, Mumbai, and Pune.

Ports

India has 12 major ports and 185 minor and intermediate ports along the country's coastline. There are also 7 shipyards under the control of the central government, 2 shipyards controlled by state governments, and 19 privately owned shipyards. The major ports handled 344.6 million tons of cargo for the financial year 2004, with Chennai, Kandla, and Vishakhapatnam carrying the greatest tonnage. Major ports can collectively handle 390 million tons of cargo annually, and port operations have improved since the mid-1990s. All major ports, except one (Ennore), are government administered, but private-sector participation in ports has increased. In 2000 there were 102 shipping companies operating in India, of which five were privately owned and based in India and one was owned by the government (Shipping Corporation of India). In 2000 there were 639 government-owned ships, including 91 oil tankers, 79 dry cargo bulk carriers, and 10 cellular container vessels.

Indian-flagged vessels carried about 15 percent of overseas cargo at Indian ports for financial year 2003.

Inland and Coastal Waterways

According to official sources, India has approximately 14,500 kilometers of inland waterways, but the transportation potential is vastly underused. More than 3,600 kilometers are navigable by large vessels, although only about 2,000 kilometers are used. For purposes of navigational development and conservation, three inland waterways have been declared national waterways: the Allahabad-Haldia portion of the Ganga-Bhagirathi-Hooghly rivers (1,620 kilometers), the Sadiya-Dhubri section of the Brahmaputra River (891 kilometers), and a combination of western canals (205 kilometers).

Civil Aviation and Airports

The government owns two airlines (Air India and Indian Airlines) and one helicopter service (Pawan Hans), and there are twelve privately owned airlines. Private airlines account for about 45 percent of domestic air traffic, and as of 2003 the government had divested more than 50 percent of the equity in both government-owned airlines. Of 288 airports, 208 have permanent-surface runways, and there are two runways of more than 3,659 meters. The Airports Authority of India administers 126 airports: 11 international, 89 domestic, and 26 for defense purposes. In 2003 these airports collectively handled approximately 500,000 flights, 40 million passengers, and 900,000 tons of cargo. Major international airports are located in Kolkata (Calcutta), Madras (Chennai), Mumbai (Bombay), New Delhi, and Thiruvananthapuram (Trivandrum). There is also international service from Bangalore, Guwahati, Hyderabad, and Mamargao, and there are major regional airports at Ahmadabad, Allahabad, Chandigarh, Kochi (Cochin), Nagpur, Pune, Srinagar, and Thiruvananthapuram.

Pipelines

In 2003 India had an estimated 5,798 kilometers of gas pipelines, 1,195 kilometers for liquid petroleum gas, 5,613 kilometers for oil, and 5,567 kilometers for refined products. India and Iran have discussed constructing a gas pipeline, but the Indian government and oil industry analysts have expressed concerns about the pipeline's security because of its proposed route through conflict-prone areas of Pakistan.

Telecommunications

India is witnessing possibly its greatest period of change in communications, with increasing shifts from government to private providers and greater public use of various technologies. From 1995 to 2003, the number of Internet users increased from 250,000 to

18.4 million. Since the late 1990s, the number of telephones, mobile phones, and personal computers has increased substantially. In 2004 there were 40.9 million telephones and 26.2 million mobile phones, and in 2003 there were an estimated 7.5 million personal computers. Some basic telephone services were opened to private-sector competition in 1994, and portions of state-owned telecommunications services have been purchased by private entities. Government-owned radio (All India Radio) and television (Doordarshan) networks have extensive national and local coverage, but domestic and international private television networks are increasingly prolific through cable and satellite. According to government figures, there were 79.4 million television households in 2001. From 1991 to 2002, the number of radios roughly doubled to an estimated 111 million, and radio remains the main source of news for most Indians.

GOVERNMENT AND POLITICS

Government Overview

India is a democratic republic with a system of government legally based on the often-amended 1950 constitution. The central government is also known as the union government, and its structure is much like the British parliamentary system, with distinct, but interrelated executive, legislative, and judicial branches. State governments are structured much like the central government, and district governments exist in a variety of forms. The Indian parliament is a bicameral legislature composed of a lower house (the Lok Sabha or House of the People), with 543 popularly elected members and 2 members appointed by the president, and an upper house (the Rajya Sabha or Council of States), with 12 appointed members and 233 members elected by state and union territory assemblies. Lok Sabha members serve five-year terms, and Rajya Sabha members serve six-year terms, with one-third of members up for election every two years. The legislature passes laws on constitutionally specified matters, such as central government finances and constitutional amendments. The two houses have the same powers, but the Rajya Sabha's power in the legislative process is subordinate to the Lok Sabha.

India has both a prime minister and a president. Members of parliament and state legislative assemblies elect the president, currently A.P.J. Abdul Kalam, who was elected in 2002. Prime ministers are leaders of the majority party in parliament but are formally appointed by the president. In 2004 Manmohan Singh became prime minister when his Indian National Congress party defeated the Bharatiya Janata Party led by Singh's predecessor as prime minister, Atal Bihari Vajpayee. Over time, political power has become increasingly concentrated in the prime minister and Council of Ministers (cabinet), although they are responsible to the parliament. The president's duties are mostly ceremonial, although the president formally approves the prime minister and also approves the Council of Ministers based on the prime minister's advice. Furthermore, all bills require presidential approval before becoming law. The vice president is ex officio chairperson of the Rajya Sabha and acts in place of the president when the president is unable to perform his or her duties.

The Supreme Court is the top legal entity, and it is composed of a chief justice appointed by the president and 25 associate judges also appointed by the president in consultation with the chief justice. The Supreme Court has numerous legal powers, such as appellate jurisdiction over all civil and criminal proceedings, with the potential of influencing interpretation of the constitution. The parliament and Supreme Court have maintained a contentious relationship on issues related to judicial review and parliamentary sovereignty. Below the Supreme Court are high courts, followed by a hierarchy of subordinate courts, and some states also have *panchayat* (village-level) courts that decide civil and criminal matters. Some high courts serve more than one state, and all are independent of state legislatures and executives. The judiciary is regarded as slow and cumbersome but is also widely respected and often takes an activist role in protecting citizens' rights.

Since independence, India has experienced a plethora of political successes and problems. Corruption, communal conflicts, and rural economic development remain difficult political issues. Furthermore, some analysts believe the government's inclusive design could undermine governing capacity and national unity as political parties and social groups press for their respective parochial interests. Yet the country maintains a democratic system of government with civil liberties that are often lacking in many poor, ethnically diverse societies. India also has an impressive record of economic development and a demonstrable commitment to correcting traditional social oppression. A wide variety of social groups have held elected office, and women, Sikhs, Muslims, and *dalits* have served as either president or prime minister. In 2004 there were 45 women elected to the Lok Sabha, and both *dalits* and indigenous groups have a certain minimum number of reserved seats in the Lok Sabha and state assemblies based on their respective percentages of the population.

Administrative Divisions

There are twenty-eight states and seven union territories including the national capital territory of New Delhi. State boundaries are often based on language or other social characteristics, and union territories tend to be geographically smaller and less populous than states. States and union territories contain 601 districts that are further subdivided into townships containing from 200 to 600 villages. The union government exercises greater control over union territories than over states, but the division of power between the union and state governments can appear blurred and even chaotic at times. Relationships between some state governments and the union government have been contentious, particularly when state governments are run by political parties that oppose the governing party or coalition in parliament. The tremendous variations in economic and social development among states suggest that state governments can have a greater influence on their populations than the union government. However, the union government still exercises considerable influence on states through numerous financial resources and its authority to assume control of states during times of emergency (called President's Rule), which the union government has done nearly 100 times since 1947.

Provincial and Local Government

Union territories have a council of ministers, a legislature, and a high court, but they are largely governed by the central or union government through a lieutenant governor or chief commissioner appointed by the prime minister. The structure of state governments largely mirrors that of the union government, with each state having a legislative assembly, chief minister, and high court. State government policies are largely implemented through state-level agencies, but union government agencies are also prevalent at local levels. District and local governments are generally weak, although some states have attempted to establish traditional village councils (*panchayats*) to address local matters.

State legislatures are usually unicameral with a legislative assembly composed of members elected for five-year terms. Bicameral state legislatures also have a legislative council that is largely advisory in its capacities, with members directly elected, indirectly elected, or nominated. States' chief ministers are the leaders of majority parties in state legislatures, and just as the prime minister is accountable to parliament, chief ministers are answerable to state legislatures. However, the popularity and party support of some chief ministers enable them to have some autonomy from their state legislature and a degree of influence that rivals that of the union government. States also have governors that are appointed by the president and accountable to the dominant political party in parliament. Although the position is largely honorific, governors do have important powers such as formal approval of chief ministers and their cabinets as well as the authority to recommend that the union government take control of a state government during times of emergency (President's Rule).

Judicial and Legal System

The legal system is derived from English common law and based on the 1950 constitution. Judges decide cases, and there is no trial by jury. Defendants can choose counsel independent of the government, and the government provides free legal counsel for defendants unable to afford such. The judiciary enforces the right to fair trial, and there are effective channels for appeal, but the judicial system is so overburdened with a case backlog that some courts barely function. In non-criminal matters, the government does not interfere with the personal status laws of Muslims and other communities on matters dealing with family law, inheritance, divorce, and discrimination against women.

The Indian constitution contains civil liberties called Fundamental Rights that are guaranteed to all citizens and include equality before the law and freedoms of speech, expression, religion, and association. Freedom of the press is not explicitly stated but is widely interpreted as included in the freedoms of speech and expression. The Fundamental Rights were also created with the objective of addressing historical social injustices and legally prohibit bonded labor, human trafficking, and discrimination based on religion, sex, race, caste, and birthplace. Still, the government has the authority to limit civil liberties in order to preserve public order, protect national security, and for other reasons.

Electoral System

The Election Commission is the independent government body that supervises parliamentary and state elections, which are massive and sometimes marred by violence. Elections for state assemblies and the Lok Sabha are held every five years unless called earlier, such as through a no-confidence vote of the government by the Lok Sabha. Indeed, elections are often held before the five-year limits because governments have often had difficulty staying in power for the full five-year term. In the 2004 general elections, there were more than 687,000 polling stations and 671.5 million voters. Since 1952, there have been 14 general elections, with voter turnout ranging from 55 to 64 percent of eligible voters. The legal voting age is 18. National and state legislative elections are similar to the British House of Commons and United States House of Representatives, in which members gain office by winning a plurality of votes in their local constituency. There are 543 parliamentary constituencies. The number of constituencies for state legislatures ranges from 32 to 403, with a total of 4,120 state constituencies nationwide.

Politics and Political Parties

From independence (1947) until 1989, the left-of-center Indian National Congress and its factions dominated national politics. In the 1990s, the center-right Bharatiya Janata Party (BJP) and the centrist Janata Dal emerged as influential political parties, although Congress returned to power in May 2004 with Manmohan Singh as prime minister. There are numerous national and state parties. Among the best known and most prominent are: Akali Dal, All-India Anna DMK (AIADMK), Asom Gana Parishad, Bahujan Samaj Party (BSP), Bharatiya Janata Party (BJP), Communist Party of India (CPI), Communist Party of India-Marxist (CPI-M), Dravida Munnetra Kazhagam (DMK), Indian National Congress, Rashtriya Janata Dal (RJD), Samajwadi Party, Samata Party, Shiv Sena, and Telugu Desam.

Since the late 1960s, minority parties in Parliament have often been majority parties in state legislatures. Since 1989, single political parties have generally failed to win a parliamentary majority. As a result, parliament is often run by coalitions of political parties. It is believed that the emergence of multiparty governments is caused by voters' frustration with political corruption and the fragmentation of electorate support among the growing number of political parties that represent specific parochial or local interests. Thus, those parties have strong support only in particular states. Furthermore, lower castes and other social groups have become more involved in politics as both voters and politicians. It remains to be seen if these trends are indicative of increasing social fragmentation as parties attempt to advance parochial interests or simply the result of a socially diverse population's increasing participation in politics.

Mass Media

India has more newspapers than any other nation, and newspaper readership annually grows by millions. There are a few state-run newspapers, but most print media are privately owned. There are more than 5,600 daily newspapers and more than 46,000 non-daily newspapers and print periodicals. In 2002 the government allowed print media to be up to 26 percent foreign owned, but the most powerful publishers are joint stock companies that frequently have other commercial and industrial holdings. Government authorities control most television channels, yet the growth of private FM and television stations has marked a shift away from mostly state-run electronic media such as Doordarshan (television) and All

India Radio. Foreign television channels are available through cable television or Indian broadcasters. An estimated 42.3 percent of Indian households have a television, and 52.2 percent of those have cable or satellite transmission. Similarly, the number of Internet users has rapidly to an estimated 18.4 million users in 2003. Article 19 of India's constitution ensures freedom of speech and expression, but Article 19 also allows the government to place "reasonable restrictions" on the exercise of those rights under various circumstances, such as maintenance of public order, state security, and public morality. India does have a high degree of press and speech freedom, and the nation is not generally regarded as a major violator of civil liberties by international human rights organizations. However, the government and police have been accused of violating journalists' civil liberties.

Foreign Relations

India's Ministry of External Affairs is the governmental body that is officially responsible for making and implementing foreign policy, although India's prime ministers have often exercised substantial influence in foreign policy decision making. India's parliament and armed forces historically have had very limited roles in the formulation of foreign policy.

India's relations with all major nations traditionally have been based on principles of nonalignment and India's own economic development. The overlapping domestic and external dimensions of India's economic development continue to illustrate that many matters related to India's ongoing formation as a nation have international security implications. Attempts to promote economic growth have pushed India from its previous emphasis on domestic self-sufficiency to a major promoter of free trade and economic liberalization. Nonalignment, however, has been seriously tested as a viable basis for foreign policy with the erosion of U.S. and Soviet tensions and with India's interest in playing an influential role in regional and world politics. The demise of India's long-term ally the Soviet Union cost India precious military and financial aid as well as international leverage. Some analysts argue that India's demonstration of nuclear capabilities in 1998 was driven as much by domestic desires to protect Indian influence and prestige internationally as by regional security concerns. Post-Cold War shifts in military power and concerns with terrorism have led India to create stronger bilateral relations with China, Israel, the United States, and other nations.

The Ministry of External Affairs has generally been most concerned with relations with neighboring Nepal, Sri Lanka, and particularly Pakistan on issues concerning unresolved borders, natural resource distribution, immigration, and insurgent activity. India has often tried to use treaties, alliances, and economic coercion to counter actions by neighbors that India regards as security threats, although China and Pakistan have generally thwarted such attempts. Indeed, India's security concerns have been most pronounced with Pakistan, as exemplified by the two countries' newfound nuclear rivalry, the 1999 Kargil War in Jammu and Kashmir, and the 2001 terrorist attack on India's parliament, which Pakistan is suspected of supporting. In spite of these difficulties, tensions between India and Pakistan have periodically thawed, and in late 2004 the two countries demonstrated surprising public interest in resolving their enduring dispute over Jammu and Kashmir.

Membership in International Organizations

India is a member of numerous international organizations including: African Development Bank, Asian Development Bank, Association of Southeast Asian Nations (dialogue partner), Bank for International Settlements, Colombo Plan, Commonwealth, Food and Agriculture Organization of the United Nations, Group of Six, Group of 15, Group of 24, Group of 77, International Atomic Energy Agency, International Bank for Reconstruction and Development, International Chamber of Commerce, International Civil Aviation Organization, International Confederation of Free Trade Unions, International Development Association, International Federation of Red Cross and Red Crescent Societies, International Finance Corporation, International Fund for Agricultural Development, International Hydrographic Organization, International Labour Organization, International Maritime Organization, International Monetary Fund, International Olympic Committee, International Organization for Migration (observer), International Organization for Standardization, International Red Cross and Red Crescent Movement, International Telecommunication Union, Interpol, Nonaligned Movement, Organisation for the Prohibition of Chemical Weapons, Organization of American States (observer), Permanent Court of Arbitration, South Asian Association for Regional Cooperation, United Nations, United Nations Conference on Trade and Development, United Nations Educational, Scientific and Cultural Organization, United Nations High Commissioner for Refugees, United Nations Industrial Development Organization, United Nations Monitoring, Verification and Inspection Commission, Universal Postal Union, World Confederation of Labor, World Customs Organization, World Federation of Trade Unions, World Health Organization, World Intellectual Property Organization, World Meteorological Organization, World Tourism Organization, and World Trade Organization.

Major International Treaties

India is a signatory to numerous international treaties including: the Antarctic Treaty, Basel Convention on the Control of Transboundary Movements of Hazardous Substances, Biological and Toxin Weapons Convention, Chemical Weapons Convention, Conference on Disarmament, Convention on Biological Diversity, Convention on International Trade in Endangered Species of Wild Flora and Fauna, Convention on Migratory Species, Convention on the Physical Protection of Nuclear Material, Convention on the Prohibition of Military or Any Other Hostile Use of Environmental Modification Techniques, Convention on Wetlands of International Importance Especially as Waterfowl Habitat, Geneva Protocol, International Atomic Energy Association Safeguards Agreement, International Convention for the Regulation of Whaling, International Plant Protection Convention, International Tropical Timber Agreement 1983, International Tropical Timber Agreement 1994, Kyoto Protocol to the United Nations Framework Convention on Climate Change, Montreal Protocol on Substances that Deplete the Ozone layer, Nuclear Safety Convention, Partial Test Ban Treaty, Protocol of 1978 Relating to the International Convention for the Prevention of Pollution from Ships, Protocol on Environmental Protection to the Antarctic Treaty, United Nations Convention on the Law of the Sea, United Nations Convention to Combat Desertification, United Nations Framework Convention on Climate Change, and Vienna Convention for the

Protection of the Ozone Layer. India is not a party to the Treaty on the NonProliferation of Nuclear Weapons (NPT) or the Missile Technology Control Regime. Indian governments have argued that the NPT does not reduce nuclear weapons proliferation by states already possessing nuclear weapons and that the NPT denies non-nuclear states the right to have nuclear weapons.

NATIONAL SECURITY

Armed Forces Overview

The prime minister and Council of Ministers formulate national security policy. Below this level is the civilian bureaucracy, which exercises important influence, primarily through the Defence Minister's Committee of the cabinet. The third tier of defense policy making is the Chiefs of Staffs Committee. These three levels are supported by intelligence organizations, scientific and technical advisory committees, defense production, and research and development groups. There are three military services—army, navy, and air force—and a number of paramilitary and reserve forces. The army has been the dominant service in terms of both percentage of budget allotted to the armed forces and percentage of persons serving in the armed forces.

The military has undergone tremendous change since the early 1990s, and the government and military have seriously appraised the military's capabilities and organization. India's great-power aspirations have been continually hindered by its capabilities, but the situation has changed with India's emergence as a nuclear power after successful nuclear tests in May 1998 (India has since pledged a unilateral moratorium on nuclear testing). The armed services' goals of force modernization (particularly the navy and air force) through new arms acquisitions and a "Revolution in Military Affairs" via information technology are constrained by budgetary, bureaucratic, personnel, and technological obstacles. Although the military has long desired to rely on domestically produced military goods, much matériel is imported. Indeed, the Defense Research and Development Organization (DRDO), the arm of the Department of Defence responsible for providing military hardware, has been criticized by both parliament and the military for failing to provide even basic equipment, and several DRDO projects have been behind schedule. The 1984 merger of the Department of Defence Production and the Department of Defence Supplies has not yet led to reliance on domestic production of military hardware.

Service chiefs and military officers continually suggest that the military should have greater input into defense policymaking and national security, and generally such a role is not viewed as a threat to civilian control of the military. Since 2001, the government has established the Defence Intelligence Agency (DIA), the Defence Acquisitions Council (DAC, which now controls the DRDO), and the National Security Council (NSC), which suggests that India has rethought its defense policymaking structure. The government has also proposed creating a Chief of Defence Staff. However, these changes have yet to make a major impact. Indeed, the NSC issued the draft nuclear doctrine but has not otherwise played an important role in defense policymaking and is criticized as an ad hoc organization.

In 2004 there were approximately 1,325,000 active-duty personnel, with 1,100,000 in the army, 55,000 in the navy (5,000 in naval aviation and 1,200 marines), and 170,000 in the air force. Reserve forces personnel totaled 535,000, and there were fourteen paramilitary forces (including the coast guard) under the control of various ministries with a total strength of 1,089,700 in 2004.

Foreign Military Relations

India's most important bilateral relationship was with the Soviet Union, whose breakup cost India both a consistent soft-currency supplier of arms and a guardian of its interests in international forums. Since the late 1990s, arms purchases from Russia have increased, and military relations between the countries have changed from a buyer-seller relationship to collaborative development of military systems and occasional joint military exercises. Furthermore, in 2000 India and Russia signed a Declaration of Strategic Relationship that addresses military and technical cooperation and "deepening service to service cooperation." India has strengthened bilateral defense links with France, Israel, Poland, South Africa, and the United States through various combinations of military acquisitions, agreements, and joint exercises. India has also attempted to project its influence beyond South Asia by engaging in occasional joint operations with Indian Ocean nations and participating in its first summit with the Association of Southeast Asian Nations in November 2002.

Furthermore, Indian peacekeeping forces have been sent to Sri Lanka from 1987 to 1990 and to the Maldives in 1988. Since 1950 Indian military and police contingents have participated in United Nations (UN) peacekeeping forces in Angola, Bosnia and Herzegovina, Cambodia, Democratic Republic of the Congo, Costa Rica, Cyprus, Dominican Republic, El Salvador, Ethiopia and Eritrea, Gaza, Guatemala, Honduras, Iraq, Korea (during the Korean War), Kuwait, Laos, Lebanon, Liberia, Mozambique, Namibia, Nicaragua, Rwanda, Sierra Leone, Somalia, Vietnam, West New Guinea (West Irian), Yemen, and Yugoslavia. India has also provided police personnel and monitors for UN peacekeeping operations in Angola, Bosnia and Herzegovina, Cambodia, Haiti, Kosovo, Mozambique, Sierra Leone, and Western Sahara.

Foreign Military Forces

The only foreign military forces in India are with the United Nations Military Observer Group in India and Pakistan (UNMOGIP), which has 45 military observers from 9 countries stationed in Jammu and Kashmir.

External Threat

External security threats come from neighboring countries and insurgents using foreign border areas as havens for activities in India. Countries such as Bangladesh, Bhutan, and Sri Lanka present no conventional military threat to India, but their inability to police and control areas bordering India has provided Indian insurgents with havens. Indian government and military officials have publicly expressed concern about the political instability in Nepal posed by the Maoist insurgents. As far as external threats posed by other countries, popular opinion tends to regard Pakistan as the principal enemy, largely because of the Kashmir conflict and Pakistan's suspected links to numerous South Asian militant groups. However, the defense establishment generally regards China as the chief external threat, because of perceived Chinese attempts to isolate India militarily and diplomatically from the rest of Asia and perceived Chinese efforts to prevent India from becoming a permanent member of the United Nations (UN) Security Council. While China-India border issues remain unresolved from the Indian point of view, Sino-Indian relations have improved as China has adopted a less intimate relationship with Pakistan.

Defense Budget

India's defense budget has grown tremendously since the early 1990s, and India accounts for more than two-thirds of South Asian military spending. India's defense budget was approximately US$16.6 billion in 2003, about 2.5 percent of gross domestic product (GDP), and the 2004 defense budget is US$19.1 billion. By contrast, the 1994 defense budget was US$7.6 billion, which was also 2.5 percent of GDP in 1994. Interestingly, as a result of inefficient equipment procurement processes, defense expenditures are often less than the defense budget (around 5 percent less).

Major Military Units

The army has an estimated 800,000 active-duty troops and 300,000 reserves. The army is structured as 12 corps, 4 field armies, and 3 armored divisions under central control and organized into 5 regional commands. The Northern regional command consists of three corps with eight infantry and five mountain divisions; the Western regional command has one armored, five infantry, and three "RAPID" divisions; the Central regional command has one corps with one armored, one infantry, and one RAPID division; the Eastern regional command has three corps with one infantry and seven mountain divisions; and the Southern regional command has two corps with one armored and three infantry divisions. The navy has an estimated 55,000 persons on active duty and an equal number of reserve troops. Navy units are structured into three area commands, and there are six naval bases with three more under construction. The air force has an estimated 170,000 active forces and 140,000 reserves. Air force units are under five regional air commands.

Major Military Equipment

The army's main equipment includes an estimated 3,898 main battle tanks, 1,600 armored infantry fighting vehicles, 317 armored personnel carriers, 4,175 towed artillery, 200 self-propelled artillery, 150 multiple rocket launchers, 2,424 air defense guns, and 100 helicopters. The navy's arsenal is composed of 1 aircraft carrier, 18 submarines, 8 destroyers, 16 frigates, 26 corvettes, 7 amphibious ships, 88 fixed-wing aircraft, and more than 100 helicopters. The air force's principal equipment consists of 679 combat aircraft of various types and 40 armed helicopters. India and its perennial rival, Pakistan, have developed nuclear weapons, ostensibly to deter foreign hostility, yet periodic fighting in Kashmir—such as the 1999 Kargil War—suggests that the theoretical logic of deterrence has not yet taken hold.

For decades, the military has aspired to domestic production of most items, but it relies heavily on imports of both simple items, such as clothing, and complex weapons systems. Observers contend that India has not done well with the production of tanks, helicopters, and submarines, but has fared better with missiles, small arms, and naval craft. Moreover, India's substantial spending on defense has stirred some debate about how much the defense industry should be privatized in order to avoid a collapse similar to that suffered by the Soviet Union. However, it is believed that the Ministry of Defence's civilian bureaucracy opposes privatization in order to protect employment in an overstaffed state bureaucracy. There has been some consideration of exporting arms to make up for budget shortfalls, but exports—and concrete efforts to increase them—remain minimal.

Military Service

The minimum age of service is 16, and the mandatory age for retirement for officers varies from 48 to 60 depending on rank. The military has expressed concern about its increasing age profile and a shortage of officers. Formal military service is completely on a volunteer basis, and India does not have—and never has had—conscription. However, a 2004 public opinion poll suggests that the Indian public is in favor of conscription.

Paramilitary Forces

Police are under the control of state governments, and the central government can assist states by providing central paramilitary forces as deemed necessary, particularly to guard coasts, borders, and sensitive military areas and to aid local police forces against insurgencies. There is also a great deal of interest in improving paramilitary training, hardware, and domestic intelligence, as paramilitary forces are often outdone by insurgents in both combat and the use of sophisticated hardware and weapons. There are 1,089,700 active paramilitary personnel (including police) and 1,027,000 voluntary reserves. The Ministry of Home Affairs controls the Central Reserve Police Force (CRPF; 167,400 active); Assam Rifles (52,500); Border Security Force (BSF; 174,000); Indo-Tibetan Border Police (ITBP; 32,400); and National Security Guard, which is composed of elements of the armed forces, CRPF, and BSF (NSG; 7,400). Other paramilitary forces include the Central Industrial Security Force (95,000), Special Protection Group (3,000), Special Frontier Force (9,000), Defence Security Corps (31,000), Railway Protection Forces (70,000), and Coast Guard (more than 8,000 with 34 patrol craft). Voluntary forces include the Home Guard (574,000) and Civil Defence (453,000). Voluntary forces typically have little military training and are used for civil disturbances and relief work.

Police

As of October 2002, there were 1,015,416 police officers in India for a national average of 1 police officer per 125 persons. Police are under the control of state governments, and, with central government permission, states are allowed to create police reserve battalions; all 13 reserve police battalions are in insurgent-prone northeastern states. State police are often assisted by—and some say depend upon—paramilitaries and the armed forces for the maintenance of internal security. An August 2000 government report on police reforms suggested that the Indian police should improve their relations with civilians, place a higher priority on crime prevention, and obtain improved infrastructure. The previous review of the nation's police was conducted in the late 1970s, and its recommendations are as yet unimplemented.

Internal Threats and Terrorism

India's top security concerns are mostly internal. Indeed, much of the national security apparatus is directed to maintaining territorial integrity as dozens of groups push for varying degrees of political or social autonomy, sometimes violently. India treats separatism with extreme concern given the possibility that successful separatism may establish a precedent that other groups might seek to follow. Internal threats can be categorized as religiously oriented conflict or ethnic violence, usually with separatist objectives. The 10-year Khalistani separatist conflict in Punjab terminated in 1994, but separatist violence periodically escalates in Indian-controlled Jammu and Kashmir. Numerous separatist insurgent groups are active in the northeast, and India has periodically expanded its military efforts in Assam against groups such as the United Liberation Front of Assam (ULFA), National Democratic Front of Bodoland (NDFB), and Bodo Security Force (BSF). Other rebel groups in Assam observe ceasefire agreements with the government. The decades-long separatist conflict in Nagaland continues with the National Socialist Council of Nagaland-Khapland (NSCN-K), although peace talks have occurred with another faction, the NSCN-IM (Isaac Muivah), after the government lifted its previous ban on the organization. In Tripura, various insurgents continue to target Bengali immigrants and Indian security forces.

Religiously oriented violence has occurred, principally among Hindus and Muslims and most notably in Ayodyha (in Uttar Pradesh) and urban areas of Gujarat and Maharashtra. While less common than separatist violence, these conflicts prompt greater popular debates on Indian history, society, and politics; there are allegations that national and state-level politicians with the Bharatiya Janata Party (BJP) have facilitated such conflicts.

Human Rights

Although human rights problems exist in India, the country is generally not regarded as among the world's serious human rights violators. Human rights problems appear to be acute in areas and periods of communal violence, and security forces, insurgents, and various ethnic-based groups have all been accused of human rights violations in Jammu and Kashmir, Gujarat, Maharashtra, Uttar Pradesh, and various northeastern states. Furthermore, Hindu organizations have been accused of attacking religious minorities—particularly Muslims and Christians—and of receiving deferential treatment and even outright support from some political parties. Both international human rights organizations and India's National Human Rights Commission have questioned the impartiality of police and judicial authorities in various locales.

On the other hand, human rights groups have praised India's September 2004 repeal of the 2002 Prevention of Terrorism Act, which both the newly elected government and international organizations criticized as enabling human rights abuses by security forces. Indian media routinely address controversial issues, such as political corruption and discrimination against women, sexual minorities, indigenous peoples, and "untouchables." However, the government has been accused of harassing and jailing journalists who investigate topics such as corruption and the situation in Kashmir. Moreover, in response to cyber-crime and cyber-terrorism perpetrated by parties in both India and Pakistan, India passed the Information Technology Act of 2000, which allows cybercafés and Internet users' homes to be searched without warrants at any time as part of criminal investigations.

In: India on the Move
Editor: Lea M. Surit, pp. 33-68

ISBN: 978-1-60021-813-2
© 2007 Nova Science Publishers, Inc.

Chapter 2

India-U.S. Relations[*]

K. Alan Kronstadt

ABSTRACT

Long considered a "strategic backwater" from Washington's perspective, South Asia has emerged in the 21st century as increasingly vital to core U.S. foreign policy interests. India, the region's dominant actor with more than one billion citizens, is now recognized as a nascent major power and "natural partner" of the United States, one that many analysts view as a potential counterweight to China's growing clout. Washington and New Delhi have since 2004 been pursuing a "strategic partnership" based on shared values such as democracy, multi-culturalism, and rule of law. Numerous economic, security, and global initiatives, including plans for "full civilian nuclear energy cooperation," are underway. This latter initiative, launched by President Bush in July 2005 and provisionally endorsed by the 109th Congress in late 2006 (P.L. 109-401), reverses three decades of U.S. nonproliferation policy. It would require, among other steps, conclusion of a peaceful nuclear agreement between the United States and India, which would itself enter into force only after a Joint Resolution of Approval by Congress. Also in 2005, the United States and India signed a ten-year defense framework agreement that calls for expanding bilateral security cooperation. Since 2002, the two countries have engaged in numerous and unprecedented combined military exercises. The issue of major U.S. arms sales to India may come before the 110th Congress. The influence of a growing and relatively wealthy Indian-American community of more than two million is reflected in Congress's largest country-specific caucus.

Further U.S. interest in South Asia focuses on ongoing tensions between India and Pakistan, a problem rooted in unfinished business from the 1947 Partition, competing claims to the Kashmir region, and, in more recent years, "cross-border terrorism" in both Kashmir and major Indian cities. In the interests of regional stability, the United States strongly encourages an ongoing India-Pakistan peace initiative and remains concerned about the potential for conflict over Kashmiri sovereignty to cause open hostilities between these two nuclear-armed countries. The United States seeks to curtail the proliferation of nuclear weapons and ballistic missiles in South Asia. Both India and Pakistan have resisted external pressure to sign the major nonproliferation treaties. In

---

[*] Excerpted from CRS Report RL33529, dated January 3, 2007.

1998, the two countries conducted nuclear tests that evoked international condemnation. Proliferation-related restrictions on U.S. aid were triggered, then later lifted through congressional-executive cooperation from 1998 to 2000. Remaining sanctions on India (and Pakistan) were removed in October 2001.

India is in the midst of major and rapid economic expansion. Many U.S. business interests view India as a lucrative market and candidate for foreign investment. The United States supports India's efforts to transform its once quasi-socialist economy through fiscal reform and market opening. Since 1991, India has taken steps in this direction, with coalition governments keeping the country on a general path of reform. Yet there is U.S. concern that such movement remains slow and inconsistent. Congress also continues to have concerns about abuses of human rights, including caste- and gender-based discrimination, and religious freedoms in India. Moreover, the spread of HIV/AIDS in India has attracted congressional attention as a serious development.

Most Recent Developments

- On December 22, two days of India-Pakistan talks on the militarized Sir Creek dispute ended with agreement to conduct a joint survey. In mid-November, the India-Pakistan "Composite Dialogue" recommenced when the Indian and Pakistani foreign secretaries held formal meetings in New Delhi, the first such meetings since New Delhi's suspension of the peace process in the wake of July 11 terrorist bombings in Bombay. New Indian Foreign Secretary Shiv Shankar Menon called the talks "very useful and constructive" and, along with Pakistani Foreign Secretary Riaz Khan, further developed the planned joint anti-terrorism mechanism mandated by Prime Minister Singh and Pakistani President Pervez Musharraf on the sidelines of a September Nonaligned Movement summit in Cuba. The foreign secretaries also reviewed the peace process and developments in Kashmir, but made no announcements on longstanding territorial disputes or the status of investigations into the Bombay bombings (in October, Prime Minister Singh said India had "credible evidence" of Pakistan's involvement in those bombings).

- On December 18, President Bush signed into law H.R. 5682, the Henry J. Hyde United States-India Peaceful Atomic Energy Cooperation Act of 2006 (P.L. 109-401), to enable civil nuclear cooperation with India. Days earlier, a conference report (H.Rept. 109-721) had been issued to accompany the bill; congressional conferees had reconciled House and Senate versions of the legislation and provided a 30-page explanatory statement. The Indian government welcomed the developments while also claiming the legislation contained "extraneous and prescriptive provisions," and Prime Minister Singh said "clearly difficult negotiations lie ahead." Vocal critics of the initiative in its current form include India's main opposition Bharatiya Janata Party, influential Left Front leaders, and some members of the country's nuclear scientific community, who express various concerns about potentially negative effects on India's scientific and foreign policy independence. (See also CRS Report RL33016, *U.S. Nuclear Cooperation With India.*)

- On December 15, Prime Minister Singh paid a visit to Tokyo, where India and Japan inked 12 bilateral agreements to forward their "strategic partnership," including negotiations toward a future free trade agreement. Tokyo withheld endorsement of India's entry into the civilian nuclear club.

- On December 8, day, Under Secretary of State Nicolas Burns met with Foreign Secretary Shiv Shankar Menon in New Delhi to discuss "progress in all the areas" of U.S.-India relations.

- On December 4, Pakistani President Musharraf said Pakistan is "against independence" for Kashmir, instead offering a four-point proposal that would lead to "self-governance," defined as "falling between autonomy and independence." Many analysts saw the proposal as being roughly in line with New Delhi's Kashmir position. Prime Minster Singh later welcomed Musharraf's proposals, saying they "contribute to the ongoing thought process."

- On November 28, a delegation of 250 American business executives arrived in Bombay on a mission to explore new opportunities to invest in India and develop new partnerships with companies there. The delegation, led by Under Secretary of Commerce Franklin Lavin, represented 180 companies from a variety of sectors and is the largest-ever to visit India.

- On November 23, Chinese President Hu Jintao ended a four-day visit to India, the first such visit by a Chinese president since 1996. Two days earlier, India and China issued a Joint Declaration which outlined a "ten-pronged strategy" to boost bilateral socio-economic ties and defense cooperation, and to "reinforce their strategic partnership." The two countries, which declared themselves "partners for mutual benefit" rather than rivals or competitors, also signed 13 pacts on a variety of bilateral initiatives. The Joint Declaration notably contained an agreement to "promote cooperation in the field of nuclear energy." Outstanding border disputes, including China's continuing claim to 35,000 square miles of Indian territory, remain unresolved.

- On November 18, Agriculture Secretary Mike Johanns was in New Delhi for meetings with top Indian officials in New Delhi to discuss trade issues and to "get the Doha talks back on track." Secretary Johanns urged India to further open its farm markets to exports from other countries.

- On November 17, Iranian Foreign Minister Manouchehr Mottaki held talks with top Indian officials in New Delhi, where he said Tehran would "very soon" begin exports to India of liquid natural gas under a $21 billion, five million tons per year deal. According to New Delhi, India and Iran agreed that "the economic potential of the relationship needed to be actualized in the maximum."

- Also on November 16, a two-day meeting of the U.S.-India Defense Policy Group ended in New Delhi, where Under Secretary of Defense Eric Edelman and other U.S. officials expressed optimism about the potential for major arms sales to India in 2007.

- On November 5, a series of bombings in the northeastern Assam state left at least 15 people dead and dozens more injured. Police blamed the separatist the United Liberation Front of Assam (ULFA). A spike in violence in the region follows New Delhi's September withdrawal from a six-week-long truce with ULFA after militants shot dead a policeman and a civilian.

CONTEXT OF THE U.S.-INDIA RELATIONSHIP

Background

U.S. and congressional interests in India cover a wide spectrum of issues, ranging from the militarized dispute with Pakistan and weapons proliferation to concerns about regional security, terrorism, human rights, health, energy, and trade and investment opportunities. In the 1990s, India-U.S. relations were particularly affected by the demise of the Soviet Union — India's main trading partner and most reliable source of economic and military assistance for most of the Cold War — and New Delhi's resulting need to diversify its international relationships. Also significant were India's adoption of significant economic policy reforms beginning in 1991, a deepening bitterness between India and Pakistan over Kashmir, and signs of a growing Indian preoccupation with China as a potential long-term strategic rival. With the fading of Cold War constraints, the United States and India began exploring the possibilities for a more normalized relationship between the world's two largest democracies. Throughout the 1990s, however, regional rivalries, separatist tendencies, and sectarian tensions continued to divert India's attention and resources from economic and social development. Fallout from these unresolved problems — particularly nuclear proliferation and human rights issues — presented irritants in bilateral relations.

India's May 1998 nuclear tests were an unwelcome surprise and seen to be a policy failure in Washington, and they spurred then-Deputy Secretary of State Strobe Talbott to launch a series of meetings with Indian External Affairs Minister Jaswant Singh in an effort to bring New Delhi more in line with U.S. arms control and nonproliferation goals. While this proximate purpose went unfulfilled, the two officials soon engaged a broader agenda on the entire scope of U.S.-India relations, eventually meeting fourteen times in seven different countries over a two-year period. The Talbott-Singh talks were considered the most extensive U.S.-India engagement up to that time and likely enabled circumstances in which the United States could play a key role in defusing the 1999 Kargil crisis, as well as laying the groundwork for a landmark U.S. presidential visit in 2000.

President Bill Clinton's March 2000 visit to South Asia seemed a major U.S. initiative to improve relations with India. One outcome was a Joint Statement in which the two countries pledged to "deepen the India-American partnership in tangible ways."[1] A U.S.-India Joint Working Group on Counterterrorism was established that year and continues to meet regularly. During his subsequent visit to the United States later in 2000, Prime Minister Atal Bihari Vajpayee addressed a joint session of Congress and issued a second Joint Statement with President Clinton agreeing to cooperate on arms control, terrorism, and HIV/AIDS.[2]

In the wake of the September 2001 terrorist attacks on the United States, India took the immediate and unprecedented step of offering to the United States full cooperation and the use of India's bases for counterterrorism operations. Engagement was accelerated after a November 2001 meeting between President Bush and Prime Minister Vajpayee, when the two leaders agreed to greatly expand U.S.-India cooperation on a wide range of issues, including regional security, space and scientific collaboration, civilian nuclear safety, and broadened economic ties.[3] Notable progress has come in the area of security cooperation, with an increasing focus on counterterrorism, joint military exercises, and arms sales. In late 2001, the U.S.-India Defense Policy Group met in New Delhi for the first time since India's 1998 nuclear tests and outlined a defense partnership based on regular and high-level policy dialogue.

India in Brief

Population: 1.1 billion; *growth rate*: 1.4% (2006 est.)

Area: 3,287,590 sq. km. (slightly more than onethird the size of the United States)

Capital: New Delhi

Head of Government: Prime Minister Manmohan Singh (Congress Party)

Ethnic Groups: Indo-Aryan 72%; Dravidian 25%; other 3%

Languages: 15 official, 13 of which are the primary tongue of at least 10 million people; Hindi is primary tongue of about 30%; English widely used

Religions: Hindu 81%; Muslim 13%; Christian 2%; Sikh 2%, other 2% (2001 census)

Life Expectancy at Birth: female 65.6 years; male 63.9 years (2006 est.)

Literacy: female 48%; male 70% (2003 est.)

Gross Domestic Product (at PPP): $4.24 trillion; *per capita*: $3,870; *growth rate* 8.5% (2006 est.)

Currency: Rupee (100 = $2.27)

Inflation: 5.6% (2006 est.)

Military Expenditures: $22.8 billion (2.9% of GDP; 2005)

U.S. Trade: exports to U.S. $21.9 billion; imports from U.S. $9.9 billion (2006 est.)

Sources: CIA World Factbook; U.S. Commerce Department; Economist Intelligence Unit; Global Insight.

Prime Minister Manmohan Singh paid a landmark July 2005 visit to Washington, where what may be the most significant joint U.S.-India statement to date was issued.[4] In March 2006, President Bush spent three days in India, discussed further strengthening a bilateral "global partnership," and issued another Joint Statement.[5] Today, the Bush Administration vows to "help India become a major world power in the 21st century," and U.S.-India relations are conducted under the rubric of three major "dialogue" areas: strategic (including global issues and defense), economic (including trade, finance, commerce, and environment), and energy. President Bush's 2002 *National Security Strategy of the United States* stated that "U.S. interests require a strong relationship with India." The 2006 version claims that, "India now is poised to shoulder global obligations in cooperation with the United States in a way befitting a major power."[6] (See also CRS Report RL33072, *U.S.-India Bilateral Agreements.*)

Recognition of India's increasing stature and importance — and of the growing political influence some 2.3 million Indian-Americans — is found in the U.S. Congress, where the India and Indian-American Caucus is now the largest of all country-specific caucuses. Over the past six years, legal Indian immigrants have come to the United States at a more rapid rate than any other group. In 2005 and 2006, the Indian-American community, relatively wealthy, geographically dispersed, and well-entrenched in several U.S. business sectors, conducted a major (and apparently successful) lobbying effort to encourage congressional passage of legislation to enable U.S.-India civil nuclear cooperation.[7]

Current U.S.-India Engagement

Following President Bush's March 2006 visit to New Delhi — the first such trip by a U.S. President in six years — U.S. diplomatic engagement with India has continued to be deep and multifaceted:

- A two-day meeting of the U.S.-India Joint Working Group on Counterterrorism was held in April in Washington, where Counterterrorism Coordinator Henry Crumpton led the U.S. delegation.
- Indian Power Minister Sushil Shinde paid an April visit to Washington for meetings with top U.S. officials.
- The fourth meeting of the U.S.-India Trade Policy Forum took place in May in New Delhi, where talks focused on trade barriers, agriculture, investment, and intellectual property rights.
- In June, the Chairman of the U.S. Joint Chiefs of Staff, Gen. Peter Pace, met with top Indian officials in New Delhi to discuss expanding U.S.-India strategic ties.
- Also in June, new U.S. Trade Representative Susan Schwab met with Indian Commerce Minister Kamal Nath in Washington, agreeing on initiatives to strengthen and deepen bilateral trade.
- In July, President Bush met with Prime Minister Singh on the sidelines of the G-8 Summit in St. Petersburg, Russia, to discuss the 7/11 Bombay bombings and planned U.S.-India civil nuclear cooperation.
- In August, a delegation of U.S. officials, including President Bush's top energy and environment advisor, visited New Delhi to meet with top Indian officials and business leaders to discuss energy security and the environment.
- Also in August, a meeting of the U.S.-India Financial and Economic Forum was held in Washington, where officials discussed Indian efforts to liberalize its financial sector, among other issues.
- In September, U.S. and Indian army troops conducted joint counterinsurgency exercises in Hawaii.
- Defense Minister Pranab Mukherjee led an Indian delegation to the U.N. General Assembly session later in September and met with top U.S. officials in New York.
- In October, a meeting of the U.S.-India CEO Forum was held in New York City. Along with numerous U.S. and Indian business leaders, high-level government

officials joining the session included Commerce Secretary Carlos Gutierrez and Assistant to the President for Economic Policy Allan Hubbard from the American side, and Commerce Minister Kamal Nath and Planning Commission Deputy Minister Montek Singh Ahluwalia from India.

- Assistant Secretary of State Richard Boucher made a lengthy visit to India in November for meetings with top Indian leaders.
- In mid-November, U.S. Under Secretary of Defense Edelman met with Defense Secretary Dutt in New Delhi for the eighth session of the U.S.-India Defense Policy Group, where officials discussed bolstering bilateral cooperation in military security, technology, and trade.
- Also in mid-November, the U.S. Environmental Protection Agency announced establishment of a Methane to Markets Partnership to promote development of coal bed and coal methane projects in India.
- Later in November, Agriculture Secretary Michael Johannes visited New Delhi to discuss bilateral and multilateral trade issues with top Indian leaders.
- In late November, Under Secretary of Commerce Franklin Lavin led a delegation of 250 American business executives to Bombay on a mission to explore new opportunities to invest in India and develop new partnerships with companies there.
- In December, Under Secretary of Commerce and Director of the U.S. Patent and Trademark Office Jon Dudas visited New Delhi to discuss intellectual property rights and copyright protections with India leaders.
- Also in December, Under Secretary of State Nicholas Burns met with Foreign Secretary Shiv Shankar Menon in New Delhi to discuss progress in all areas of U.S.-India relations. (See also CRS Report RL33072, *U.S.-India Bilateral Agreements.*)

India's Regional Relations

India is geographically dominant in both South Asia and the Indian Ocean region. While all of South Asia's smaller continental states (Pakistan, Bangladesh, Nepal, and Bhutan) share borders with India, none share borders with each other. The country possesses the region's largest economy and, with more than one billion inhabitants, is by far the most populous on the Asian Subcontinent. The United States has a keen interest in South Asian stability, perhaps especially with regard to the India-Pakistan nuclear weapons dyad, and so closely monitors India's regional relationships.

Pakistan

Decades of militarized tensions and territorial disputes between India and Pakistan have seriously hamstrung economic and social development in both countries while also precluding establishment of effective regional economic or security institutions. Seemingly incompatible national identities contributed to the nuclearization of the Asian Subcontinent, with the nuclear weapons capabilities of both countries becoming overt in 1998. Since that time, a central aspect of U.S. policy in South Asia has been prevention of interstate conflict that could lead to nuclear war. In 2004, New Delhi and Islamabad launched their most recent comprehensive effort to reduce tensions and resolve outstanding disputes.

Current Status

The India-Pakistan peace initiative continues, with officials from both countries (and the United States) offering a generally positive assessment of the ongoing dialogue. In May 2006, India and Pakistan agreed to open a second Kashmiri bus route and to allow new truck service to facilitate trade in Kashmir (the new bus service began in June). Subsequent "Composite Dialogue" talks were held to discuss militarized territorial disputes, terrorism and narcotics, and cultural exchanges, but high hopes for a settlement of differences over the Siachen Glacier were dashed when a May session ended without progress. June talks on the Tubal navigation project/Wullar barrage water dispute similarly ended without forward movement.

Compounding tensions, separatist-related violence spiked in Indian Kashmir in the spring and summer of 2006, and included a May massacre of 35 Hindu villagers by suspected Islamic militants. Grenade attacks on tourist buses correlated with a late May roundtable meeting of Prime Minister Singh and Kashmiri leaders, leaving at least two dozen civilians dead and devastating the Valley's recently revitalized tourist industry. Significant incidents of attempted "cross-border infiltration" of Islamic militants at the Kashmiri Line of Control continue and top Indian leaders renewed their complaints that Islamabad is taking insufficient action to quell terrorist activities on Pakistan-controlled territory.

The serial bombing of Bombay commuter trains on July 11, 2006, killed nearly 200 people and injured many hundreds more. With suspicions regarding the involvement of Pakistan-based groups, New Delhi suspended talks with Islamabad pending an investigation. However, at a September meeting on the sidelines of a Nonaligned Movement summit in Cuba, Prime Minister Singh and Pakistani President Musharraf announced a resumption of formal peace negotiations and also decided to implement a joint anti-terrorism mechanism. Weeks later, Bombay's top police official said the 7/11 train bombings were planned by Pakistan's intelligence services and, in October, Prime Minister Singh himself said India had "credible evidence" of Pakistani involvement.

To date, India is not known to have gone public with or shared with Pakistan any incriminating evidence of Pakistani government involvement in the Bombay bombings. In November 2006, Composite Dialogue resumed with its third round of foreign secretary-level talks when Foreign Secretary Shiv Shankar Menon hosted a New Delhi visit by his Pakistani counterpart, Riaz Khan. No progress was made on outstanding territorial disputes, but the two officials did give shape to a joint anti-terrorism mechanism proposed in September. Such a mechanism is controversial in India, with some analysts skeptical about the efficacy of institutional engagement with Pakistan in this issue-area even as Islamabad is suspected of complicity in anti-India terrorism. The India-Pakistan peace process is slated to continue in early 2007 when External Affairs Minister Pranab Mukherjee is to visit Pakistan.

Background

Three wars — in 1947-48, 1965, and 1971 — and a constant state of military preparedness on both sides of the border have marked six decades of bitter rivalry between India and Pakistan. The bloody and acrimonious nature of the 1947 partition of British India and continuing violence in Kashmir remain major sources of interstate tensions. Despite the existence of widespread poverty across South Asia, both India and Pakistan have built large defense establishments —including nuclear weapons capability and ballistic missile programs — at the cost of economic and social development. The nuclear weapons capabilities of the two countries became overt in May 1998, magnifying greatly the potential dangers of a fourth

India-Pakistan war. Although a bilateral peace process has been underway for nearly three years, little substantive progress has been made toward resolving the Kashmir issue, and New Delhi continues to be rankled by what it calls Islamabad's insufficient effort to end Islamic militancy that affects India.

The Kashmir problem is itself rooted in claims by both countries to the former princely state, now divided by a military Line of Control (LOC) into the Indian state of Jammu and Kashmir and Pakistan-controlled Azad [Free] Kashmir (see "The Kashmir Issue," below). Normal relations between New Delhi and Islamabad were severed in December 2001 after a terrorist attack on the Indian Parliament was blamed on Pakistan-supported Islamic militants. Other lethal attacks on Indian civilians spurred Indian leaders to call for a "decisive war," but intense international diplomatic engagement, including multiple trips to the region by high-level U.S. officials, apparently persuaded India to refrain from attacking.[8] In October 2002, the two countries ended a tense, ten-month military standoff at their shared border, but there remained no high-level diplomatic dialogue between India and Pakistan (a July 2001 summit meeting in the Indian city of Agra had failed to produce any movement toward a settlement of the bilateral dispute).

In April 2003, Prime Minister Vajpayee extended a symbolic "hand of friendship" to Pakistan. The initiative resulted in slow, but perceptible progress in confidence-building, and within months full diplomatic relations between the two countries were restored. September 2003 saw an exchange of heated rhetoric by the Indian prime minister and the Pakistani president at the U.N. General Assembly; some analysts concluded that the peace initiative was moribund. Yet New Delhi soon reinvigorated the process by proposing confidence-building through people-to-people contacts. Islamabad responded positively and, in November, took its own initiatives, most significantly the offer of a cease-fire along the Kashmir LOC. A major breakthrough in bilateral relations came at the close of a January 2004 summit session of the South Asian Association for Regional Cooperation in Islamabad. After a meeting between Vajpayee and Pakistani President Musharraf — their first since July 2001 — the two leaders agreed to re-engage a "composite dialogue" to bring about "peaceful settlement of all bilateral issues, including Jammu and Kashmir, to the satisfaction of both sides."

A May 2004 change of governments in New Delhi had no effect on the expressed commitment of both sides to carry on the process of mid- and high-level discussions, and the new Indian Prime Minister, Manmohan Singh, met with President Musharraf in September 2004 in New York, where the two leaders agreed to explore possible options for a "peaceful, negotiated settlement" of the Kashmir issue "in a sincere manner and purposeful spirit." After Musharraf's April 2005 visit to New Delhi, India and Pakistan released a joint statement calling their bilateral peace process "irreversible." Some analysts believe that increased people-to-people contacts have significantly altered public perceptions in both countries and may have acquired permanent momentum. Others are less optimistic about the respective governments' long-term commitment to dispute resolution. Moreover, an apparent new U.S. embrace of India has fueled Pakistan's anxieties about the regional balance of power.

China

India and China together account for one-third of the world's population, and are seen to be rising 21st century powers and potential strategic rivals. The two countries fought a brief but intense border war in 1962 that left China in control of large swaths of territory still claimed by India. Today, India accuses China of illegitimately occupying nearly 15,000 square miles of Indian territory in Kashmir, while China lays claim to 35,000 square miles in the northeastern Indian state of Arunachal Pradesh. The 1962 clash ended a previously friendly relationship between the two leaders of the Cold War "nonaligned movement" and left many Indians feeling shocked and betrayed. While Sino-Indian relations have warmed considerably in recent years, the two countries have yet to reach a final boundary agreement. Adding to New Delhi's sense of insecurity have been suspicions regarding China's long-term nuclear weapons capabilities and strategic intentions in South and Southeast Asia. In fact, a strategic orientation focused on China appears to have affected the course and scope of New Delhi's own nuclear weapons and ballistic missile programs. Beijing's military and economic support for Pakistan —support that is widely understood to have included WMD-related transfers — is a major and ongoing source of friction; past Chinese support for Pakistan's Kashmir position has added to the discomfort of Indian leaders. New Delhi takes note of Beijing's security relations with neighboring Burma and the construction of military facilities on the Indian Ocean. The two countries also have competed for energy resources to feed their rapidly growing economies; India's relative poverty puts New Delhi at a significant disadvantage in such competition.

Analysts taking a realist perspective view China as an external balancer in the South Asian subsystem, with Beijing's material support for Islamabad allowing Pakistan to challenge the aspiring regional hegemony of a more powerful India. Many observers, especially in India, see Chinese support for Pakistan as a key aspect of Beijing's perceived policy of "encirclement" or constraint of India as a means of preventing or delaying New Delhi's ability to challenge Beijing's region-wide influence.

Despite historic and strategic frictions, high-level exchanges between India and China regularly include statements that there exists no fundamental conflict of interest between the two countries. During a landmark 1993 visit to Beijing, Prime Minister Narasimha Rao signed an agreement to reduce troops and maintain peace along the Line of Actual Control that divides the two countries' forces at the disputed border. A total of 30 rounds of border talks and joint working group meetings aimed at reaching a final settlement have been held since 1981, with New Delhi and Beijing agreeing to move forward in other issue-areas even as territorial claims remain unresolved.

A 2003 visit to Beijing by Prime Minister Vajpayee was viewed as marking a period of much improved relations. In late 2004, India's army chief visited Beijing to discuss deepening bilateral defense cooperation and a first-ever India-China strategic dialogue was later held in New Delhi. Military-to-military contacts have included modest but unprecedented combined naval and army exercises. During Chinese Prime Minister Wen Jiabao's April 2005 visit to New Delhi, India and China inked 11 new agreements and vowed to launch a "strategic partnership" that will include broadened defense links and efforts to expand economic relations.[9] In a move that eased border tensions, China formally recognized Indian sovereignty over the former kingdom of Sikkim, and India reiterated its view that Tibet is a part of China. Moreover, in 2006, dubbed the "Year of India-China Friendship," the two countries formally agreed to cooperate in securing overseas oil resources. In July of that year, India and China reopened the Nathu La border crossing for local trade. The Himalayan pass had been closed since the 1962 war. Sino-India trade relations are blossoming — bilateral commerce was worth nearly $19 billion in 2005, almost an eight-fold increase over the 1999 value. In fact, China may soon supplant the United States as India's largest trading partner.

Indo-Chinese relations further warmed in November 2006, when Chinese President Hu Jintao made a trip to India., the first such visit by a Chinese president since 1996. There India and China issued a Joint Declaration outlining a "ten-pronged strategy" to boost bilateral socio-economic ties and defense cooperation, and to "reinforce their strategic partnership." The two countries, which declared themselves "partners for mutual benefit" rather than rivals or competitors, also signed 13 new pacts on a variety of bilateral initiatives. The Joint Declaration notably contained an agreement to "promote cooperation in the field of nuclear energy," although no details have been provided on what form such cooperation might take.

Other Countries

India takes an active role in assisting reconstruction efforts in Afghanistan, having committed $650 million to this cause, as well as contributing personnel and opening numerous consulates there (much to the dismay of Pakistan, which fears strategic encirclement and takes note of India's past support for Afghan Tajik and Uzbek militias). Among Indian assistance to Afghanistan are funding for a new $111 million power station, an $84 million road-building project, a $77 million damn project, and construction of Kabul's new $67 Parliament building, to be completed in 2010. The United States has welcomed India's role in Afghanistan.

To the north, New Delhi called King Gyanendra's February 2005 power seizure in Nepal "a serious setback for the cause of democracy," but India renewed nonlethal military aid to the Royal Nepali Army only months later. India remains seriously concerned about political instability in Kathmandu and the cross-border infiltration of Maoist militants from Nepal. The United States seeks continued Indian attention to the need for a restoration of democracy in Nepal.

To the east, and despite India's key role in the creation of neighboring Bangladesh in 1971, New Delhi's relations with Dhaka have been fraught with tensions related mainly to the cross-border infiltration of Islamic and separatist militants, and huge numbers of illegal migrants into India. The two countries' border forces engage in periodic gunbattles and India is completing construction of a fence along the entire shared border. Still, New Delhi and Dhaka have cooperated on counterterrorism efforts and talks on energy cooperation continue.

Further to the east, India is pursuing closer relations with the repressive regime in neighboring Burma, with an interest in energy cooperation and to counterbalance China's influence there. Such engagement seeks to achieve economic integration of India's northeast region and western Burma, as well as bolstering energy security. International human rights groups have criticized New Delhi's military interactions with Rangoon. The Bush Administration has urged India to be more active in pressing for democracy in Burma.

In the island nation of Sri Lanka off India's southeastern coast, a Tamil Hindu minority has been fighting a separatist war against the Sinhalese Buddhist majority since 1983. The violent conflict has again become serious in 2006, causing some three thousand deaths. More than 60 million Indian Tamils live in southern India. India's 1987 intervention to assist in enforcing a peace accord resulted in the deaths of more than 1,200 Indian troops and led to the 1991 assassination of former Indian Prime Minister Rajiv Gandhi by Tamil militants. Since that time, New Delhi has maintained friendly relations with Colombo while refraining from any deep engagement in third-party peace efforts. The Indian Navy played a key role in providing disaster relief to Sri Lanka following the catastrophic December 2004 Indian Ocean tsunami.

Political Setting

India is the world's most populous democracy and remains firmly committed to representative government and rule of law. U.S. policymakers commonly identify in the Indian political system shared core values, and this has facilitated increasingly friendly relations between the U.S. and Indian governments.

National Elections

India, with a robust and working democratic system, is a federal republic where the bulk of executive power rests with the prime minister and his or her cabinet (the Indian president is a ceremonial chief of state with limited executive powers). As a nation-state, India presents a vast mosaic of hundreds of different ethnic groups, religious sects, and social castes. Most of India's prime ministers have come from the country's Hindi-speaking northern regions and all but two have been upper-caste Hindus. The 543-seat Lok Sabha (People's House) is the locus of national power, with directly elected representatives from each of the country's 28 states and 7 union territories. A smaller upper house, the Rajya Sabha (Council of States), may review, but not veto, most legislation, and has no power over the prime minister or the cabinet. National and state legislators are elected to five-year terms.

National elections in October 1999 had secured ruling power for a Bharatiya Janata Party (BJP)-led coalition government headed by Prime Minister Vajpayee. That outcome decisively ended the historic dominance of the Nehru-Gandhi-led Congress Party, which was relegated to sitting in opposition at the national level (its members continued to lead many state governments). However, a surprise Congress resurgence under Sonia Gandhi in May 2004 national elections brought to power a new left-leaning coalition government led by former finance minister and Oxford-educated economist Manmohan Singh, a Sikh and India's first-ever non-Hindu prime minister. Many analysts attributed Congress's 2004 resurgence to the resentment of rural and poverty-stricken urban voters who felt left out of the "India shining" campaign of a BJP more associated with urban, middle-class interests. Others saw in the results a rejection of the Hindu nationalism associated with the BJP. (See CRS Report RL32465, *India's 2004 National Elections.*)

The Congress Party

Congress's electoral strength reached a nadir in 1999, when the party won only 110 Lok Sabha seats. Observers attributed the poor showing to a number of factors, including perceptions that party leader Sonia Gandhi lacked the experience to lead the country and the failure of Congress to make strong pre-election alliances (as had the BJP). Support for Congress had been in fairly steady decline following the 1984 assassination of Prime Minister Indira Gandhi and the 1991 assassination of her son, Prime Minister Rajiv Gandhi. Sonia Gandhi, Rajiv's Italian-born, Catholic widow, refrained from active politics until the 1998 elections. She later made efforts to revitalize the party by phasing out older leaders and attracting more women and lower castes — efforts that appear to have paid off in 2004. Today, Congress again occupies more parliamentary seats (145) than any other party and, through unprecedented alliances with powerful regional parties, it again leads India's government under the United Progressive Alliance (UPA) coalition. As party chief and UPA chair, Sonia Gandhi is believed to wield considerable influence over the ruling coalition's policy decision-making process.[10]

The Bharatiya Janata Party (BJP)

With the rise of Hindu nationalism, the BJP rapidly increased its parliamentary strength during the 1980s. In 1993, the party's image was tarnished among some, burnished for others, by its alleged complicity in serious communal violence in Bombay and elsewhere. Some hold elements of the BJP, as the political arm of extremist Hindu groups, responsible for the incidents (the party has advocated "Hindutva," or an India based on Hindu culture, and views this as key to nation-building). While leading a national coalition from 1998-2004, the BJP worked — with only limited success — to change its image from right-wing Hindu fundamentalist to conservative and secular, although 2002 communal rioting in Gujarat again damaged the party's credentials as a moderate organization. The BJP-led National Democratic Alliance was overseen by party notable Prime Minister Atal Vajpayee, whose widespread personal popularity helped to keep the BJP in power. Since 2004, the BJP has been weakened by leadership disputes, criticism from Hindu nationalists, and controversy involving party president Lal Advani (in December 2005, Advani ceded his leadership post and Vajpayee announced his retirement from politics). In 2006, senior BJP leader Pramod Mahajan was shot and killed in a family dispute.[11]

Regional Parties

The influence of regional and caste-based parties has become an increasingly important variable in Indian politics; the May 2004 national elections saw such parties receiving nearly half of all votes cast. Never before 2004 had the Congress Party entered into pre-poll alliances at the national level, and numerous analysts attributed Congress's success to precisely this new tack, especially thorough arrangements with the Bihar-based Rashtriya Janata Dal and Tamil Nadu's Dravida Munnetra Kazhagam. The newfound power of both large and smaller regional parties, alike, is seen to be reflected in the UPA's ministerial appointments, and in the Congress-led coalition's professed attention to rural issues and center-state relations. Two significant regional parties currently independent of both the ruling coalition and the BJP-led opposition are the Samajwadi Party, a largely Muslim- and lower caste-based organization highly influential in Uttar Pradesh, and the Bahujan Samaj Party of Bihar, which also represents mainly lower-caste constituents. State assembly elections in Uttar Pradesh — home to more than 170 million Indians — are slated for February 2007 and may be an important indicator of national political trends, especially in gauging satisfaction with the current center coalition.

BILATERAL ISSUES

"Next Steps in Strategic Partnership" and Beyond

The now-concluded Next Steps in Strategic Partnership (NSSP) initiative encompassed several major issues in India-U.S. relations. The Indian government has long pressed the United States to ease restrictions on the export to India of dual-use high-technology goods (those with military applications), as well as to increase civilian nuclear and civilian space cooperation. These three key issues came to be known as the "trinity," and top Indian officials insisted that progress in these areas was necessary to provide tangible evidence of a changed U.S.-India relationship. There were later references to a "quartet" when the issue of missile defense was included. In January 2004, President Bush and Prime Minister Vajpayee issued a joint statement declaring that the U.S.-India "strategic partnership" included expanding cooperation in the "trinity" areas, as well as expanding dialogue on missile defense.[12] This initiative was dubbed as the NSSP and involved a series of reciprocal steps.

In July 2005, the State Department announced successful completion of the NSSP, allowing for expanded bilateral commercial satellite cooperation, removal/revision of some U.S. export license requirements for certain dual-use and civil nuclear items. Taken together, the July 2005 U.S.-India Joint Statement and a June 2005 U.S.-India Defense Framework Agreement include provisions for moving forward in all four NSSP issue-areas.[13] Many observers saw in the NSSP evidence of a major and positive shift in the U.S. strategic orientation toward India, a shift later illuminated more starkly with the Bush Administration's intention to initiate full civil nuclear cooperation with India. (See also CRS Report RL33072, *U.S.-India Bilateral Agreements and 'Global Partnership.'*)

Civil Nuclear Cooperation

India's status as a non-signatory to the 1968 Nuclear Nonproliferation Treaty (NPT) has kept it from accessing most nuclear-related materials and fuels on the international market for more than three decades. New Delhi's 1974 "peaceful nuclear explosion" spurred the U.S.-led creation of the Nuclear Suppliers Group (NSG) — an international export control regime for nuclear-related trade — and the U.S. government further tightened its own export laws with the Nuclear Nonproliferation Act of 1978. New Delhi has long railed at a "nuclear apartheid" created by apparent double standards inherent in the NPT, which allows certain states to legitimately employ nuclear deterrents while other states cannot.

The Bush Administration Policy Shift

Differences over nuclear policy bedeviled U.S.-India ties for decades and — given New Delhi's lingering resentments — have presented a major psychological obstacle to more expansive bilateral relations. In a major policy shift, the July 2005 U.S.-India Joint Statement notably asserted that, "as a responsible state with advanced nuclear technology, India should acquire the same benefits and advantages as other such states," and President Bush vowed to work on achieving "full civilian nuclear energy cooperation with India." As a reversal of three decades of U.S. nonproliferation policy, such proposed cooperation stirred controversy and required changes in both U.S. law and in NSG guidelines. India reciprocally agreed to take its own steps, including identifying and separating its civilian and military nuclear facilities in a phased manner and placing the former under international safeguards. Some in Congress express concern that civil nuclear cooperation with India might allow that country to advance its military nuclear projects and be harmful to broader U.S. nonproliferation efforts. While the Bush Administration previously had insisted that such cooperation would take place only within the limits set by multilateral nonproliferation regimes, the Administration later actively sought adjustments to U.S. laws and policies, and has approached the NSG in an effort to adjust that regime's guidelines, which are set by member consensus.

In March 2006, President Bush and Prime Minister Singh issued a Joint Statement that included an announcement of "successful completion of India's [nuclear facility] separation plan."[14] After months of complex and difficult negotiations, the Indian government had presented a plan to separate its civilian and military nuclear facilities as per the July 2005 Joint Statement. The separation plan would require India to move 14 of its 22 reactors into permanent international oversight by the year 2014 and place all future civilian reactors under permanent safeguards. Shortly thereafter, legislation to waive the application of certain requirements under the Atomic Energy Act of 1954 with respect to India was, at the President's request, introduced in the U.S. Congress.

Potential Benefits and Costs

Secretary of State Rice appeared before key Senate and House committees in April 2006 to press the Bush Administration's case for civil nuclear cooperation with India. The Administration offered five main justifications for making changes in U.S. law to allow for such cooperation, contending that doing so would

- benefit U.S. security by bringing India "into the nonproliferation mainstream;"
- benefit U.S. consumers by reducing pressures on global energy markets, especially carbon-based fuels;
- benefit the environment by reducing carbon emissions/greenhouse gases;
- benefit U.S. business interests through sales to India of nuclear reactors, fuel, and support services; and
- benefit progress of the broader U.S.-India "global partnership."[15]

Many leading American experts on South Asian affairs joined the Administration in urging Congress to support the new policy, placing particular emphasis on the "necessary" role it would play in promoting a U.S.-India global partnership.[16]

Further hearings in the Senate (April 26) and House (May 11) saw a total of fifteen independent analysts weigh in on the potential benefits and/or problems that might accrue from such cooperation. Some experts opined that the Administration's optimism, perhaps especially as related to the potential effects on global energy markets and carbon emissions, could not be supported through realistic projections. Numerous nonproliferation experts, scientists, and former U.S. government officials warned that the Bush Administration's initiative was ill-considered, arguing that it would facilitate an increase in the size of India's nuclear arsenal, potentially leading to a nuclear arms race in Asia, and would undermine the global nonproliferation regime and cause significant damage to key U.S. security interests.[17]

The U.S. Chamber of Commerce, which, along with the U.S.-India Business Council, lobbied vigorously in favor of President Bush's initiative, speculated that civil nuclear cooperation with India could generate contracts for American businesses worth up to $100 billion, as well as generate up to 27,000 new American jobs each year for a decade.[18] However, foreign companies such as Russia's Atomstroyexport and France's Areva may be better poised to take advantage of the Indian market. Moreover, U.S. nuclear suppliers will likely balk at entering the Indian market in the absence of nuclear liability protection, which New Delhi does not offer at present.

Geopolitical Motives

In the realm of geopolitics, much of the Administration's argument for moving forward with the U.S.-India nuclear initiative appears rooted in an anticipation/expectation that New Delhi will in coming years and decades make policy choices that are more congruent with U.S. regional and global interests (a desire for such congruence is, in fact, written into P.L. 109-401). Proponents suggest that this U.S. "gesture" will have significant and lasting psychological and symbolic effects in addition to the strictly material ones, and that Indian leaders require such a gesture in order to feel confident in the United States as a reliable partner on the world stage.[19] Skeptics aver that the potential strategic benefits of the nuclear initiative are being over-sold. Indeed, centuries of Indian anti-colonial sentiments and oftentimes prickly, independent foreign policy choices are unlikely to be set aside in the short run, meaning that the anticipated geopolitical benefits of civil nuclear cooperation with India remain speculative and at least somewhat dependent upon unknowable global political developments.

Congressional Action

After months of consideration, the House International Relations Committee and Senate Foreign Affairs Committee both took action on relevant legislation in late June 2006, passing modified versions of the Administration's proposals by wide margins. The new House and Senate bills (H.R. 5682 and S. 3709) made significant procedural changes to the Administration's proposal, changes that sought to retain congressional oversight of the negotiation process, in part by requiring the Administration to gain future congressional approval of a completed peaceful nuclear cooperation agreement with India (this is often referred to as a "123 Agreement," as it is negotiated under the conditions set forth in Section 123 of the Atomic Energy Act).

During the final months of its tenure, the 109th Congress demonstrated widespread bipartisan support for the Administration's new policy initiative by passing enabling legislation through both chambers (in July 2006, the House passed H.R. 5682 by a vote of 359-68; in November, the Senate passed an amended version of the same bill by a vote of 85-12). Numerous so-called "killer amendments" were rejected by both chambers (Indian government and Bush Administration officials had warned that certain proposed new provisions, such as those requiring that India halt its fissile material production or end its military relations with Iran, would trigger New Delhi's withdrawal from the entire negotiation).

In a December 2006 "lame duck" session, congressional conferees reconciled the House and Senate versions of the legislation and provided a 30-page explanatory statement (H.Rept. 109-721). On December 18, President Bush signed the Henry J. Hyde United States-India

Peaceful Atomic Energy Cooperation Act of 2006 into law (P.L. 109-401), calling it a "historic agreement" that would help the United States and India meet the energy and security challenges of the 21st century. The President also issued a signing statement asserting that his approval of the Act "does not constitute [his] adoption of the statements of policy as U.S. foreign policy" and that he will construe such policy statements as "advisory." Some Members of Congress later expressed concern that President Bush would seek to disregard Congress's will.[20]

Civil nuclear cooperation with India cannot commence until Washington and New Delhi finalize a peaceful nuclear cooperation agreement, until the NSG allows for such cooperation, and until New Delhi concludes its own safeguards agreement with the International Atomic Energy Agency. (See CRS Report RL33016, *U.S. Nuclear Cooperation With India.*)

Indian Concerns

Almost immediately upon the release of the July 2005 Joint Statement, key Indian political figures and members of the country's insular nuclear scientific community issued strong criticisms of the U.S.-India civil nuclear initiative; critics continue to be vocal to this day. Former Prime Minister Vajpayee, along with many leading figures in his Bharatiya Janata Party (BJP), insisted that the deal as envisioned would place unreasonable and unduly expensive demands on India, particularly with regard to the separation of nuclear facilities. In reaction to the U.S. Congress's passage of enabling legislation in late 2006, the BJP listed numerous continuing objections, and went so far as to call the deal "unacceptable" and aimed at "capping, rolling back, and eventually eliminating India's nuclear weapons capability."[21] Many analysts view the BJP's opposition as political rather than substantive, especially in light of the fact that the 2004 NSSP initiative was launched during the BJP's tenure.

India's influential communist parties, whose Left Front provides crucial support to the Congress-led ruling coalition in New Delhi, have focused their ire on geopolitical aspects of the civil nuclear initiative. In December 2006, the leader of India's main communist party said the U.S.-India civil nuclear deal was "not acceptable" as it would "seriously undermine India's independent foreign policy." Previously, the Left Front had called India's two IAEA votes on Iran a "capitulation" to U.S. pressure. Indian leftists thus have been at the forefront of political resistance to India's becoming a "junior partner" of the United States.

Equally stinging and perhaps more substantive criticism has come from several key Indian scientists, whose perspectives on the technical details of the civil nuclear initiative are considered highly credible. India's nuclear scientific community, mostly barred from collaboration with international civil nuclear enterprises as well as direct access to key technologies, has worked for decades in relative isolation, making its members both proud of their singular accomplishments and sensitive to any signs of foreign "interference." Many view the enabling legislation passed by the U.S. Congress as being more about nonproliferation and less about energy cooperation. They consider it both intrusive on and preclusive of their activities.

The seven major criticisms of existing plans for U.S.-India civil nuclear cooperation made by Indian commentators may be summarized as follows:

- Intra-U.S. government certification and reporting requirements are overly rigorous;
- India's unilateral moratorium on nuclear tests is being codified into a bilateral obligation;

- India is being denied nuclear reprocessing technologies warranted under "full cooperation;"
- India has not been given assurances that it will receive uninterrupted fuel supplies in perpetuity;
- The United States is retaining the right to carry out its own "intrusive" end-use verifications;
- India is being expected to adhere to multilateral protocols, including the Proliferation Security Initiative, the Missile Technology Control Regime, and the Waasenaar Arrangement, which it has declined to accept in the past; and
- Language on securing India's assistance with U.S. efforts to prevent Iran from obtaining weapons of mass destruction limits New Delhi's foreign policy independence.[22]

Prime Minister Singh has stood firm against such wide-ranging and high-profile criticisms, repeatedly assuring his Parliament that relevant negotiations with the United States have not altered basic Indian policies or affected New Delhi's independence on matters of national interest. Within this context, however, Singh has expressed serious concern about the points listed above.[23] Regardless of the legally binding or non-binding nature of certain controversial sections of the U.S. legislation, New Delhi has found many of them to be either "prescriptive" in ways incompatible with the provisions of the July 2005 and March 2006 Joint Statements, or "extraneous" and inappropriate to engagements "among friends."[24]

Civil Space Cooperation

India has long sought access to American space technology; such access has since the 1980s been limited by U.S. and international "red lines" meant to prevent assistance that could benefit India's military missile programs. India's space-launch vehicle technology was obtained largely from foreign sources, including the United States, and forms the basis of its intermediate-range Agni ballistic missile booster, as well as its suspected Surya intercontinental ballistic missile program. The NSSP called for enhanced U.S.-India cooperation on the peaceful uses of space technology, and the July 2005 Joint Statement called for closer ties in space exploration, satellite navigation and launch, and in the commercial space arena. Conferences on India-U.S. space science and commerce were held in Bangalore (headquarters of the Indian Space Research Organization) in 2004 and 2005. During President Bush's March 2006 visit to India, the two countries committed to move forward with agreements that will permit the launch of U.S. satellites and satellites containing U.S. components by Indian space launch vehicles and, two months later, they agreed to include two U.S. scientific instruments on India's Chandrayaan lunar mission planned for 2007.

High-Technology Trade

U.S. Commerce Department officials have sought to dispel "trade-deterring myths" about limits on dual-use trade by noting that only about 1% of total U.S. trade value with India is subject to licensing requirements and that the great majority of dual-use licensing applications for India are approved (more than 90% in FY2005). July 2003 saw the inaugural session of the U.S.-India High-Technology Cooperation Group (HTCG), where officials discussed a wide range of issues relevant to creating the conditions for more robust bilateral high technology commerce; the fourth HTCG meeting was held in New Delhi in November 2005 (in early 2005, the inaugural session of the U.S.-India High-Technology Defense Working Group was held under HTCG auspices).[25]

Since 1998, a number of Indian entities have been subjected to case-by-case licensing requirements and appear on the U.S. export control "Entity List" of foreign end users involved in weapons proliferation activities. In September 2004, as part of NSSP implementation, the United States modified some export licensing policies and removed the Indian Space Research Organization (ISRO) headquarters from the Entity List. Further adjustments came in August 2005 when six more subordinate entities were removed. Indian entities remaining on the Entity List are four subordinates of the ISRO, four subordinates of the Defense Research and Development Organization, one Department of Atomic Energy entity, and Bharat Dynamics Limited, a missile production agency.[26]

Security Issues

U.S.-India Security Cooperation

Defense cooperation between the United States and India is in the early stages of development (unlike U.S.-Pakistan military ties, which date back to the 1950s). Since September 2001, and despite a concurrent U.S. rapprochement with Pakistan, U.S.-India security cooperation has flourished. The India-U.S. Defense Policy Group (DPG) — moribund since India's 1998 nuclear tests and ensuing U.S. sanctions — was revived in late 2001 and meets annually; U.S. diplomats call military cooperation among the most important aspects of transformed bilateral relations. In June 2005, the United States and India signed a ten-year defense pact outlining planned collaboration in multilateral operations, expanded two-way defense trade, increasing opportunities for technology transfers and co-production, expanded collaboration related to missile defense, and establishment of a bilateral Defense Procurement and Production Group. The United States views defense cooperation with India in the context of "common principles and shared national interests" such as defeating terrorism, preventing weapons proliferation, and maintaining regional stability. Many analysts laud increased U.S.-India security ties as providing an alleged "hedge" against or "counterbalance" to growing Chinese influence in Asia.

Since early 2002, the United States and India have held a series of unprecedented and increasingly substantive combined exercises involving all military services. "Cope India" air exercises have provided the U.S. military with its first look at Russian-built Su-30MKIs; in 2004, mock air combat saw Indian pilots in late-model Russian-built fighters hold off American pilots flying older F-15Cs, and Indian successes were repeated versus U.S. F-16s in 2005. U.S. and Indian special forces soldiers have held joint exercises near the India-China border, and major annual "Malabar" joint naval exercises are held off the Indian coast (the sixth and most recent in October 2006). Despite these developments, there remain indications that the perceptions and expectations of top U.S. and Indian military leaders are divergent on several key issues, including India's regional role, approaches to countering terrorism, and U.S.-Pakistan relations.

Along with increasing military-to-military ties, the issue of U.S. arms sales to India has taken a higher profile. In 2002, the Pentagon negotiated a sale to India of 12 counter-battery radar sets (or "Firefinder" radars) worth a total of $190 million. India also purchased $29 million worth of counterterrorism equipment for its special forces and has received sophisticated U.S.-made electronic ground sensors to help stem the tide of militant infiltration in the Kashmir region. In 2004, Congress was notified of a possible sale to India involving up to $40 million worth of aircraft self-protection systems to be mounted on the Boeing 737s that carry the Indian head of state. The State Department has authorized Israel to sell to India the jointly developed U.S.-Israeli Phalcon airborne early warning system, an expensive asset that some analysts believe may tilt the regional strategic balance even further in India's favor. In August 2006, New Delhi approved a $44 million plan to purchase the USS Trenton, a decommissioned American amphibious transport dock. The ship, which will become the second largest in the Indian navy, is set to fly the Indian flag in early 2007, possibly carrying six surplus Sikorsky UH-3H Sea King helicopters India seeks to purchase for another $39 million.

The Indian government reportedly possesses an extensive list of desired U.S.-made weapons, including PAC-3 anti-missile systems, electronic warfare systems, and possibly even combat aircraft. The March 2005 unveiling of the Bush Administration's "new strategy for South Asia" included assertions that the United States welcomed Indian requests for information on the possible purchase of F-16 or F/A-18 multi-role fighters, and indicated that Washington is "ready to discuss the sale of transformative systems in areas such as command and control, early warning, and missile defense." American defense firms eagerly pursue new and expanded business ties with India. Still, some top Indian officials express concern that the United States is a "fickle" partner that may not always be relied upon to provide the reciprocity, sensitivity, and high-technology transfers sought by New Delhi.[27] (In February 2006, the Indian Navy declined an offer to lease two U.S. P-3C maritime reconnaissance aircraft, calling the arrangements "expensive.")

In a controversial turn, the Indian government has sought to purchase a sophisticated anti-missile platform, the Arrow Weapon System, from Israel. Because the United States took the lead in the system's development, the U.S. government has veto power over any Israeli exports of the Arrow. Although Defense Department officials are seen to support the sale as meshing with President Bush's policy of cooperating with friendly countries on missile defense, State Department officials are reported to opposed the transfer, believing that it would send the wrong signal to other weapons-exporting states at a time when the U.S. is seeking to discourage international weapons proliferation. Indications are that a U.S. interest in maintaining a strategic balance on the subcontinent, along with U.S. obligations under the Missile Technology Control Regime, may preclude any approval of the Arrow sale.

Joint U.S.-India military exercises and arms sales negotiations can cause disquiet in Pakistan, where there is concern that induction of advanced weapons systems into the region could disrupt the "strategic balance" there. Islamabad worries that its already disadvantageous conventional military status vis-à-vis New Delhi will be further eroded by India's acquisition of sophisticated "force multipliers." In fact, numerous observers identify a pro-India drift in the U.S. government's strategic orientation in South Asia. Yet Washington regularly lauds Islamabad's role as a key ally in the U.S.-led counterterrorism coalition and assures Pakistan that it will take no actions to disrupt strategic balance on the subcontinent. (See also CRS Report RL33072, *U.S.-India Bilateral Agreements*, and CRS Report RL33515, *Combat Aircraft Sales to South Asia: Potential Implications*.)

Nuclear Weapons and Missile Proliferation

Some policy analysts consider the apparent arms race between India and Pakistan as posing perhaps the most likely prospect for the future use of nuclear weapons by states. In May 1998, India conducted five underground nuclear tests, breaking a self-imposed, 24-year moratorium on such testing. Despite international efforts to dissuade it, Pakistan quickly followed. The tests created a global storm of criticism and represented a serious setback for two decades of U.S. nuclear nonproliferation efforts in South Asia. Following the tests, President Clinton imposed full restrictions on non-humanitarian aid to both India and Pakistan as mandated under Section 102 of the Arms Export Control Act. India currently is believed to have enough fissile material, mainly plutonium, for 55-115 nuclear weapons; Pakistan, with a program focused on enriched uranium, may be capable of building a similar number. Both countries have aircraft capable of delivering nuclear bombs. India's military has inducted short- and intermediate-range ballistic missiles, while Pakistan itself possesses short- and medium-range missiles (allegedly acquired from China and North Korea). All are assumed to be capable of delivering nuclear warheads over significant distances.

Proliferation in South Asia is part of a chain of rivalries — India seeking to achieve deterrence against China, and Pakistan seeking to gain an "equalizer" against a conventionally stronger India. In 1999, a quasi-governmental Indian body released a Draft Nuclear Doctrine for India calling for a "minimum credible deterrent" (MCD) based upon a triad of delivery systems and pledging that India will not be the first to use nuclear weapons in a conflict. In January 2003, New Delhi announced creation of a Nuclear Command Authority. After the body's first session in September 2003, participants· vowed to "consolidate India's nuclear deterrent." India thus appears to be taking the next steps toward operationalizing its nuclear weapons capability. (See also CRS Report RL32115, *Missile Proliferation and the Strategic Balance in South Asia*, and CRS Report RS21237, *Indian and Pakistani Nuclear Weapons*.)

U.S. Nonproliferation Efforts and Congressional Action

Soon after the May 1998 nuclear tests in South Asia, Congress acted to ease aid sanctions through a series of legislative measures.[28] In September 2001, President Bush waived remaining sanctions on India pursuant to P.L. 106-79. During the 1990s, the U.S. security focus in South Asia sought to minimize damage to the nonproliferation regime, prevent escalation of an arms race, and promote Indo-Pakistani bilateral dialogue. In light of these goals, the Clinton Administration set out "benchmarks" for India and Pakistan based on the contents of U.N. Security Council Resolution 1172, which condemned the two countries' nuclear tests. These included signing and ratifying the Comprehensive Nuclear Test Ban Treaty (CTBT); halting all further production of fissile material and participating in Fissile Material Cutoff Treaty negotiations; limiting development and deployment of WMD delivery vehicles; and implementing strict export controls on sensitive WMD materials and technologies.

Progress in each of these areas has been limited, and the Bush Administration quickly set aside the benchmark framework. Along with security concerns, the governments of both India and Pakistan faced the prestige factor attached to their nuclear programs and domestic resistance to relinquishing what are perceived to be potent symbols of national power. Neither has signed the CTBT, and both appear to be producing weapons-grade fissile materials. (India has consistently rejected the CTBT, as well as the Nuclear Nonproliferation Treaty, as discriminatory, calling instead for a global nuclear disarmament regime. Although both India and Pakistan currently observe self-imposed moratoria on nuclear testing, they continue to resist signing the CTBT — a position made more tenable by U.S. Senate's rejection of the treaty in 1999.) The status of weaponization and deployment is unclear, though there are indications that this is occurring at a slow but steady pace. Section 1601 of P.L. 107-228 outlined U.S. nonproliferation objectives for South Asia. Some Members of Congress identify "contradictions" in U.S. nonproliferation policy toward South Asia, particularly as related to the Senate's rejection of the CTBT and U.S. plans to build new nuclear weapons. In May 2006, the United States presented in Geneva a draft global treaty to ban future production of fissile material (a Fissile Material Cutoff Treaty) that it hopes will be supported by India. Some analysts speculated that the move was meant to bolster U.S. congressional support for proposed U.S.-India civil nuclear cooperation.

India-Iran Relations

India's relations with Iran traditionally have been positive and, in 2003, the two countries launched a bilateral "strategic partnership."[29] Many in the U.S. Congress have voiced concern that New Delhi's policies toward Tehran's controversial nuclear program may not be congruent with those of Washington, although these concerns were eased when India voted with the United States (and the majority) at the International Atomic Energy Agency sessions of September 2005 and February 2006. In each of the past three years, the United States has sanctioned Indian scientists and chemical companies for transferring to Iran WMD-related equipment and/or technology (most sanctions have been chemical-related, but one scientist was alleged to have aided Iran's nuclear program); New Delhi called the moves unjustified. Included in legislation to enable U.S.-India civil nuclear cooperation (P.L. 109-141) was a non-binding assertion that U.S. policy should "secure India's full and active participation" in U.S. efforts to prevent Iran from acquiring weapons of mass destruction.[30] Some in Congress also have noted with alarm reports of contacts between the Indian and Iranian militaries, although such contacts may be insubstantial.[31]

There are further U.S. concerns that India will seek energy resources from Iran, thus benefitting financially a country the United States is seeking to isolate. Indian firms have in recent years taken long-term contracts for purchase of Iranian gas and oil. Purchases could be worth many billions of dollars, but thus far differences over pricing have precluded sales. Building upon growing energy ties is the proposed construction of a pipeline to deliver Iranian natural gas to India through Pakistan. The Bush Administration has expressed strong opposition to any gas pipeline projects involving Iran, but top Indian officials insist the project is in India's national interest and they remain "fully committed" to the multi-billion-dollar venture, which may begin construction in 2007. The Iran-Libya Sanctions Act (P.L. 107-24) required the President to impose sanctions on foreign companies that make an "investment" of more than $20 million in one year in Iran's energy sector. The 109th Congress extended this provision in the Iran Freedom Support Act (P.L. 109-293). To date, no firms have been sanctioned under these Acts. (See also CRS Report RS22486, *India-Iran Relations and U.S. Interests*, and CRS Report RS20871, *The Iran-Libya Sanctions Act*.)

India's Economy and U.S. Concerns

Overview

India is in the midst of a major and rapid economic expansion, with an economy projected to be the world's third largest in coming decades. Although there is widespread and serious poverty in the country, observers believe long-term economic potential is tremendous, and recent strides in the technology sector have brought international attention to such high-tech centers as Bangalore and Hyderabad. However, many analysts and business leaders, along with U.S. government officials, point to excessive regulatory and bureaucratic structures as a hindrance to the realization of India's full economic potential. The high cost of capital (rooted in large government budget deficits) and an "abysmal" infrastructure also draw negative appraisals as obstacles to growth. Constant comparisons with the progress of the Chinese economy show India lagging in rates of growth and foreign investment, and in the removal of trade barriers.

India's per capita GDP is still less than $800 ($3,510 when accounting for purchasing power parity). The highly-touted information technology and business processing industries only employ about one-third of one percent of India's work force and, while optimists vaunt an Indian "middle class" of some 300 million people, a roughly equal number of Indians subsist on less than $1 per day.[32] Yet, even with the existence of ongoing problems, the current growth rate of India's increasingly service-driven economy is among the highest in the world and has brought the benefits of development to many millions of citizens. The U.N. Development Program ranked India 126th out of 177 countries on its 2006 human development index, up from 127th in both 2004 and 2005.

After enjoying an average growth rate above 6% for the 1990s, India's economy cooled with the global economic downturn after 2000. Yet sluggish Cold War-era "Hindu rates of growth" became a thing of the past. For the fiscal year ending March 2006, real change in GDP was 8.5%, the second-fastest rate of growth among the world's 20 largest economies. Robust growth in the services and industry sectors continues, but is moderated by a fluctuating agricultural sector (low productivity levels in this sector, which accounts for about one-fifth of the country's GDP, are a drag on overall growth). Estimated growth for the current fiscal year is about 8.7% and short-term estimates are encouraging, predicting expansion well above 7% for the next two years. A major upswing in services is expected to lead; this sector now accounts for more than half of India's GDP. Consumer price inflation has risen (a year-on-year rate above 7% in October 2006), but is predicted to again drop to between 5% and 6% in 2007. As of June 2006, India's foreign exchange reserves were at a record $163 billion. The soaring Bombay Stock Exchange tripled in value from 2001-2006, then apparently overheated with the worst-ever daily decline of its benchmark Sensex index on May 22, 2006, when almost 11% of its total value was lost. The market has since stabilized and apparently recovered, reaching new highs in the closing months of 2006.

A major U.S. concern with regard to India is the scope and pace of reforms in what has been that country's quasi-socialist economy. Economic reforms begun in 1991, under the Congress-led government of Prime Minister Rao and his finance minister, current Prime Minister Manmohan Singh, boosted growth and led to major new inbound foreign investment in the mid-1990s. Reform efforts stagnated, however, under weak coalition governments later in the decade, and combined with the 1997 Asian financial crisis and international sanctions on India (as a result of its 1998 nuclear tests) to further dampen the economic outlook.

Following the 1999 parliamentary elections, the BJP-led government launched second-generation economic reforms, including major deregulation, privatization, and tariff-reducing measures.

Once seen as favoring domestic business and diffident about foreign involvement, New Delhi appears to gradually be embracing globalization and has sought to reassure foreign investors with promises of transparent and nondiscriminatory policies. In February 2006, a top International Monetary Fund official said that India's continued rapid economic growth will be facilitated only by enhanced Indian integration with the global economy through continued reforms and infrastructure improvements. A November 2006 World Bank report identified the country's main economic challenges as

- improving the delivery of core public services such as healthcare, education, power and water supply for all India's citizens;
- making growth more inclusive by diminishing existing disparities, accelerating agricultural growth, improving th job market, and helping lagging states grow faster;
- sustaining growth by addressing its fiscal and trade deficits, and pushing ahead with reforms that facilitate growth, and;
- addressing HIV/AIDS before the epidemic spreads to the general public.

Trade and Investment

As India's largest trade and investment partner, the United States strongly supports New Delhi's continuing economic reform policies; a U.S.-India Trade Policy Forum was created in November 2005 to expand bilateral economic engagement and provide a venue for discussing multilateral trade issues. India was the 22nd largest export market for U.S. goods in 2005 (up from 24th the previous year). Levels of U.S.-India trade, while relatively low, are blossoming; the total value of bilateral trade has doubled since 2001 and the two governments intend to see it doubled again by 2009. U.S. exports to India in 2006 had an estimated value of $9.9 billion (up 24% over 2005), with aircraft; business and telecommunications equipment; pearls, gemstones, and jewelry; fertilizer; and chemicals as leading categories. Imports from India in 2006 totaled an estimated $21.9 billion (up 17% over 2005). Leading imports included cotton apparel; textiles; and pearls, gemstones, and jewelry. Annual foreign direct investment to India from all countries rose from about $100 million in 1990 to an estimated $7.4 billion for 2005 and more than $11 billion in 2006. About one-third of these investments was made by U.S. firms; in recent months and years, the major U.S.-based companies Microsoft, Dell, Oracle, and IBM announced plans for multi-billion-dollar investments in India. Strong portfolio investment added another $10 billion in 2005. India has moved to raise limits on foreign investment in several key sectors, although U.S. officials prod New Delhi to make more rapid and more substantial changes to foreign investment ceilings, especially in the retail, financial services, and banking sectors.

During his March 2006 visit to Delhi, President Bush noted India's "dramatic progress" in economic reform while insisting "there's more work to be done," especially in lifting caps on foreign investment, making regulations more transparent, and continuing to lower tariffs. That same month, the U.S.-India CEO Forum —composed of ten chief executives from each country representing a cross-section of key industrial sectors — issued a report identifying India's poor infrastructure and dense bureaucracy as key impediments to increased bilateral trade and investment relations.[33]

Barriers to Trade and Investment

Despite significant tariff reductions and other measures taken by India to improve market access, according to the 2006 report of the United States Trade Representative (USTR), a number of foreign trade barriers remain, including high tariffs, especially in the agricultural sector. The USTR asserts that "substantial expansion of U.S.-India trade will depend on continued and significant additional Indian liberalization."[34] The Commerce Department likewise encourages New Delhi to continue lowering tariffs as a means of fostering trade and development.

India's extensive trade and investment barriers have been criticized by U.S. government officials and business leaders as an impediment to its own economic development, as well as to stronger U.S.-India ties. For example, in 2004, the U.S. Ambassador to India told a Delhi audience that "the U.S. is one of the world's most open economies and India is one of the most closed." Later that year, U.S. Under Secretary of State Alan Larson opined that "trade and investment flows between the U.S. and India are far below where they should and can be," adding that "the picture for U.S. investment is also lackluster." He identified the primary reason for the suboptimal situation as "the slow pace of economic reform in India."[35]

Inadequate intellectual property rights protection is another long-standing issue between the United States and India. The USTR places India on its Special 301 Priority Watch List for "inadequate laws and ineffective enforcement" in this area. The International Intellectual Property Alliance, a coalition of U.S. copyright-based industries, estimated U.S. losses of $443 million due to trade piracy in India in 2005, three-quarters of this in the categories of business and entertainment software (estimated loss amounts for 2005 do not include motion picture piracy, which in 2004 was estimated to have cost some $80 million).[36] In December 2006, Under Secretary of Commerce and Director of the U.S. Patent and Trademark Office Jon Dudas told a New Delhi audience that "further modifications are necessary" in India's intellectual property rights protection regime and that India's copyright laws are "insufficient in many aspects." He also warned that "piracy and counterfeiting rates will continue to rise without effective enforcement."[37]

While the past two decades have seen a major transformation of the Indian economy, it remains relatively closed in many aspects. The Heritage Foundation's *2006 Index of Economic Freedom* — which may overemphasize the value of absolute growth and downplay broader quality-of-life measurements — again rated India as being "mostly unfree," highlighting especially restrictive trade policies, heavy government involvement in the banking and finance sector, demanding regulatory structures, and a high level of "black market" activity.[38] The Vancouver-based Fraser Institute provides a more positive assessment of economic freedom in India, while also faulting excessive restrictions on capital markets and regulations on business.[39] Corruption also plays a role: Berlin-based Transparency International placed India 70th out of 163 countries in its 2006 "corruption perceptions index." The group's 2006 "bribery index" found India to be the worst offender among the world's top 30 exporting countries.[40] (See also CRS Report RS21502, *India-U.S. Economic Relations.*)

Multilateral Trade Negotiations

In July 2006, the World Trade Organization's "Doha Round" of multilateral trade negotiations were suspended indefinitely due to disagreement among the WTO's six core group members —which include the United States and India — over methods to reduce trade-distorting domestic subsidies, eliminate export subsidies, and increase market access for agricultural products. The United States and other developed countries seek substantial tariff reductions in the developing world. India, like other members of the "G-20" group of developing states, has sought more market access for its goods and services in the developed countries, while claiming that developing countries should be given additional time to liberalize their own markets. In particular, India is resistant to opening its markets to subsidized agricultural products from developed countries, claiming this would result in further depopulation of the countryside. India's Commerce Minister, Kamal Nath, blamed U.S. intransigence for the Doha Round's collapse. In November 2006, during a visit to New Delhi to discuss trade issues with top Indian leaders, U.S. Agriculture Secretary Mike Johanns urged India to match "ambitious" U.S. offers and "lead the way toward unlocking the Doha negotiations by offering real market access."[41] (See also CRS Report RL32060, *World Trade Organization Negotiations: The Doha Development Agenda*, and CRS Report RL33144, *WTO Doha Round: The Agricultural Negotiations.*)

The Energy Sector

India's continued economic growth and security are intimately linked to the supply of energy resources. Indeed, Indian leaders insist that energy security is an essential component of the country's development agenda, calling for an integrated national energy policy, diversification of energy supplies, greater energy efficiency, and rationalization of pricing mechanisms. The country's relatively poor natural energy resource endowment and poorly functioning energy market are widely viewed as major constraints on the country's continued rapid economic growth. Estimates indicate that maintaining recent rates of growth will require that India increase its commercial energy supplies by 4%-6% annually in coming years.[42] The U.S. government has committed to assist India in promoting the development of stable and efficient energy markets there; a U.S.-India Energy Dialogue was launched in July 2005 to provide a forum for bolstering bilateral energy cooperation.[43]

India is the world's fifth largest energy consumer and may become third by the middle of this century. Overall power generation in the country more than doubled from 1991 to 2005.[44] Coal is the country's leading commercial energy source, accounting for more than half of national demand. India is the world's third most productive coal producer, and domestic supplies satisfy most demand (however, most of India's coal is a low-grade, high-ash variety of low efficiency). Oil consumption accounts for some one-third of India's total energy consumption; about 70% of this oil is imported (at a rate of 1.7 million barrels per day in 2005), mostly from the West Asia/Middle East region. India's domestic natural gas supply is not likely to keep pace with demand, and the country will have to import much of its natural gas, either via pipeline or as liquefied natural gas. Hydropower, especially abundant in the country's northeast and near the border with Nepal, supplies about 5% of energy needs. Nuclear power, which Indian government officials and some experts say is a sector in dire need of expansion, currently accounts for only 1% of the country's energy supplies and less than 3% of total electricity generation.[45] Even optimistic projections suggest that nuclear power will provide less than 10% of India's generation capacity in 25 years.[46] One-fifth of the country's power is consumed by farmers' irrigation systems, making the farm lobby a powerful obstacle to curtailing subsidies provided by State Electricity Boards, which collectively lose $4.5 billion annually. Moreover, as much as 42% of India's electricity is said to disappear though "transmission losses," i.e., theft.[47]

Regional Dissidence and Human Rights

The United States maintains an ongoing interest in India's domestic stability and the respect for internationally recognized human rights there. The U.S. Congress has held hearings in which such issues are discussed. As a vast mosaic of ethnicities, languages, cultures, and religions, India can be difficult to govern. Internal instability resulting from diversity is further complicated by colonial legacies such as international borders that separate members of the same ethnic groups, creating flashpoints for regional dissidence and separatism. Beyond the Kashmir problem, separatist insurgents in remote and underdeveloped northeast regions confound New Delhi and create international tensions by operating out of neighboring Bangladesh, Burma, Bhutan, and Nepal. Maoist rebels continue to operate in numerous states. India also has suffered outbreaks of serious communal violence between Hindus and Muslims, especially in the western Gujarat state. (See also CRS Report RL32259, *Terrorism in South Asia*.)

India's domestic security is a serious issue beyond the Jammu and Kashmir state: in April 2006, Prime Minister Singh identified a worsening Maoist insurgency as "the single biggest internal security challenge" ever faced by India. Lethal attacks by these "Naxalites" continue and have included June and December landmine explosions that left a total of 26 policemen dead in the eastern Jharkhand state. Three days of communal rioting followed the demolition of a Muslim shrine in the Gujarat state in May and left six people dead and dozens more injured. More than 1,000 Indian army troops were deployed to quell the violence. Later communal clashes between Hindus and Muslims in the Uttar Pradesh state left two children dead and more than 100 homes destroyed by fire. As for militant separatism in the northeast, serious violence has flared anew in the Assam state following the collapse of negotiations with the United Liberation Front of Assam, which is designated as a "group of concern" by the U.S. State Department.

The Kashmir Issue

Although India suffers from several militant regional separatist movements, the Kashmir issue has proven the most lethal and intractable. Conflict over Kashmiri sovereignty also has brought global attention to a potential "flashpoint" for interstate war between nuclear-armed powers. The problem is rooted in competing claims to the former princely state, divided since 1948 by a military Line of Control (LOC) separating India's Jammu and Kashmir and Pakistan-controlled Azad [Free] Kashmir. India and Pakistan fought full-scale wars over Kashmir in 1947-48 and 1965. Some Kashmiris seek independence from both countries. Spurred by a perception of rigged state elections in 1989, an ongoing separatist war between Islamic militants and their supporters and Indian security forces in Indian-held Kashmir has claimed perhaps 66,000 lives.

Some separatist groups, such as the Jammu and Kashmir Liberation Front (JKLF), continue to seek an independent or autonomous Kashmir. Others, including the militant Hizbul Mujahideen (HuM), seek union with Pakistan. In 1993, the All Parties Hurriyat [Freedom] Conference was formed as an umbrella organization for groups opposed to Indian rule in Kashmir. The Hurriyat membership of more than 20 political and religious groups has included the JKLF (now a political group) and Jamaat-e-Islami (the political wing of the HuM). The Hurriyat Conference, which states that it is committed to seeking dialogue with the Indian government on a broad range of issues, calls for a tripartite conference on Kashmir, including Pakistan, India, and representatives of the Kashmiri people. Hurriyat leaders demand Kashmiri representation at any talks between India and Pakistan on Kashmir. The Hurriyat formally split in 2003 after a dispute between hardliners allied with Islamabad and those favoring negotiation with New Delhi. Subsequent efforts to reunify the group failed. In September 2005, the Congress-led government renewed high-level contact with moderate Hurriyat leaders begun by the previous BJP-led coalition. New Delhi vowed to pull troops out of Kashmir if militant infiltrations and violence there cease, but to date only nominal troop withdrawals have come in response to a somewhat improved security situation in the region.

India blames Pakistan for supporting "cross-border terrorism" and for fueling a separatist rebellion in the Muslim-majority Kashmir Valley with arms, training, and militants. Islamabad, for its part, claims to provide only diplomatic and moral support to what it calls "freedom fighters" who resist Indian rule and suffer alleged human rights abuses in the region. New Delhi insists that the dispute should not be "internationalized" through involvement by third-party mediators and India is widely believed to be satisfied with the territorial status quo. In 1999, a bloody, six-week-long battle near the LOC at Kargil cost more than one thousand lives and included Pakistani army troops crossing into Indian-controlled territory. Islamabad has sought to bring external major power persuasion to bear on India, especially from the United States. The longstanding U.S. position on Kashmir is that the issue must be resolved through negotiations between India and Pakistan while taking into account the wishes of the Kashmiri people.

The Northeast

Since the time of India's foundation, numerous militant groups have fought for greater ethnic autonomy, tribal rights, or independence in the country's northeast region. Some of the tribal struggles in the small states known as the Seven Sisters are centuries old. It is estimated that more than 50,000 people have been killed in such fighting since 1948, including some 10,000 deaths in 15 years of fighting in the Assam state. The United Liberation Front of Assam (ULFA), the National Liberation Front of Tripura, the National Democratic Front of Bodoland (NDFB), and the United National Liberation Front (seeking an independent Manipur) are among the groups at war with the central government. In April 2005, the U.S. State Department's Counterterrorism Office named ULFA in its list of "other groups of concern," the first time an Indian separatist group outside Kashmir was so named.[48] A series of bombings left at least 15 people dead and dozens more injured in Assam in November 2006; police blamed ULFA rebels for the attacks.

New Delhi has at times blamed Bangladesh, Burma, Nepal, and Bhutan for "sheltering" one or more of these groups beyond the reach of Indian security forces, and New Delhi has launched joint counter-insurgency operations with some of its neighbors. India also has accused Pakistan's intelligence agency of training and equipping militants. Bhutan launched major military operations against suspected rebel camps on Bhutanese territory in 2003 and appeared to have routed the ULFA and NDFB. In 2004, five leading separatist groups from the region rejected New Delhi's offer of unconditional talks, saying talks can only take place under U.N. mediation and if the sovereignty issue was on the table. Later, in what seemed a blow to the new Congress-led government's domestic security policies, a spate of lethal violence in Assam and Nagaland was blamed on ULFA and NDFB militants who had re-established their bases in Bhutan. Major Indian army operations in late 2004 may have overrun Manipur separatist bases near the Burmese border. New Delhi's hesitant year-long efforts at negotiation with ULFA rebels and a six-week-old cease-fire in Assam collapsed in October 2006, leading to a spike of lethal violence that included multiple bombings the final months of 2006.

Maoist Insurgency

Also operating in India are "Naxalites" — Maoist insurgents ostensibly engaged in violent struggle on behalf of landless laborers and tribals. These groups, most active in inland areas of east-central India, claim to be battling oppression and exploitation in order to create a classless society. Their opponents call them terrorists and extortionists. The groups get their name from Naxalbari, a West Bengal village and site of a militant peasant uprising in 1967. In April 2006, Prime Minister Singh identified a worsening Maoist insurgency as "the single biggest internal security challenge" ever faced by India, saying it threatened India's democracy and "way of life." The U.S. State Department's *Country Reports on Terrorism 2005* warned that attacks by Maoist terrorists in India are "growing in sophistication and lethality and may pose a long-term threat."[49] Naxalites now operate in half of India's 28 states and related violence caused nearly 1,000 deaths in 2005.

The most notable of these outfits are the People's War Group (PWG), mainly active in the southern Andhra Pradesh state, and the Maoist Communist Center of West Bengal and Bihar. In 2004, the two groups merged to form the Communist Party of India (Maoist). Both appear on the U.S. State Department's list of "groups of concern" and both are designated as terrorist groups by New Delhi, which claims there are nearly 10,000 Maoist militants active in the country. PWG fighters were behind a 2003 landmine attack that nearly killed the chief minster of Andhra Pradesh. In 2004, that state's government lifted an 11-year-old ban on the PWG, but the Maoists soon withdrew from ensuing peace talks, accusing the state government of breaking a cease-fire agreement. Violent attacks on government forces then escalated in 2005 and continued with even greater frequency in 2006.

The Indian government has since May 2005 sponsored a grassroots anti-Maoist effort. This "Salwa Jundum" ("Campaign for Peace" or, literally, "purification hunt") militia, especially active in the Chhattisgarh state, is viewed by some as an effective countervailing people's movement, but others label it a vigilante group that has engaged in its own coercive and violent tactics against innocent tribals. New Delhi has also expressed concern that indigenous Maoists are increasing their links with Nepali communists that recently ended their war with the Kathmandu government. Many analysts see abundant evidence that Naxalite activity is spreading and becoming more audacious in the face of incoherent and insufficient Indian government policies to halt it.

Hindu-Muslim Tensions

Some elements of India's Hindu majority have at times engaged in violent conflict with the country's Muslim minority. In late 1992, a huge mob of Hindu activists in the western city of Ayodhya demolished a 16th century mosque said to have been built at the birth site of the Hindu god Rama. Ensuing communal riots in cities across India left many hundreds dead. Bombay was especially hard hit and was the site of coordinated 1993 terrorist bombings believed to have been a retaliatory strike by Muslims. In early 2002, another group of Hindu activists returning by train to the western state of Gujarat after a visit to the site of the now razed Babri Mosque (and a proposed Hindu temple) were attacked by a Muslim mob in the town of Godhra; 58 were killed. Up to 2,000 people died in the fearsome communal rioting that followed, most of them Muslims. The BJP-led state and national governments came under fire for inaction; some observers saw evidence of state government complicity in anti-Muslim attacks.

The U.S. State Department and human rights groups have been critical of New Delhi's largely ineffectual efforts to bring those responsible to justice; some of these criticisms were echoed by the Indian Supreme Court in 2003. In March 2005, the State Department made a controversial decision to deny a U.S. visa to Gujarat Chief Minster Narendra Modi under a U.S. law barring entry for foreign government officials found to be complicit in severe violations of religious freedom. The decision was strongly criticized in India. Sporadic incidents of communal violence continued to destroy both lives and property in 2006.

Human Rights

According to the U.S. State Department's *India: Country Report on Human Rights Practices, 2005*, the Indian government "generally respected the human rights of its citizens; however, numerous serious problems remained." These included extensive societal violence against women; extrajudicial killings, including faked encounter killings; excessive use of force by security forces, arbitrary arrests, and incommunicado detentions in Kashmir and several northeastern states; torture and rape by agents of the government; poor prison conditions and lengthy pretrial detentions without charge; forced prostitution; child prostitution and female infanticide; human trafficking; and caste-based discrimination and violence, among others. Terrorist attacks and kidnapings also remained grievous problems, especially in Kashmir and the northeastern states.[50] New York-based Human Rights Watch's latest annual report noted "important positive steps" by the Indian government in 2005 with respect to human rights, but also reviewed the persistence of problems such as abuses by security forces and a failure to contain violent religious extremism.[51]

The State Department's Bureau of Democracy, Human Rights, and Labor has claimed that India's human right abuses "are generated by a traditionally hierarchical social structure, deeply rooted tensions among the country's many ethnic and religious communities, violent secessionist movements and the authorities' attempts to repress them, and deficient police methods and training."[52] India's 1958 Armed Forces Special Powers Act, which gives security forces wide leeway to act with impunity in conflict zones, has been called a facilitator of "grave human rights abuses" in several Indian states. India generally denies international human rights groups official access to Kashmir and other sensitive areas. State's 2005-2006 report on *Supporting Human Rights and Democracy* calls India "a vibrant democracy with strong constitutional human rights protections," but also asserts that "poor enforcement of laws, widespread corruption, a lack of accountability, and the severely overburdened court system weakened the delivery of justice."[53]

Human Trafficking

The State Department's June 2006 report on trafficking in persons said that New Delhi "does not fully comply with the minimum standards for the elimination of trafficking; however, it is making significant efforts to do so" and it placed India on the "Tier 2 Watch List" for the third consecutive year "due to its failure to show evidence of increasing efforts to address trafficking in persons." New Delhi later downplayed the claims and said the report was "not helpful." The trafficking of women and children is identified as a serious problem in India.[54]

Religious Freedom

An officially secular nation, India has a long tradition of religious tolerance (with occasional lapses), which is protected under its constitution. The population includes a Hindu majority of 82% as well as a large Muslim minority of some 150 million (14%). Christians, Sikhs, Buddhists, Jains, and others total less than 4%. Although freedom of religion is protected by the Indian government, human rights groups have noted that India's religious tolerance is susceptible to attack by religious extremists.

In its annual report on international religious freedom released in November 2005, the State Department found that the status of religious freedom in India had "improved in a number of ways ... yet serious problems remained." It lauded the New Delhi government for demonstrating a commitment to policies of religious inclusion, while claiming that "the government sometimes in the recent past did not act swiftly enough to counter societal attacks against religious minorities and attempts by some leaders of state and local governments to limit religious freedom."[55] A May 2006 report of the U.S. Commission on International Religious Freedom lauds continued improvements since the May 2004 election of the Congress-led coalition, but warns that concerns about religious freedom in India remain. These include ongoing attacks against religious minorities, perpetrated mainly by Hindu activists and most often in states with BJP-led governments. The Commission also continues to criticize allegedly insufficient state efforts to pursue justice in cases related to 2002 communal rioting in Gujarat.[56]

HIV/AIDS

The United Nations estimates that 5.7 million Indians are infected with HIV/AIDS, giving India the largest such population worldwide (India overtook South Africa in this category in 2006). Due to the country's large population, prevalence rates among adults remain below 1%. India's AIDS epidemic has become generalized in four states in the country's south (Andhra Pradesh, Tamil Nadu, Karnataka, and Maharashtra) and two in the northeast (Manipur and Nagaland). According to USAID, these six states account for 80% of the country's reported AIDS cases.[57] India first launched its AIDS control program in 1992; New Delhi boosted related funding to about $120 million in the most recent fiscal year. As part of its foreign assistance program in India, the U.S. government supports integrated HIV/AIDS prevention, treatment, and support services in high prevalence states. Stigma, gender inequalities, and discrimination present major obstacles to controlling India's HIV/AIDS epidemic. In the country's traditional society, open discussion of sexuality and risk of infection is rare, making education and awareness difficult. Analysts have said substantially greater resources are needed to address HIV/AIDS in India than are currently available.[58] (See also CRS Report RL33771, *Trends in U.S. Global AIDS Spending: FY2000-FY2007*.)

U.S. Assistance

Economic

According to the U.S. Agency for International Development (USAID), India has more people living in abject poverty (some 385 million) than do Latin America and Africa combined. From 1947 through 2005, the United States provided nearly $15 billion in economic loans and grants to India. USAID programs in India, budgeted at about $68 million in FY2006, concentrate on five areas: (1) *economic growth* (increased transparency and efficiency in the mobilization and allocation of resources); (2) *health* (improved overall health with a greater integration of food assistance, reproductive services, and the prevention of HIV/AIDS and other infectious diseases); (3) *disaster management*; (4) *energy and environment* (improved access to clean energy and water; the reduction of public subsidies through improved cost recovery); and (5) *opportunity and equity* (improved access to elementary education, and justice and other social and economic services for vulnerable groups, especially women and children).[59]

Security

The United States has provided about $161 million in military assistance to India since 1947, more than 90% of it distributed from 1962-1966. In recent years, modest security-related assistance has emphasized export control enhancements and military training. Earlier Bush Administration requests for Foreign Military Financing were later withdrawn, with the two countries agreeing to pursue commercial sales programs. The Pentagon reports military sales agreements with India worth $288 million in FY2002-FY2005.

Table 1. U.S. Assistance to India, FY2001-FY2007
(in millions of dollars)

Program or Account	FY2001 Actual	FY2002 Actual	FY2003 Actual	FY2004 Actual	FY2005 Actual	FY2006 Est.	FY2007 Request
CSH	24.6	41.7	47.4	47.8	53.2	47.7	48.4
DA	28.8	29.2	34.5	22.5	24.9	10.9	10.0
ESF	5.0	7.0	10.5	14.9	14.9	5.0	6.5
IMET	0.5	1.0	1.0	1.4	1.5	1.2	1.5
NADR	0.9	0.9	1.0	0.7	4.2	2.4	1.5
Subtotal	$59.8	$79.8	$94.4	$106.2	$98.7	$67.2	$67.9
Food Aid*	78.3	105.7	44.8	30.8	26.1	43.0	—
Total	$138.1	$185.5	$139.2	$137.0	$124.8	$110.2	$67.9

Sources: U.S. Departments of State and Agriculture; U.S. Agency for International Development.
Abbreviations:
CSH: Child Survival and Health
DA: Development Assistance
ESF: Economic Support Fund
IMET: International Military Education and Training
NADR: Nonproliferation, Anti-Terrorism, Demining, and Related (mainly export control assistance, but includes anti-terrorism assistance for FY2007)
* P.L.480 Title II (grants) and Section 416(b) of the Agricultural Act of 1949, as amended (surplus donations). Food aid totals do not include freight costs.

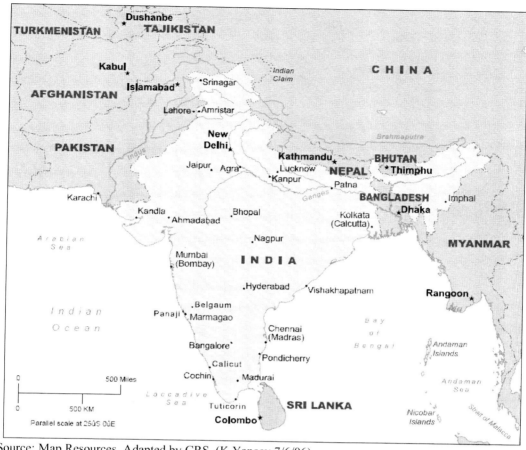

Source: Map Resources. Adapted by CRS. (K.Yancey 7/6/06).

Figure 1. Map of India.

REFERENCES

[1]   See [http://www.usindiafriendship.net/archives/usindiavision/delhideclaration.htm].
[2]   See [http://clinton4.nara.gov/WH/new/html/Wed_Oct_4_105959_2000.html].
[3]   See [http://www.state.gov/p/sca/rls/rm/6057.htm].
[4]   See [http://www.whitehouse.gov/news/releases/2005/07/20050718-6.html].
[5]   See [http://www.whitehouse.gov/news/releases/2006/03/20060302-5.html].
[6]   See   [http://www.comw.org/qdr/fulltext/nss2002.pdf]   and   [http://www.comw.org/
       qdr/fulltext/nss2006.pdf].
[7]   Walter Andersen, "The Indian-American Community Comes Into Its Political Own,"
       India Abroad, Sep. 1, 2006; "Indian Community Burgeoning in America," Associated
       Press, Oct. 22, 2006.
[8]   See Polly Nayak and Michael Krepon, "US Crisis Management in South Asia's Twin
       Peaks Crisis" at [http://www.stimson.org/southasia/pdf/USCrisisManagement.pdf].

[9] See John Lancaster, "India, China Hoping to 'Reshape the World Order' Together," *Washington Post*, Apr. 12, 2005, at [http://www.washingtonpost.com/wp-dyn/articles/A43053-2005Apr11.html].

[10] See Indian National Congress at [http://www.congress.org.in].

[11] See Bharatiya Janata Party at [http://www.bjp.org].

[12] See [http://www.whitehouse.gov/news/releases/2004/01/20040112-1.html].

[13] See [http://www.whitehouse.gov/news/releases/2005/07/20050718-6.html] and [http://www.indianembassy.org/press_release/2005/June/31.htm].

[14] See [http://www.whitehouse.gov/news/releases/2006/03/20060302-5.html].

[15] See "U.S.-India Civil Nuclear Cooperation Initiative Fact Sheet," U.S. Department of State, at [http://www.state.gov/r/pa/scp/2006/62904.htm]; Condoleezza Rice, "Our Opportunity With India," *Washington Post*, Mar. 13, 2006.

[16] See, for example, an open letter Congress at [http://www.indianembassy.org/newsite/press_release/2006/Mar/30.asp].

[17] See, for example, open letters to Congress at [http://fas.org/ intt2006/X3e_FDC01218.pdf]; [http://www. armscontrol.org/ pdf/20060912_ India_Ltr_Congress.pdf]; and [http:// www.armscontrol. org/pdf/ 20051118_ India_Ltr_Congress.pdf].

[18] See Sridhar Krishnaswami, "'Indo-US N-deal a Historic Opportunity,'" Rediff India Abroad, Mar. 22, 2006, at [http://www.rediff.com/news/2006/mar/22ndeal.htm].

[19] Some believe that offering U.S. support for a permanent Indian seat on the U.N. Security Council (UNSC) might have been a more appropriate and more readily delivered gesture. For example, the former Chairman of the House International Relations Subcommittee on Asia and the Pacific, Representative Jim Leach, called U.S. support for India's permanent seat on the UNSC a "self-apparent gesture" (House Committee on International Relations Hearing, "The U.S. and India: An Emerging Entente?," Sep. 8, 2005).

[20] See [http://www.whitehouse.gov/news/releases/2006/12/20061218-1.html]; [http://www.whitehouse.gov/news/releases/2006/12/20061218-12.html]; Carol Giacomo, "Bush India Statement Raises Congress Concerns," Reuters, Dec. 21, 2006).

[21] See "Press Statement of the BJP on the Indo-US Nuclear Deal," Dec. 10, 2006, at [http://www.bjp.org].

[22] Ibid.; M.R. Srinavasan, "India May Lose Control of Its Nuclear Future," *Frontline* (Madras), Dec. 14, 2006; "India's Top Scientists Oppose US Deal," Agence France Presse," Dec. 16, 2006; V. Sudarshan, "Not Much Frisson," *Outlook* (Delhi), Dec. 25, 2006.

[23] See "Excerpts from PM's Reply to Discussion in Rajya Sabha on Civil Nuclear Energy Cooperation with the United States," Aug. 17, 2006, at [http://www.carnegieendowment.org/static/npp/Singh_speech_Aug_2006.pdf].

[24] Author interview with Indian government officials, New Delhi, Sep.13, 2006.

[25] See U.S. Department of Commerce, Bureau of Industry and Security fact sheets at [http://www.bis.doc.gov/InternationalPrograms/IndiaCooperation.htm] and [http://www.bis.doc.gov/InternationalPrograms/IndiaICoopPresentation.htm].

[26] See [http://www.bis.doc.gov/Entities].

[27] See, for example, "Defense Firms Seek Sales in India," *Chicago Tribune*, Dec. 21, 2006.

[28] The India-Pakistan Relief Act of 1998 (in P.L. 105-277) authorized a one-year sanctions waiver exercised by President Clinton in November 1998. The Department of Defense Appropriations Act, 2000 (P.L. 106-79) gave the President permanent authority after October 1999 to waive nuclear-test- related sanctions applied against India and Pakistan. On October 27, 1999, President Clinton waived economic sanctions on India (Pakistan remained under sanctions as a result of an October 1999 military coup). (See CRS Report RS20995, *India and Pakistan: U.S. Economic Sanctions.*)

[29] See text of the January 2003 "New Delhi Declaration" at [http://meaindia.nic.in/declarestatement/2003/01/25jd1.htm].

[30] Although President Bush indicated he has not adopted the law's statements of policy as U.S. foreign policy, this provision has rankled many in New Delhi who view it as an "extraneous" constraint on India's foreign policy independence. In their explanatory statement accompanying P.L. 109-401, congressional conferees repeatedly emphasized their belief that securing India's assistance on this matter was "critical" (H.Rept. 109-721).

[31] See, for example, Vivek Raghuvanshi and Gopal Ratnam, "Indian Navy Trains Iranian Sailors," *Defense News*, Mar. 27, 2006; "India-Iran Military Ties Growing," *Strategic Affairs*, June 16, 2001; "Rice Downplays India's Iran Links," CNN.com, Apr. 6, 2006.

[32] A December 2006 study by the Indian Ministry of Statistics found that more than 200 million citizens in rural areas subsist on less than 12 rupees (about 27 cents) per day.

[33] See "U.S.-India Strategic Economic Partnership," U.S.-India CEO Forum, Mar. 2006 at [http://planningcommission.nic.in/reports/genrep/USIndia.pdf].

[34] See [http://www.ustr.gov/Document_Library/Reports_Publications/Section_Index.html].

[35] See [http://www.state.gov/e/rls/rm/2004/36345.htm].

[36] See [http://www.iipa.com/rbc/2006/2006SPEC301INDIA.pdf].

[37] See [http://newdelhi.usembassy.gov/pr120706.html]. Bush Administration policy is at [http://mumbai.usconsulate.gov/chris_israel.html].

[38] See [http://www.heritage.org/research/features/index/country.cfm?id=India].

[39] See [http://www.fraserinstitute.ca/admin/books/chapterfiles/3aEFW2006ch3A-K.pdf#].

[40] See [http://www.transparency.org].

[41] "India Blames U.S. for Failure of WTO Talks," *Hindu* (Madras), July 26, 2006; Secretary Johanns at [http://newdelhi.usembassy.gov/pr112106b.html].

[42] See Vibhuti Hate, "India's Energy Dilemma," Center for Strategic and International Studies, Sep. 7, 2006, at [http://www.csis.org/media/csis/pubs/sam98.pdf].

[43] See U.S. Department of State fact sheet at [http://www.state.gov/p/sca/rls/fs/2005/49724.htm]. In May 2006, the Senate Foreign Relations Committee passed S. 1950, to promote global energy security through increased cooperation between the United States and India on non-nuclear energy-related issues, but the full Senate took no action on the bill.

[44] See [http://powermin.nic.in/reports/pdf/ar05_06.pdf].

[45] Data from U.S. Department of Energy, Energy Information Administration, Dec. 2005 at [http://www.eia.doe.gov/emeu/cabs/india.html]; Tanvi Madan, "India," Brookings Institution Energy Security Series Report, Nov. 2006 at [http://www.brookings.edu/fp/research/energy/2006india.pdf].

[46] John Stephenson and Peter Tynan, "Will the U.S.-India Civil Nuclear Cooperation Initiative Light India?," Nov. 13, 2006, at [http://www.dalberg.com/npec.pdf].

[47] Mark Gregory, "India Struggles With Power Theft," BBC News, Mar. 15, 2006.

[48] See [http://www.state.gov/s/ct/rls/crt/2005/65275.htm].

[49] See [http://www.state.gov/s/ct/rls/crt/2005/64345.htm].

[50] See [http://www.state.gov/g/drl/rls/hrrpt/2005/61707.htm].

[51] See [http://hrw.org/wr2k6/wr2006.pdf].

[52] *Supporting Human Rights and Democracy: The U.S. Record 2002 -2003*," U.S. Department of State, at [http://www.state.gov/g/drl/rls/shrd/2002/21760.htm].

[53] See [http://www.state.gov/g/drl/rls/shrd/2005/63948.htm].

[54] See [http://www.state.gov/g/tip/rls/tiprpt/2006/65989.htm].

[55] See [http://www.state.gov/g/drl/rls/irf/2006/71440.htm].

[56] See [http://www.uscirf.gov/countries/publications/currentreport/index.html].

[57] See "Health Profile: India," U.S. Agency for International Development, at [http://www.usaid.gov/our_work/global_health/aids/Countries/ane/india_05.pdf].

[58] See, for example, Pramit Mitra and Teresita Schaffer, "Public Health and International Security: The Case of India," July 2006 at [http://www.csis.org/media/csis/pubs/060731_aids_india.pdf].

[59] See USAID India at [http://www.usaid.gov/in].

In: India on the Move
Editor: Lea M. Surit, pp. 69-100

ISBN: 978-1-60021-813-2
© 2007 Nova Science Publishers, Inc.

Chapter 3

U.S. NUCLEAR COOPERATION WITH INDIA: ISSUES FOR CONGRESS[*]

Sharon Squassoni

ABSTRACT

On July 18, 2005, President Bush announced he would "work to achieve full civil nuclear energy cooperation with India" and would "also seek agreement from Congress to adjust U.S. laws and policies," in the context of a broader, global partnership with India to promote stability, democracy, prosperity and peace. Administration officials have promoted nuclear cooperation with India as a way to reduce India's carbon dioxide emissions and its dependence on oil, bring India into the "nonproliferation mainstream" and create jobs for U.S. industry.

India, which has not signed the Nuclear Nonproliferation Treaty (NPT) and does not have International Atomic Energy Agency safeguards on all nuclear material in peaceful nuclear activities, exploded a "peaceful" nuclear device in 1974, convincing the world of the need for greater restrictions on nuclear trade. The United States created the Nuclear Suppliers Group (NSG) as a direct response to India's test, halted nuclear exports to India a few years later, and worked to convince other states to do the same. India tested nuclear weapons again in 1998.

Nonproliferation experts have argued that the potential costs of nuclear cooperation with India to U.S. and global nonproliferation policy may far exceed the benefits. At a time when the United States has called for all states to strengthen their domestic export control laws and for tighter multilateral controls, U.S. nuclear cooperation with India would require loosening its own nuclear export legislation, as well as creating a NSG exception. This is at odds with nearly three decades of U.S. nonproliferation policy and practice. Some believe the proposed agreement undercuts the basic bargain of the NPT, could undermine hard-won restrictions on nuclear supply, and could prompt some suppliers, like China, to justify supplying other states outside the NPT regime, like Pakistan. Others contend that allowing India access to the international uranium market will free up its domestic uranium sources to make more nuclear weapons.

U.S. nuclear cooperation is governed by the Atomic Energy Act (AEA). The Administration proposed legislation in 2006 that, in addition to providing waivers of

---

[*] Excerpted from CRS Report RL33016, dated December 22, 2006.

relevant provisions of the AEA (Sections 123 a. (2), 128, and 129), would have allowed an agreement to enter into force without a vote from Congress, as though it conformed to AEA requirements. In late July, the House passed H.R. 5682, which provided the necessary waivers but retained the prerogative of Congress to vote on the actual cooperation agreement later. The Senate passed its version of H.R. 5682 on November 16, 2006, and on December 7, the House approved the conference report. The Senate approved the conference report by unanimous consent early on December 9, and President Bush signed the bill into law (P.L. 109-401) on December 18. The law requires that the following, among other things, must occur before nuclear cooperation can proceed: submission of a finalized text of a cooperation agreement to Congress, approval of an IAEA safeguards agreement by the IAEA Board of Governors, consensus agreement within the NSG to make an exception for India, and passage of a joint resolution of approval of the agreement by the Congress.

RECENT DEVELOPMENTS

On December 8, 2006, the House agreed to the conference report on H.R. 5682, the "Henry J. Hyde United States-India Peaceful Atomic Energy Cooperation Act of 2006," by a vote of 330-59. The Senate agreed by unanimous consent to the conference report in the early hours of December 9, 2006. On December 18, President Bush signed the bill into law (P.L. 109-401.)[1] In his signing statement, President Bush noted that the act "will strengthen the strategic relationship between the United States and India."[2] With respect to particular provisions, President Bush stated that the executive branch would construe two sections of the bill as "advisory" only: policy statements in Section 103 and the restriction contained in Section 104 (d) (2) on transferring items to India that would not meet NSG guidelines. On the first, the President cited the Constitution's "commitment to the presidency of the authority to conduct the Nation's foreign affairs;" on the second, the President raised the question of whether the provision "unconstitutionally delegated legislative power to an international body." In other words, the President was questioning whether Congress were ceding authority to approve U.S. exports to the Nuclear Suppliers Group. However, U.S. officials, including Secretary of State Rice, have formally told Congress multiple times that the United States government would abide by NSG guidelines. The President's signing statement also noted that the executive branch would construe "provisions of the Act that mandate, regulate, or prohibit submission of information to the Congress, an international organization, or the public, such as sections 104, 109, 261, 271, 272, 273, 274, and 275, in a manner consistent with the President's constitutional authority to protect and control information that could impair foreign relations, national security, the deliberative processes of the Executive, or the performance of the Executive's constitutional duties."

Many steps are still ahead before nuclear cooperation can occur. P.L. 109-401 contains seven requirements that must be met for the President to exercise his waiver authority, and to present the final cooperation agreement to Congress for its approval. The agreement itself cannot enter into force without a joint resolution of approval from Congress. The seven requirements are 1) provision of a credible separation plan for India's nuclear facilities; 2) approval by the IAEA Board of Governors of India's new nuclear safeguards agreement; 3) substantial progress toward concluding an Additional Protocol; 4) India's active support for the conclusion of a treaty to ban fissile material production for nuclear weapons; 5) India's support for U.S. and international efforts to halt the spread of sensitive nuclear fuel cycle technologies (enrichment and reprocessing); 6) India taking necessary steps to secure nuclear and other sensitive materials and technologies through adherence to multilateral control regimes (like NSG and MTCR); and 7) a consensus decision by the NSG to make an exception for India.

Negotiations between the United States and India on the cooperation agreement reportedly have not progressed in the past six months, and negotiations between India and the International Atomic Energy Agency (IAEA) on a safeguards agreement reportedly also have made little progress. Although U.S. officials offered draft decision language to Nuclear Suppliers Group (NSG) members in March 2006 on a broad exception for India, members discussed the issue but did not agree to take up a decision at the May 2006 plenary. Similarly, the NSG did not take up a decision at the October 2006 Consultative Group meeting. However, since passage of P.L. 109-401, some observers believe that there may be greater incentives for progress in each of these areas than before.

BACKGROUND

The United States actively promoted nuclear energy cooperation with India from the mid-1950s, building nuclear power reactors (Tarapur), providing heavy water for the CIRUS research reactor, and allowing Indian scientists to study at U.S. nuclear laboratories. Although India was active in negotiations of the 1968 Nuclear Nonproliferation Treaty (NPT), India refused to join the NPT on grounds that it was discriminatory. The "peaceful" nuclear test in 1974 demonstrated that nuclear technology transferred for peaceful purposes could be used to produce nuclear weapons.[3] In the United States, the Congress responded by passing the Nuclear NonProliferation Act of 1978 (NNPA, P.L. 95-242), which imposed tough new requirements for U.S. nuclear exports to non-nuclear-weapon states — full-scope safeguards and termination of exports if such a state detonates a nuclear explosive device or engages in activities related to acquiring or manufacturing nuclear weapons, among other things.[4] Internationally, the United States created the Nuclear Suppliers Group (NSG) in 1975 to implement nuclear export controls. The NSG published guidelines in 1978 "to apply to nuclear transfers for peaceful purposes to help ensure that such transfers would not be diverted to unsafeguarded nuclear fuel cycle or nuclear explosive activities."[5]

Conditioning U.S. nuclear exports on non-nuclear-weapon states having full-scope safeguards created a problem particularly for India's reactors at Tarapur, which were built by U.S. firms and fuelled by U.S. low-enriched uranium, pursuant to a 1963 nuclear cooperation agreement. After passage of the NNPA, the Carter Administration exported two more uranium shipments under executive order after the Nuclear Regulatory Commission (NRC) refused to approve an export license on nonproliferation conditions. Although the House voted to disapprove the President's determination, the Senate voted 46 to 48 on a resolution of disapproval. After 1980, all nuclear exports from the United States to India were cut off under the terms of the NNPA. France supplied fuel under the terms of the U.S. agreement with India until France also adopted a full-scope safeguards requirement (1995). After the NSG adopted the full-scope safeguards condition in 1992, China picked up the slack, and Russia supplied fuel from 2001 to 2004.[6] The issue of LEU fuel for Tarapur became one of pride for the Indians, particularly since their other reactors use natural uranium and they reportedly do not have the enrichment capability to supply Tarapur with fuel. Although the NPT requires safeguards on items going to non-nuclear weapon states, it does not explicitly prohibit nuclear commerce with states outside the NPT. In 1995, at the NPT Extension Conference, states supported the principle that non-NPT parties should not be eligible for the same kinds of assistance as NPT parties in good standing.

GLOBAL PARTNERSHIP[7]

The Bush Administration had been considering a strategic partnership with India as early as 2001. Indian officials identified their growing energy needs as an area for cooperation, particularly in nuclear energy. The U.S.-India 2004 Next Steps in Strategic Partnership (NSSP) initiative included expanded cooperation in civil nuclear technology as one of three goals. Phase I of the NSSP, completed in September 2004, required addressing proliferation concerns and ensuring compliance with U.S. export controls.[8]

On July 18, 2005, President Bush announced the creation of a global partnership with India in a joint statement with Prime Minister Manmohan Singh.[9] Noting the "significance of civilian nuclear energy for meeting growing global energy demands in a cleaner and more efficient manner," President Bush said he would "work to achieve full civil nuclear energy cooperation with India" and would "also seek agreement from Congress to adjust U.S. laws and policies."

The Joint Statement noted that the United States "will work with friends and allies to adjust international regimes to enable full civil nuclear energy cooperation and trade with India, including but not limited to expeditious consideration of fuel supplies for safeguarded nuclear reactors at Tarapur." The United States committed to encouraging its partners to consider this request — a reversal in the U.S. position, which has been to ban fuel to Tarapur — and to consulting with its partners on Indian participation in ITER (collaboration on fusion research) and in the Generation IV International Forum for future reactor design.

Prime Minister Singh conveyed that India "would take on the same responsibilities and practices and acquire the same benefits and advantages as other leading countries with advanced nuclear technology, such as the United States."[10] India agreed to:

- identify and separate its civilian and military nuclear facilities and programs;
- declare its civilian facilities to the International Atomic Energy Agency (IAEA);
- voluntarily place civilian facilities under IAEA safeguards; ! sign an Additional Protocol for civilian facilities;
- continue its unilateral nuclear test moratorium;
- work with the United States to conclude a Fissile Material Cut Off Treaty (FMCT);[11]
- refrain from transferring enrichment and reprocessing technologies to states that do not have them, as well as support international efforts to limit their spread;
- secure its nuclear materials and technology through comprehensive export control legislation and through harmonization and adherence to Missile Technology Control Regime (MTCR) and NSG guidelines.

ISSUES FOR CONSIDERATION

The Atomic Energy Act of 1954, as amended, requires Congressional approval and oversight of peaceful nuclear cooperation agreements (details described below). As Senator Lugar has noted, "Ultimately the entire Congress ... must determine what effect the Joint Statement will have on U.S. efforts to halt the proliferation of weapons of mass destruction."[12] Congress held eight hearings in 2005 and 2006 on the global partnership and has consulted with the Administration on various aspects of the U.S.-India nuclear agreement.[13] The discussion of potential issues for consideration is drawn in part from the hearings and from the emerging debate.

Strategy vs. Tactics

The Bush Administration has described its "desire to transform relations with India" as "founded upon a strategic vision that transcends even today's most pressing security concerns."[14] There is clearly broad support for cultivating a close relationship with India, yet some members of Congress have suggested that civil nuclear cooperation may not be the most appropriate vehicle for advancing our relationship. In a House International Relations Committee hearing on September 8, 2005, Congressman Jim Leach stated,

> I don't know any member of Congress that doesn't want to have a warming of relations with the government of India.... I also don't know many members of Congress who are pushing for the precise commitment that the administration has made.[15]

Congressman Leach suggested instead that U.S. support for a permanent seat for India on the United Nations Security Council might have been a more appropriate gesture.

Other observers outside of Congress have questioned whether U.S. energy assistance should focus on expanding nuclear power, in contrast to other energy alternatives. Henry Sokolski, of the Nonproliferation Policy Education Center, has argued that Indian energy needs might be better met through free market allocation, including improved efficiency. He asserts that nuclear power is the least leveraged of India's options to meet India's energy needs, given that it currently provides only 2.7% of installed electrical capacity.[16] India's projections of its nuclear energy needs are predicated on an estimated annual growth rate of 8%, which some observers believe may be unrealistic.[17] One well-known Indian commentator, Brahma Chellaney, argued in the *International Herald Tribune* that the premise that India should meet its rapidly expanding energy needs through importing nuclear power reactors was flawed. Chellaney argued that a better approach for India would be to secure clean-coal and renewable energy technologies.[18]

The Senate Foreign Relations Committee's November 2, 2005 hearing sought, among other things, to answer the question of why civil nuclear cooperation was so important to the U.S.-Indian strategic relationship. Under Secretary of State Nicholas Burns told Committee members that "India had made this the central issue in the new partnership developing between our countries."[19]

Impact on U.S. Nonproliferation Policies

The Administration has characterized civil nuclear cooperation with India as a "win" for nonproliferation because it would bring India into the "nonproliferation mainstream." In short, the Administration is proposing that India should be courted as an *ally* in U.S. (not global) nonproliferation policy, rather than continue as a *target* of U.S. (and global) nonproliferation policy. India should become an ally for three reasons: past policies have not worked; India has a relatively good nonproliferation record anyway, and India could be a useful ally in the nonproliferation regime.

Some observers, however, are concerned that India may not support U.S. nonproliferation policies sufficiently to warrant nuclear cooperation, particularly where the United States faces its greatest nuclear proliferation threat: Iran. For example, at the September 8 HIRC hearing, several members of Congress questioned whether the United States had obtained assurances from India of its support on Iran before it issued the July 18 joint statement.

Iran

Two factors may present challenges to Indian support for U.S. policies toward Iran. First, India has a growing strategic relationship with Iran, not limited to its interest in a proposed $7.4 billion, 2800-km-long gas pipeline between Iran, Pakistan, and India. Second, India has a strong tradition of foreign policy independence, as a long-time leader of the Non-Aligned Movement (NAM) states and as a vigorous opponent of the discriminatory nature of the Nuclear Nonproliferation Treaty.[20] One witness before the House International Relations Committee hearing on November 16, 2005, suggested that opposition from the United States on the gas pipeline project is considered to be "interference with India's autonomy in foreign relations, as well as disregard for its security and energy needs."[21]

On Iran's nuclear program, Indian officials have stated they do not support a nuclear weapons option for Iran. However, they did not agree with the United States on the urgency of reporting Iran's nuclear program to the U.N. Security Council, which the United States has proposed since 2003, nor on the need to limit Iran's nuclear fuel cycle development. When the IAEA Board of Governors passed a resolution (GOV/2005/77) on September 24, 2005, finding Iran in noncompliance with its safeguards agreement, India voted with the United States, provoking significant domestic dissent. However, the resolution was weak by traditional standards of noncompliance resolutions: it did not pass by consensus (Venezuela voted against it and 12 countries abstained) and it did not refer the matter immediately to the Security Council. According to Indian Foreign Secretary Shyam Saran, India voted for the resolution and against the majority of NAM states which abstained, because it felt obligated after having pressured the EU-3 to omit reference to immediate referral to the U.N. Security Council.[22] Moreover, India explained its vote this way:

> In our Explanation of Vote, we have clearly expressed our opposition to Iran being declared as noncompliant with its safeguards agreements. Nor do we agree that the current situation could constitute a threat to international peace and security. Nevertheless, the resolution does not refer the matter to the Security Council and has agreed that outstanding issues be dealt with under the aegis of the IAEA itself. This is in line with our position and therefore, we have extended our support.[23]

On February 4, 2006, following Iran's resumption of some uranium enrichment research and development, the IAEA Board of Governors met in an emergency session and voted to report Iran's noncompliance to the U.N. Security Council.[24] India voted with the United States to report Iran, although this followed a controversial remark to the press the previous week by U.S. Ambassador to India, David Mulford, that India would have to support the United States on Iran in Vienna or the U.S. Congress would not support the peaceful nuclear cooperation agreement.[25]

Iran may also test India's support for curtailing peaceful nuclear programs. India has always been an advocate of states' rights to develop the peaceful uses of nuclear energy and for thirty years has derided the NPT and nonproliferation policies as discriminatory. The official Iranian press agency reported Prime Minister Singh as telling President Ahmadinejad on September 22, 2005, that solutions to Iran's nuclear problem should be based on the principle that Iran as an NPT member should retain its lawful rights.[26] On September 26, 2005, Foreign Secretary Saran told the press that "With respect to Iran's right to peaceful uses of nuclear energy, that is something which we have ourselves no reservations about."[27] In September 2006, India joined in the 118-nation Nonaligned Movement (NAM) summit statement that expressed support for Iran's "choices and decisions in the field of peaceful uses of nuclear technology and its fuel cycle policies."[28]

Reported Indian Transfers of WMD-Related Items to Iran[29]

Concerns about India's relationship with Iran extend, for some, to the transfer of WMD-related items. Entities in India and Iran appear to have engaged in very limited nuclear, chemical and missile-related transfers over the years. There are no publicly available indications of activities related to biological weapons. In the early 1990s, when Iran actively sought nuclear-related assistance and technology from many foreign sources, India appears to have played only a minor role in contrast to other states. India signed an agreement in November 1991 to provide a 10 megawatt research reactor to Tehran, but cancelled under pressure from the United States. Nonetheless, India reportedly trained Iranian nuclear scientists in the 1990s.[30] More recently, India's Foreign Minister Jaswant Singh stated in December 2003 that India "has and would continue to help Iran in its controversial bid to generate nuclear energy."[31]

In September 2004, the United States imposed sanctions on two Indian nuclear scientists, Dr. Y.S.R. Prasad and Dr. C. Surendar, under the Iran Nonproliferation Act. Indian officials protested, stating that cooperation had taken place under the auspices of the IAEA Technical Cooperation program. Other reports suggest that the scientists, who had served as Chairman and Managing Director of the Nuclear Power Corporation of India, Ltd. (NPCIL), which runs India's power reactors, passed information to Iran on tritium extraction from heavy water reactors.[32] Sanctions were lifted on Dr. Surendar in 2005.

In the chemical area, there is one confirmed transfer of 60 tons of thionyl chloride, a chemical that can be used in the production of mustard gas, from India to Iran in March 1989.[33] Other shipments in that time-frame reportedly were halted under U.S. pressure. India does not appear in the CIA's unclassified nonproliferation report to Congress as a supplier of chemical-weapons-related exports to Iran since the report began publication in 1997. India signed the Chemical Weapons Convention in 1993 and deposited its instrument of ratification until 1996. However, in December 2005, the United States imposed sanctions on Sabero Organic Chemicals Gujarat Ltd and Sandhya Organic Chemicals Pvt. Ltd, pursuant to the Iran Nonproliferation Act of 2000. In July 2006, the United States imposed sanctions on Balaji Amines and Prachi Poly Products, chemical manufacturers, pursuant to the Iran and Syrian Nonproliferation Act.[34]

Restricting Enrichment and Reprocessing

One of India's commitments in the July 18 statement was to refrain from transferring enrichment and reprocessing technologies to states that do not already have those technologies and to support international efforts to limit their spread. To some observers, U.S. efforts to restrict development of certain aspects of the nuclear fuel cycle (enrichment and reprocessing) that are most useful in a nuclear weapons development program are seen as creating a new category of "have-nots" — those states that can have some peaceful nuclear technology but cannot be trusted with it all. In other words, states like Japan, Germany, and Brazil might be trusted with sensitive technologies, but states like Iran and North Korea cannot be trusted. Historically, India has supported states' inalienable right to all peaceful uses of nuclear energy.

David Albright, president of the Institute for Science and International Security, published a report on March 10, 2006 that asserted that India had potentially exported centrifuge enrichment-related technology by virtue of tendering public offers and providing blueprints for technology to interested parties.[35] It is not clear whether Indian procurement practices facilitate transfer of technology, but the U.S. nuclear cooperation agreement will have no impact on those procurement practices. One question that arises is how India will be treated with respect to the U.S. policy restricting the expansion of enrichment and reprocessing technology. Is India a technology holder or not? On the one hand, the State Department asserted in responses to questions for the record from Senator Lugar that the United States will not engage in reprocessing or enrichment technology cooperation with India.[36] On the other hand, some observers have suggested that other NSG members may be interested in such cooperation with India and may not place as stringent requirements on India.

Other Priorities

In his February 11, 2004, speech, President Bush outlined several counterproliferation priorities, including expanding the Proliferation Security Initiative; strengthening laws and international controls against weapons of mass destruction (WMD) and missile proliferation (ultimately resulting in adoption of UNSCR 1540); expanding the G8 Global Partnership; and strengthening IAEA safeguards through universal adoption of the Additional Protocol. Ambassador Joseph has noted that India's adherence to NSG and MTCR guidelines would help ensure that WMD and missile-related technologies would not be transferred. Although India's adoption of the Additional Protocol would contribute to its universalization, there are few proliferation benefits to be realized from the adoption of such a protocol in a nuclear weapons state. Finally, although the United States reportedly has asked India to endorse PSI, that endorsement has not been forthcoming.

Impact on the Nonproliferation Regime

India has long stood outside the nonproliferation regime and this initiative raises questions about whether a partial solution can be beneficial or detrimental. Some considerations include cohesion within the Nuclear Suppliers Group, effect on nonnuclear weapon member states of the NPT, potential missed opportunities to strengthen the nuclear nonproliferation regime, and whether U.S. nuclear cooperation might in any way assist, encourage, or induce India to manufacture nuclear weapons, in possible violation of our Article I obligation under the NPT.

NSG Cohesion

Cohesion within the Nuclear Suppliers Group (NSG) is critical to effective implementation of export controls. As noted earlier, the NSG has followed the U.S. lead on requiring full-scope safeguards as a condition of nuclear supply. During the September 8, 2005 hearing, House International Relations Committee Chairman Henry Hyde noted that "Many of us are strong supporters of the NSG and would not want to see it weakened or destroyed." Chairman Hyde asked whether the administration could assure the Committee that

> ...no matter what else happens, that the administration will continue to abide by NSG guidelines, and if you are unable to gain consensus within the NSG for the amendments you need, you will not implement the new India policy in violation of NSG guidelines.

Ambassador Joseph told the Committee that "we intend to take no action that would undercut the effectiveness of the NSG," and further, that the Administration did not intend to change the consensus procedure or even change the NSG full-scope safeguards condition of nuclear supply.[37] The House-passed H.R. 5682 specified a requirement for NSG consensus, while the Senate-passed H.R. 5682 required NSG consensus and limited the decision to India, implicitly prohibiting a similar exception for Pakistan or Israel.

Dissent within the NSG could be counterproductive to achieving other objectives the United States is pursuing in nuclear nonproliferation, such as restricting the fuel cycle, disarming North Korea, and restraining Iran, all of which rely on the considerable support of friends and allies. Moreover, harmonizing export controls has played a key role in Bush counter- and non-proliferation policies in the last few years and is particularly important for interdiction efforts. U.S.-India cooperation could prompt other suppliers, like China, to justify supplying other nonnuclear-weapon states, like Pakistan. China, which joined the NSG in 2004, has shared some negative views on the nuclear cooperation agreement, and reportedly favors an NSG decision based on criteria, not just an exception for India.[38] Russia, which only halted fuel supplies to the Indian Tarapur reactors in December 2004 at the insistence of the NSG, has already stepped into the breach by resuming fuel supplies to Tarapur under the guise of the safety exception, reportedly to the dismay of many NSG members.[39]

Effect on NPT Member States

India has complained for years that it has been excluded from regular nuclear commerce because of its status outside the NPT. Some observers believe this is a good thing and shows that the policy works. Others believe that a new paradigm is needed for India because it will not join the NPT as a non-nuclear weapon state. One observer argued in a 2005 law review journal that India could join the NPT as a non-nuclear weapon state and not give up its nuclear weapons, primarily because the NPT defines "nuclear weapon states" but does not define non-nuclear weapon states and because the treaty does not expressly prohibit non-nuclear weapon states from possessing nuclear weapons, just from acquiring, manufacturing, receiving transfers of or control of nuclear weapons and not to seek or receive any assistance in manufacturing nuclear weapons.[40] However, that approach would require India to stop producing fissile material for nuclear weapons and place all nuclear material (except that which is in its nuclear weapons) under IAEA safeguards.

The NPT is basically a two-way bargain. Non-nuclear-weapon states under the NPT give up the option of developing nuclear weapons in exchange for the promise of peaceful nuclear cooperation. Nuclear weapon states under the NPT were not required immediately to disarm, but to commit to eventual disarmament. India, as a state outside the NPT, is bound by neither of these commitments. Some observers may see the offer of nuclear cooperation previously reserved for states under the NPT with full-scope safeguards not only as undermining the agreements made by nonnuclear weapon states, but also the commitments made by nuclear weapon states to eventually disarm. In this view, India's continued unilateral testing moratorium is insufficient, compared with signing the Comprehensive Test Ban Treaty and its support for FMCT negotiations is insufficient compared with capping its nuclear weapons fissile material production now, as four of the five nuclear weapon states formally have done. Some have suggested that the absence of an Indian cap on fissile material production for weapons may make it difficult for China to declare it has halted fissile material production for weapons. Others have suggested that, absent a cap on fissile material production, it would be difficult to ensure that peaceful nuclear cooperation was not indirectly assisting or encouraging India's nuclear weapons program.

The proliferation shocks of the 1990s, when the Iraqi and North Korean clandestine nuclear weapons programs surfaced, led to the strengthening of the NPT and export control regimes. At the 1995 NPT Review and Extension Conference, NPT parties affirmed the NSG's decision to require full-scope safeguards for nuclear exports, supporting the principle that non-NPT parties should not be eligible for the same kinds of assistance as NPT parties in good standing. At the 2000 conference, NPT parties again supported that principle. According to the U.S. ambassador to the conference at that time, "Reinforcement of this guideline is important given some who have questioned whether this principle should be relaxed for India and Pakistan, which have not accepted full-scope IAEA safeguards. The answer from NPT parties is clearly no."[41]

In the past 10 years, virtually all states agreed to strengthen the nonproliferation regime, sacrificing some sovereignty by allowing additional, intrusive inspections under the Additional Protocol. In the wake of revelations in 2004 about Pakistani scientist A.Q. Khan's nuclear black market sales, non-nuclear weapon states under the NPT are also being asked to consider further restrictions on their sovereignty by voluntarily restricting their access to sensitive nuclear technologies like uranium enrichment and reprocessing. If some states view the U.S.-Indian nuclear cooperation agreement as a breach of faith in the basic bargain of the NPT, they might be less inclined to accept additional sacrifices, to the detriment of the nonproliferation regime.

Missed Opportunities

Ambassador Joseph described the nuclear initiative as representing "a substantial net gain for nonproliferation. It is a win for our strategic relationship, a win for energy security, and a win for nonproliferation." Ambassador Joseph said he was "convinced that the nonproliferation regime will emerge stronger as a result."[42]

However, some observers have suggested the United States asked for too little. For example, Fred McGoldrick, Harold Bengelsdorf and Lawrence Scheinman, argued in the October 2005 issue of *Arms Control Today* that

> It is open to serious doubt whether the proposed Indian concessions were significant enough to justify the accommodations promised by the United States and whether the steps the United States and India agreed to take in the civil nuclear area will, on balance, be supportive of global nonproliferation efforts...If the Bush Administration is able to implement the joint declaration without significant modification, it will have given the Indians a great deal —acknowledgment as a de facto nuclear weapon state and access to the international nuclear energy market — in return for largely symbolic concessions in the nonproliferation area.[43]

Robert Einhorn, of the Center for Strategic and International Studies, told members of the House International Relations Committee on October 26, 2005, that several of the steps pledged by India are "simply reaffirmations of existing positions."[44] The Indian embassy itself, not surprisingly, has downplayed the depth and breadth of its nonproliferation commitments, describing all but its safeguards commitments under the July 18 statement in the following way:

> A number of existing policies were also reiterated by India, among them a unilateral moratorium on nuclear testing, working towards conclusion of a multilateral Fissile Material Cut-off Treaty, non-transfer of enrichment and reprocessing technologies, securing nuclear materials and technology through export control, and harmonisation with MTCR and NSG guidelines.[45]

India has had a self-imposed nuclear test moratorium for years, although supporters of this agreement note that this agreement would bind India bilaterally to honoring that pledge. If the NSG used a similar criterion in approving exports, it could further strengthen that pledge. India has supported FMCT negotiations for years, despite continuing to produce fissile material for use in nuclear weapons. Since the pace of FMCT negotiations has been glacial, support for negotiations could allow India to continue producing fissile material indefinitely. Moreover, the draft treaty on FMCT tabled by the United States in Geneva on May 18, 2006, would not require India's accession for the treaty to enter into force, thus lessening the pressure on India to join. Prime Minister Singh told his Parliament on August 17, 2006 that "India is willing to join only a non discriminatory, multilaterally negotiated and internationally verifiable FMCT."[46] Unfortunately, this conflicts with the U.S. draft proposal, which contains no verification measures.

The most far-reaching of the commitments is to separate civilian and military facilities, declare civilian facilities, and place them under safeguards. Administration officials have pointed to this aspect of the agreement as a nonproliferation "plus." Yet, allowing India broad latitude in determining which of its facilities to put under international safeguards is a privilege accorded currently only to nuclear weapon states under the NPT. Although the United States "in no way recognizes India as an NPT nuclear weapons state," excluding military facilities from inspections is a tacit recognition of their legitimacy.

IAEA Director General Dr. ElBaradei said that he has "always advocated concrete and practical steps towards the universal application of IAEA safeguards."[47] In remarks to the Carnegie Endowment's Nonproliferation Conference in November 2005, Dr. ElBaradei cited additional safety benefits of putting more Indian facilities under safeguards. However, it should be noted that the NSG already has an exception to its full-scope safeguards requirement for safety-related items.

The Administration has asserted that India has an "exceptional" record of nonproliferation and despite a few isolated sanctions, most of the evidence supports the view that India has exercised restraint in export controls.[48] As such, however, India's promise to refrain from transferring enrichment and reprocessing technologies to states that do not have them, as well as its promise to adhere to NSG guidelines, may be little more than a formality.

Many observers have noted that there are no measures in this global partnership to restrain India's nuclear weapons program. Many have suggested that the United States should have asked India to halt fissile material production for weapons. Ambassador Bob Joseph stated that the United States remains "committed to achieving Indian curtailment of fissile material production, and we have strongly encouraged a move in this direction. We stand willing to explore options that might serve this objective, but we will not insist on it for purposes of this civil nuclear initiative."[49] Indian officials, on the other hand, have taken pains to point out that "There is no commitment at all to cease production of fissile material ahead of the conclusion of such a multilateral [FMCT] treaty."[50] Prime Minister Singh told the parliament in August 2006 that "Our position on this matter is unambiguous. We are not willing to accept a moratorium on the production of fissile material."[51] Other observers have noted that although India committed to a test ban, it did not commit to signing the Comprehensive Test Ban Treaty. Still other observers have suggested that if India insists on being treated as a nuclear weapon state, it should undertake responsibilities similar to those of the other nuclear weapon states, for example, placing fissile material excess to defense needs under safeguards. Many believe that real limits on India's nuclear weapons program would constitute a "win" for nonproliferation.

U.S. NPT Article I Obligations

Given that India will continue to make nuclear weapons, but is considered under the NPT to be a non-nuclear weapon state, the question arises as to whether U.S. assistance might in any way "assist, encourage, or induce any non-nuclear weapon state to manufacture or otherwise acquire nuclear weapons or other nuclear explosive devices, or control over such weapons or explosive devices."[52] In testimony before the House International Relations Committee, David Albright of ISIS stated that "Without India halting production of fissile material for its nuclear weapons programs, nuclear assistance, particularly any in the areas involving the fuel cycle, would likely spill over to India's nuclear weapons program."[53]

Three areas raise potential concerns: whether the separation plan is adequate to ensure that cooperation does not in any way assist in the development or production of nuclear weapons; whether cooperation confers nuclear weapons state status on India, with an unintended consequence of encouraging the Indian nuclear weapons program; and whether opening up the international uranium market frees up India's domestic uranium for use in its weapons program.

Administration officials have defended the separation plan as credible and defensible because it covers more than just a token number of Indian facilities, provides for safeguards in perpetuity, and includes upstream and downstream facilities.[54] The conclusion that the plan calls for safeguards in perpetuity, as described in greater detail below, may be premature. Until India negotiates and the IAEA Board of Governors approves a safeguards agreement, it is unclear that safeguards will be applied in perpetuity to India's eight indigenous reactors that have been declared. More importantly, while IAEA safeguards ensure that nuclear material is not diverted, there are no procedures or measures in place to ensure that information, technology and know-how are not transferred from the civil sector to the military sector. This could become a key loophole, particularly because the separation plan places eight indigenous power reactors under safeguards, while leaving at least eight indigenous power reactors outside of safeguards. Without additional measures to prevent the transfer of personnel or knowledge from the safeguarded program to the unsafeguarded program, there would be little assurance that assistance to the safeguarded program could not migrate to the military program. For example, U.S. assistance to one of the eight indigenous power reactors, whether focused on nuclear safety, improving operational efficiency, or extending its lifetime, could easily be applied by Indian personnel to one of the similar, but unsafeguarded indigenous power reactors. Some Indian commentators have suggested that the United States has little technology to offer India, and others have doubted whether U.S. assistance would be provided to those indigenous power reactors.

A second area that raises concerns is whether nuclear cooperation confers nuclear weapon state status on India, which could encourage its weapons program. Senator Lugar noted in a hearing on November 2, 2005 that "Prior to the July 18 joint statement India had repeatedly sought unsuccessfully to be recognized as an official nuclear weapons state, a status the NPT reserves only for the United States, China, France, Russia and the United Kingdom. Opponents argue that granting India such status will undermine the essential bargain that is at the core of NPT, namely, that only by foregoing nuclear weapons can a country gain civilian nuclear assistance." Dr. Ashton Carter, testifying at that SFRC hearing, stated that:

> India obtained *de-facto* recognition of its nuclear weapons status. The United States will behave, and urge others to behave, as if India were a nuclear weapons state under the NPT. We won't deny it most civil nuclear technology or commerce. We won't require it to put all of its nuclear facilities under IAEA safeguards — only those it declares to be civil. Beyond these technicalities, nuclear recognition confers an enormous political benefit on India.

Secretary of State Rice, in response to a question for the record in April 2006 on India's nuclear weapon state status, stated that "While India has nuclear weapons and we must deal with this fact in a realistic, pragmatic manner, we do not recognize India as a nuclear weapon state or seek to legitimize India's nuclear weapons program." However, other officials' statements appear to lend more support to India. Under Secretary of State Nicholas Burns told reporters on March 2, 2006, that "...India is a nuclear weapons power, and India will preserve part of its nuclear industry to service its nuclear weapons program."[55]

Mohamed ElBaradei, Director General of the IAEA, views the U.S.-India deal as "neutral" because "it does not confer any 'status', legal or otherwise, on India as a possessor of nuclear weapons."[56] Nonetheless, a successful U.S. effort to gain an exemption in U.S. nuclear cooperation law would place India in the company of only four other nations — the United Kingdom, France, China, and Russia — all *de jure* nuclear weapon states. Many observers believe that this legitimizes India's nuclear weapons program by providing *de facto* recognition. Indian official statements repeatedly have used the term "advanced nuclear states" as synonymous with nuclear weapon states; India's separation plan compares Indian nuclear capabilities only to those of other nuclear weapon states. Prime Minister Singh told the Parliament in August 2006 that

> The July Statement did not refer to India as a Nuclear Weapons State because that has a particular connotation in the NPT, but it explicitly acknowledged the existence of India's military nuclear facilities. It also meant that India would not attract full-scope safeguards such as those applied to non-nuclear weapon states that are signatories to the NPT and there would be no curbs on continuation of India's nuclear weapon related activities. In these important respects, India would be very much on par with the five Nuclear Weapon States who are signatories to the NPT. Similarly, the Separation Plan provided for an India specific safeguards agreement with the IAEA with assurances of uninterrupted supply of fuel to reactors together with India's right to take corrective measures in the event fuel supplies are interrupted. We have made clear to the US that India's strategic programme is totally outside the purview of the July Statement, and we oppose any legislative provisions that mandate scrutiny of our nuclear weapons programme or our unsafeguarded nuclear facilities.

Finally, critics of U.S.-Indian nuclear cooperation have argued that giving India access to the international uranium market would free up India's domestic uranium resources for its weapons program.[57] India's leading strategist K. Subrahmanyam suggested as much in a December 12, 2005 article in *The Times of India*:

> Given India's uranium ore crunch and the need to build up our minimum credible nuclear deterrent arsenal as fast as possible, it is to India's advantage to categorize as many power reactors as possible as civilian ones to be refueled by imported uranium and conserve our native uranium fuel for weapon-grade plutonium production."[58]

Secretary Rice countered the critics in the House International Relations Committee hearing on April 5, 2006:

> ...Clearly this agreement does not constrain India's nuclear weapons program... Neither, however, ... does it enhance India's capability to build nuclear weapons. India has about, by most estimates, 50,000 tons or so of uranium in its reserves. That means that the very small percentage of that that would be needed for a military program, they could get, certainly, without this agreement I would note that we do not believe that the constraint on India's nuclear program is the availability or absence of nuclear material. With 50,000 tons of uranium available to them, only a very small percentage of that would be needed for a military program..

Secretary Rice seemed to be suggesting that having more uranium would not encourage or assist India's nuclear weapons program because it already had the fissile material it needed. If, as Secretary Rice suggests, India's military requirements are dwarfed by civilian requirements, then finding international sources for civilian requirements could result in a windfall for the weapons program. However, the question for the United States is not whether India intends to ramp up its weapons program with freed-up uranium, but whether U.S. and other states' actions create a new capability for India to do so.

A report by Ashley Tellis, a Bush Administration advisor who helped negotiate parts of the agreement with India, echoes Secretary Rice's arguments.[59] Tellis states that India does not seek to maximize its nuclear arsenal, that uranium shortages are exaggerated and transient, and that nuclear weapons require much less uranium than civilian power reactors. Tellis poses the question of whether U.S. assistance allows India to do something it can't do now, and whether India would, as a result of U.S. cooperation, ramp up its weapons program, and concludes that it would not. However, such conclusions are ultimately speculative, given the secrecy of India's weapons program.

For the purpose of identifying whether the United States is complying with its Article I obligations, the appropriate question is whether U.S. assistance encourages India's nuclear weapons program. There is no question that opening the international uranium market to India will result in more indigenous Indian uranium available for weapons, because it will not be consumed by India's newly safeguarded reactors. In the view of many nonproliferation analysts, the key to ensuring that civilian nuclear cooperation does not assist India's weapons program is to insist on India halting its fissile material production for weapons. That would narrow the area of concern to technology transfer to the weapons and delivery systems themselves, rather than fissile material production in reactors, enrichment facilities, and reprocessing plants.

Among others, Henry Sokolski suggested in the *Wall Street Journal* that "If we want to keep this aid from freeing up India's domestic nuclear resources to make more bombs...we have to get serious about India capping its nuclear weapons program."

It is worth noting that even before the NPT entered into force, negotiators recognized that a state outside the NPT could preserve its domestic uranium sources for a possible weapons program as long as it agreed to accept IAEA safeguards on the items it imported. In the late 1960s, however, Congress was more concerned about ensuring that the United States could supply its allies outside the treaty, such as Japan and Germany, with nuclear fuel. According to Mason Willrich's history of the NPT,

> As long as India does not become a party to the Non-Proliferation Treaty, it can continue to import from the parties nuclear materials and equipment subject to safeguards for use in its civil nuclear power program. This would free its indigenous resources, particularly its limited uranium supply, for possible concentration on a nuclear weapons program.[60]

KEY STEPS

There are several key steps to take before a nuclear cooperation agreement can be implemented with India. Although P.L. 109-401 allows the President certain authorities to waive restrictions in the Atomic Energy Act, at least seven actions must occur before the agreement for cooperation can enter into force. India took the first step by identifying civilian nuclear facilities in March 2006 and began preliminary negotiations with the IAEA on a safeguards arrangement. In mid-2006, U.S. officials began negotiations with India on the peaceful nuclear cooperation agreement itself and consultations with NSG members. After a safeguards agreement has been concluded, an agreement for cooperation has been finalized, NSG approval has been obtained, and all the other relevant determinations are made, the executive branch must bring the final agreement for cooperation back to Congress for a joint resolution of approval.

Separation Plan and Safeguards[61]

U.S. and Indian officials agreed on India's separation plan in March 2006. The key elements of India's separation plan are:[62]

- 8 indigenous Indian power reactors will be placed under an India-specific safeguards agreement, bringing the total number of power reactors under safeguards to 14 of 22 (6 are already under safeguards)[63]
- Future power reactors may also be placed under safeguards, if India declares them as civilian
- Some facilities in the Nuclear Fuel Complex (e.g., fuel fabrication) will be specified as civilian in 2008.
- 9 research facilities and 3 heavy water plants would be declared as civilian, but are "safeguards-irrelevant."
- The following facilities and activities were not on the separation list:
- 8 indigenous Indian power reactors
- Fast Breeder test Reactor (FTBR) and Prototype Fast Breeder Reactors (PFBR) under construction
- Enrichment facilities
- Spent fuel reprocessing facilities (except for the existing safeguards on the Power Reactor Fuel Reprocessing (PREFRE) plant)
- Research reactors: CIRUS (which will be shut down in 2010), Dhruva, Advanced Heavy Water Reactor
- 3 heavy water plants
- Various military-related plants (e.g., prototype naval reactor).

India's Implementation Document noted that facilities were excluded from the civilian list if they were located in a larger hub of strategic significance, even if they were not normally engaged in activities of strategic significance, calling into question whether the plan really will result in a "separation" of civilian and military facilities. Moreover, the plan stated that electricity grid connectivity is not relevant to the separation exercise and that grid connectivity would be necessary "irrespective of whether the reactor concerned is civilian or not civilian." This means that "military" reactors will continue to provide civilian electricity.

In addition, the statement in the Implementation Document that the India-specific safeguards agreement will provide "for safeguards to guard against withdrawal of safeguarded nuclear material from civilian use at any time as well as for providing for corrective measures that India may take to ensure uninterrupted operation of its civilian reactors in the event of disruption of foreign fuel supplies" raises questions about whether the Indian interpretation of safeguards in perpetuity mirrors the U.S. interpretation. Corrective measures are not defined, but probably mean the use of unsafeguarded nuclear material in an indigenous reactor. In that case, there could be periods of time when such reactors, using unsafeguarded nuclear material, would not necessarily be inspected. Moreover, IAEA safeguards agreements for states outside the NPT (INFCIRC-66 type) do not require safeguards in perpetuity for reactors that a state voluntarily places under safeguards, although they can be written that way.[64] According to one IAEA official, since 1974, the duration of 66-type agreements has been tied to actual use of supplied material or items, rather than fixed periods of time,[65] which would support the concept of lifting safeguards on the reactors once they are no longer using safeguarded material.

Another question that arises is whether India, in the absence of full-scope safeguards, can provide sufficient confidence that U.S. peaceful nuclear technology will not be diverted to nuclear weapons purposes, as many believe it was in 1974.[66] In response to a question for the record submitted by Senator Lugar on April 5, 2006 on whether exports of nuclear material or reactors from the United States would in any way assist India's nuclear weapons program, the Administration noted that "Any items sent to India would be subject to safeguards, and implementation of the Additional Protocol would provide further assurances of the non-diversion of such items or material."[67] However, the Additional Protocol provides assurances of absence of undeclared activities, rather than of the non-diversion of safeguarded items, contrary to Secretary Rice's assertions.

The application of "permanent" safeguards on the facilities declared to be civilian could make the separation more meaningful.[68] Early in the process, Indian officials had suggested they would adopt a strictly voluntary safeguards arrangement, such as those in force for nuclear weapon states wherein facilities can be put on and taken off of lists of eligible facilities. In his November 2, 2005 testimony before the Senate Foreign Relations Committee, Under Secretary Joseph stated that the United States "would not view a voluntary offer arrangement as defensible from a nonproliferation standpoint or consistent with the Joint Statement, and therefore do not believe it would constitute an acceptable safeguards arrangement." He also asserted that safeguards must be applied in perpetuity.[69] This stems from a U.S. legal obligation under Section 123 a. (1) of the Atomic Energy Act to maintain safeguards with respect to all U.S. materials and equipment transferred pursuant to the agreement *as long as that material or equipment remains under the jurisdiction of the cooperating party, irrespective of whether the agreement is terminated or suspended* [emphasis added]. Although it is likely that safeguards will be applied in perpetuity to anything the United States transfers, it may not be as likely that safeguards will be applied in perpetuity to those indigenous reactors India places under safeguards, for the reasons described above. The safeguards agreement, yet to be negotiated between India and the IAEA, will determine whether that is the case.

Administration officials repeatedly have stressed that India's separation plan must be credible, transparent, and defensible from a nonproliferation standpoint,[70] and that "the resultant safeguards must contribute to our nonproliferation goals."[71] To those observers who interpreted that statement to mean that a separation plan would need to take into account India's past commitments (e.g., use of purportedly "peaceful" nuclear reactors like CIRUS to produce plutonium for nuclear weapons) and the impact on its nuclear weapons program (e.g., capping India's fissile material production), the separation plan may not appear credible. To those observers who interpreted "credible" to mean that all power reactors that supplied electricity would be declared civilian because they have a civilian use, the separation plan also may not appear credible. Secretary Rice has stressed, however, that more reactors under safeguards means more transparency, more physical security, better nuclear safety, and therefore increased safety for the United States.[72] Even so, some observers may argue that types of facilities safeguarded are critical in assessing whether the plan is defensible from a nonproliferation standpoint. For example, in terms of preventing terrorist access to fissile material, safeguarding facilities like reprocessing and enrichment plants and breeder reactors could be viewed as providing a significant nonproliferation benefit because the materials produced by these plants are a few steps closer to potential use in a bomb. In addition, safeguards on enrichment, reprocessing plants, and breeder reactors would support the 2002 U.S. National Strategy to Combat Weapons of Mass Destruction, in which the United States pledged to "continue to discourage the worldwide accumulation of separated plutonium and to minimize the use of highly-enriched uranium."[73]

NSG Support

U.S. officials have consulted both formally and informally with NSG members thus far.[74] The United Kingdom, Russia and France have all supported an exception to the NSG's full-scope safeguards requirement for exports to India. In September 2005, France issued a joint statement with India that it would work with NSG partners to enable nuclear cooperation with India to go forward, and Prime Ministers Chirac and Singh signed a nuclear cooperation declaration with India in February 2006.[75] Other responses have been mixed, especially from Sweden and Canada. Some states, including Ireland, Sweden, Norway, and the Netherlands, reportedly have raised questions. Canada reportedly told U.S. officials that it welcomed U.S. steps to addressing what has been a thorny issue in the NPT — nuclear weapon states outside the regime — but had hoped the United States would have placed more conditions on the agreement, particularly an Indian freeze on production of fissile material for nuclear weapons.[76] The draft decision tabled by U.S. officials on March 23, 2006 reportedly sought an exception for India to the NSG requirements of full-scope safeguards, notwithstanding the exceptions for safety assistance and for those agreements signed before the full-scope safeguards requirement came into effect in 1992. It did not contain, reportedly, any restrictions on enrichment or reprocessing cooperation, nor on heavy water or HEU or plutonium sales.

In October 2005, the NSG held a Consultative Group meeting at which some members reportedly stressed the need for limits on cooperation, such as no enrichment or reprocessing cooperation, no heavy water cooperation, and no exports of highly enriched uranium or plutonium. In late March 2006, NSG members held another Consultative Group meeting, at which the United States presented a draft decision for potential discussion at the NSG plenary in May 2006. Member states did not agree to put the draft decision on the May agenda, but continued discussions.[77] Likewise, the October 2006 Consultative Group meeting did not yield an NSG decision.

Consulting with Congress

Under existing law (Atomic Energy Act of 1954; P.L. 95-242; 42 U.S.C. § 2153 et seq.) all significant nuclear cooperation requires an agreement for cooperation.[78]

The Nuclear Non-Proliferation Act of 1978 (NNPA) amended the Atomic Energy Act of 1954 to include, among other things, a requirement for full-scope safeguards for significant nuclear exports non-nuclear weapon states.[79]

At issue are the requirements for full-scope nuclear safeguards contained in Section 123 a. (2) for approval of an agreement for cooperation and in Section 128 for licensing nuclear exports. India, a non-party to the Nuclear Nonproliferation Treaty (NPT), does not have full-scope safeguards, nor is it ever expected to adopt full-scope safeguards, since it has a nuclear weapons program that would preclude them. Also at issue is the requirement in Section 129 to stop exports if a non-nuclear weapon state has detonated a nuclear device after 1978, among other things. India detonated several nuclear devices in 1998.

These three sections of the AEA provide mechanisms for the President to waive those requirements and sanctions (in Section 129), which are spelled out in more detail below. The sections also provide legislative vetoes, in the form of concurrent resolutions, of the presidential determinations. In 1983, however, the Supreme Court decided in *INS v. Chadha* that legislative veto provisions that do not satisfy the bicameralism and presentment requirements of Article I of the Constitution were unconstitutional. In 1985, some parts of the AEA were amended to provide for joint resolutions of approval or disapproval (e.g., Section 123 d.). The *Chadha* decision affects how Congress would disapprove of such presidential determinations under existing law and therefore affects the impact of the Administration's proposed legislation.

Agreements for Cooperation

Section 123 of the AEA (42 U.S.C. 2153) specifies what must happen before nuclear cooperation can take place.

- Section 123 a. states that the proposed agreement shall include the terms, conditions, duration, nature, and scope of cooperation and lists nine criteria that the agreement must meet. It also contains provisions for the President to exempt an agreement from any of the nine criteria, and includes details on the kinds of information the executive branch must provide to Congress;
- Section 123 b. specifies the process for submitting the text of the agreement to Congress;
- Section 123 c. specifies how Congress approves cooperation agreements that are limited in scope (e.g., do not transfer nuclear material or cover reactors larger than 5 MWe.).[80]
- Section 123 d. specifies how Congress approves agreements that do cover significant nuclear cooperation (transfer of nuclear material or reactors larger than 5 MWe), including exempted agreements.

The United States has 23 agreements for cooperation in place now, and had an agreement with India from 1963 to 1993. Such agreements for cooperation are "framework" agreements — they do not guarantee that cooperation will take place or that nuclear material will be transferred, but rather set the terms of reference and provide authorization for cooperation. The 1963 U.S.-India cooperation agreement is anomalous in that it did guarantee fuel for the Tarapur reactors, even though other U.S. nuclear cooperation agreements reportedly have not included any such guarantees.[81]

Section 123 a. lists nine criteria that an agreement must meet unless the President determines an exemption is necessary. These are listed in Section 123 a., paragraphs (1) through (9), 42 U.S.C. 2153. They are guarantees that (1) safeguards on nuclear material and equipment transferred continue in perpetuity; (2) full-scope safeguards are applied in non-nuclear weapon states; (3) nothing transferred is used for any nuclear explosive device or for any other military purpose; (4) the United States has the right of return if the cooperating state detonates a nuclear explosive device or terminates or abrogates an International Atomic Energy Agency (IAEA) safeguards agreement; (5) there is no transfer of material or classified data without U.S. consent; (6) physical security is maintained; (7) there is no enrichment or reprocessing by the recipient state without prior approval; (8) storage is approved by United States for plutonium and highly enriched uranium; and (9) anything produced through cooperation is subject to all of the above requirements.

In the case of India, the most difficult of these requirements to meet is the full-scope safeguards requirement for non-nuclear weapon states (Sec. 123 a. (2)). India is considered to be a non-nuclear weapon state because it did not, as defined by the Nuclear Nonproliferation Treaty, explode a nuclear device before January 1, 1967.[82] The President may exempt an agreement for cooperation from any of the requirements in Section 123 a. if he determines that meeting the requirement would be "seriously prejudicial to the achievement of U.S. non-proliferation objectives or otherwise jeopardize the common defense and security." An exempted agreement would not become effective "unless the Congress adopts, and there is enacted, a joint resolution stating that the Congress does favor such agreement."[83] In other words, both chambers of Congress must approve the agreement if it does not contain all of the Section 123 a. requirements.

If Congress votes to approve an agreement for cooperation that was exempted because the recipient state did not have full-scope safeguards (Section 123 a. (2)), such approval would essentially waive the Nuclear Regulatory Commission's (NRC) obligation to consider full-scope safeguards as an export license authorization criterion under Section 128. However, Congress would still have the authority to review one export license authorization approximately every 12 months after the agreement for cooperation has entered into force. (See discussion below) Section 123 d., in part, states the following:

> if Congress fails to disapprove a proposed agreement for cooperation which exempts the recipient nation from the requirement set forth in subsection 123 a. (2), such failure to act shall constitute a failure to adopt a resolution of disapproval pursuant to subsection 128 b. (3) for purposes of the Commission's consideration of applications and requests under section 126 a. (2) and there shall be no congressional review pursuant to section 128 of any subsequent license or authorization with respect to that state until the first such license or authorization which is issued after twelve months from the elapse of the sixty-day period in which the agreement for cooperation in question is reviewed by the Congress.[84]

Export Licensing

In addition to specifying criteria for framework agreements, the AEA sets out procedures for licensing exports (Sections 126, 127, and 128 codified as amended at 42 U.S.C. 2155, 2156, 2157). The Nuclear Regulatory Commission (NRC) is required to meet criteria in Sections 127 and 128 in authorizing export licenses; Section 128 contains the requirement for full-scope safeguards for non-nuclear weapon states. Section 126 b. (2) contains a provision for the President to authorize an export in the event that the NRC deems that the export would not meet Section 127 and 128 criteria. The President must determine "that failure to approve an export would be seriously prejudicial to the achievement of U.S. nonproliferation objectives or otherwise jeopardize the common defense and security." The President would submit his executive order, along with a detailed assessment and other documentation, to Congress for 60 days of continuous session.

After 60 days of continuous session, the export would go through unless Congress passes a concurrent resolution of disapproval.[85]

In the case of exports pursuant to an exempted agreement for cooperation (i.e., exempted from the full-scope safeguards requirement), as described above, the NRC would not have to meet the full-scope safeguards requirement in assessing whether it could issue export licenses (Section 128 b. (3)). Congress would review one license every 12 months. If Congress passed a resolution of disapproval, no further exports could be made during that Congress.[86]

In both cases, Section 128 contains a provision for the President to waive termination of exports by notifying the Congress that the state has adopted full-scope safeguards or that the state has made significant progress toward full-scope safeguards, or that U.S. foreign policy interests dictate reconsideration. Such a determination would become effective unless Congress disagrees with the President's determination.[87]

Termination of Cooperation

Section 129 of the AEA (42 U.S.C. 2158) requires ending exports of nuclear materials and equipment or sensitive nuclear technology to any non-nuclear-weapon state that, after March 10, 1978, the President determines to have:

- detonated a nuclear explosive device;
- terminated or abrogated IAEA safeguards;
- materially violated an IAEA safeguards agreement; or
- engaged in activities involving source or special nuclear material and having "direct significance" for the manufacture or acquisition of nuclear explosive devices, and "has failed to take steps which, in the President's judgment, represent sufficient progress toward terminating such activities."

In addition, Section 129 would also halt exports to any nation the President determines:

- to have materially violated the terms of an agreement for cooperation with the U.S.;
- assisted, encouraged, or induced any other non-nuclear weapon state to obtain nuclear explosives or the materials and technologies needed to manufacture them; or
- re-transferred or entered into an agreement for exporting reprocessing equipment, materials or technology to another non-nuclear weapons state.

The President can waive termination if he determines that "cessation of such exports would be seriously prejudicial to the achievement of United States nonproliferation objectives or otherwise jeopardize the common defense and security." The President must submit his determination to Congress, which is then referred to the House International Relations Committee and the Senate Foreign Relations Committee for 60 days of continuous session. The determination becomes effective unless Congress opposes it.[8]

EVOLUTION OF P.L. 109-401[89]

On March 9, 2006, the Administration submitted its proposed legislation to Representative Hyde and Senator Lugar, and on March 16, 2006, Representatives Hyde and Lantos introduced H.R. 4974, and Senator Lugar introduced S. 2429. Following public hearings and committee mark-ups, the House passed H.R. 5682 on July 26, 2006 by a vote of 359 to 68 and the Senate passed its version of H.R. 5682, substituting the text of the amended S. 3709, on November 16, 2006 by a vote of 85 to 12. One issue that held up the Senate bill was the inclusion, in Title II, of the implementing legislation for the U.S. Additional Protocol — an agreement between the United States and the IAEA to provide for enhanced information, access, and inspection tools for IAEA inspectors as they inspect U.S. nuclear and other facilities under the U.S. voluntary safeguards agreement.

The House and Senate version of the H.R. 5682 were remarkably similar, with four differences.[90] The Senate version contained an additional requirement for the President to execute his waiver authority, an amendment introduced by Senator Harkin and adopted by unanimous consent that the President determine that India is "fully and actively participating in U.S. and international efforts to dissuade, sanction and contain Iran for its nuclear program." This provision was watered down into a reporting requirement in the conference report. The Senate version also had two unique sections related to the cooperation agreement, Sections 106 and 107, both of which appear in the conference report. Section 106 (now Section 104 (d) (4)) prohibits exports of equipment, material or technology related for uranium enrichment, spent fuel reprocessing or heavy water production unless conducted in a multinational facility participating in a project approved by the International Atomic Energy Agency (IAEA) or in a facility participating in a bilateral or multilateral project to develop a proliferation-resistant fuel cycle. Section 107 (now Section 104 (d) (5)) would establish a program to monitor that U.S. technology is being used appropriately by Indian recipients. Finally, the Senate version also contained the implementing legislation for the U.S. Additional Protocol in Title II, which was retained in the conference report.

P.L. 109-401 allows the President to

- exempt a proposed agreement for cooperation with India from the full-scope safeguards requirement of Section 123 a. (2) of the Atomic Energy Act;
- exempt an agreement from any export review by the Congress under Section 128 of the AEA;
- exempt the agreement from restrictions resulting from India's nuclear weapons activities under Section 129 a. (1) (D) of the AEA, and exempt the agreement from a cutoff in exports because of India's 1998 nuclear test.

It does not exempt the agreement from a future cutoff in exports if India tests a nuclear explosive device again. For the President to exercise his waiver authority, seven requirements, as outlined earlier, must be met. P.L. 109-401 contains numerous statements of policy and reporting requirements, as well as restrictions on certain kinds of transfers. There are specific prohibitions on (as outlined in Section 104 (d)): (1) transfers that would violate U.S. obligations under Article 1 of the NPT not to in any way assist any country to manufacture or otherwise acquire nuclear weapons; (2) transfers that would violate NSG guidelines in force at the time; (3) a cutoff in exports if India is found to have violated NSG or MTCR guidelines; 4) enrichment and reprocessing cooperation, except to "a multinational facility participating in an IAEA-approved program to provide alternatives to national fuel cycle capabilities; or... a facility participating in, and the export, reexport, transfer, or retransfer is associated with, a bilateral or multinational program to develop a proliferation-resistant fuel cycle." Additionally, the law provides for a nuclear export accountability program (formerly Section 107 of the Senate version of H.R. 5682).

President's Signing Statement

In President Bush's signing statement, he noted that the act "will strengthen the strategic relationship between the United States and India."[91] With respect to particular provisions, President Bush stated that the executive branch would construe two sections of the bill as "advisory" only: policy statements in Section 103 and the restriction contained in Section 104 (d) (2) on transferring items to India that would not meet NSG guidelines. On the first, the President cited the Constitution's "commitment to the presidency of the authority to conduct the Nation's foreign affairs"; on the second, the President raised the question of whether the provision "unconstitutionally delegated legislative power to an international body." In other words, the President was questioning whether Congress were ceding authority to approve U.S. exports to the Nuclear Suppliers Group. However, U.S. officials, including Secretary of State Rice, have formally told Congress multiple times that the United States government would abide by NSG guidelines. The President's signing statement also noted that the executive branch would construe "provisions of the Act that mandate, regulate, or prohibit submission of information to the Congress, an international organization, or the public, such as sections 104, 109, 261, 271, 272, 273, 274, and 275, in a manner consistent with the President's constitutional authority to protect and control information that could impair foreign relations, national security, the deliberative processes of the Executive, or the performance of the Executive's constitutional duties." This seems to suggest that the executive branch might limit the scope of reporting required by Congress in those sections, not just on national security grounds, but to protect executive branch processes or performance. The implications of the approach outlined in this signing statement will not be clear until the executive branch produces (or does not produce, as the case may be) required reports.

POTENTIAL ISSUES FOR CONGRESS

It may be some time before all the requirements are met for the executive branch to bring a final cooperation agreement before Congress again. When that happens, Congress will have another opportunity to consider the specific parameters of cooperation. In addition to meeting the requirements set out in P.L. 109-401, Congress may want to assess how well the actual agreement meets the other nonproliferation requirements of the Atomic Energy Act (other than full-scope safeguards). Some substantive questions could include whether the Indian safeguards agreement meets the U.S. requirements for perpetuity; whether U.S. assistance could benefit India's nuclear weapons program and whether India's nonproliferation record, as described in the Nuclear Nonproliferation Nonproliferation Assessment Statement, contains anything that causes concern for Members, or would have a negative impact on U.S. national security.

Although joint resolutions of approval for nuclear cooperation agreements receive expedited consideration, significant concerns about the agreement could result in the passage of a joint resolution of approval with conditions, as happened in the case of the 1985 U.S. nuclear cooperation agreement with China. In P.L. 93-183, Congress required the President to certify that (a) reciprocal arrangements would ensure that nuclear materials, facilities or components would be used solely for peaceful purposes; (b) China was not violating paragraph 2 of Section 129 (particularly with respect to assisting non-nuclear weapon states in a nuclear weapons program); and (c) that U.S. approval for subsequent potential Chinese requests to enrich, reprocess or alter in any form material provided under the agreement would not be automatic. A presidential certification on the three matters was not made until January 12, 1998.

APPENDIX: FREQUENTLY ASKED QUESTIONS ABOUT U.S.-INDIA NUCLEAR COOPERATION

Is there a signed peaceful nuclear cooperation agreement?

No. The United States and India must negotiate the text of a peaceful nuclear cooperation agreement (pursuant to the Atomic Energy Act). That agreement is required to specify the terms, conditions, duration, nature and scope of cooperation. Negotiating that agreement could last anywhere from months to a year or more.

What was the agreement signed on March 2, 2006?

In July 2005, India committed to identifying and separating its civilian and military nuclear facilities and programs. On March 2, 2006, U.S. and Indian officials agreed upon a "separation" plan.

Is membership in the Nuclear Nonproliferation Treaty (NPT) necessary to sign a peaceful nuclear cooperation agreement?

No, but the Nuclear Nonproliferation Act of 1978 made comprehensive International Atomic Energy Agency (IAEA) safeguards a requirement for nuclear cooperation with non-nuclear weapon states.

What are comprehensive IAEA safeguards?

States that join the NPT as non-nuclear weapon states are obligated to sign an agreement with the IAEA to safeguard all the nuclear material in their state and under their jurisdiction. These are called "comprehensive" or "full-scope" nuclear safeguards, or INFCIRC/153-type safeguards.

Does India have IAEA safeguards now on some nuclear facilities?

India has facility-specific (INFCIRC/66-type) safeguards on two U.S.-supplied reactors at Tarapur, two Canadian-supplied reactors at Rajasthan, and has concluded a safeguards agreement for two Russian-supplied reactors under construction at Kudankulam. India also applies intermittent safeguards at its reprocessing plant at Tarapur when safeguarded fuel is present.

If India has nuclear weapons, why isn't it considered a nuclear weapons state?

The Nuclear Nonproliferation Treaty (NPT) defined nuclear weapons states as those states that had detonated a nuclear explosive device before January 1, 1967. Those states are the United States, the United Kingdom, Russia, France, and China. U.S. law follows the NPT definition.

Which laws is the Administration seeking to adjust?

The Atomic Energy Act (P.L. 83-703) does not prohibit nuclear cooperation with India, but has three provisions that contain restrictions. The first is Section 123, which requires non-nuclear weapon state recipients of U.S. nuclear cooperation to have full-scope safeguards, among other requirements. The second is Section 128, which requires full-scope safeguards to license nuclear exports. The third is Section 129, which would terminate nuclear exports if a non-nuclear weapon state has conducted a nuclear test after 1978 or continues a nuclear weapons program without steps to terminate such activities.

What facilities did India designate as civilian?

In a statement to the Indian Parliament on March 7, 2006, India identified 14 out of 22 power reactors to declare as civilian; some facilities at the fuel fabrication complex to be identified in the future; some spent fuel storage; 3 heavy water plants (which are not required to be safeguarded); and several research facilities (which are not required to be safeguarded). India has stated that the 14 plants equal 65% of its total nuclear electricity capacity (known as megawattage). However, six of those plants are already covered by existing IAEA safeguards agreements.

On May 11, 2006, Indian officials provided more details. The eight indigenous power reactors to be safeguarded include RAPS 3, 4, 5, and 6 (at Rajasthan); two at Uttar Pradesh (NAPS 1, 2); and two at Gujrat (KAPS 1, 2). The safeguards will be phased in beginning in 2007 and completed by 2014. Other facilities (so-called "upstream") were also identified in May, to include a uranium oxide plant, two ceramic fuel fabrication plants, an enriched uranium oxide plant, an enriched fuel fabrication plant and the Gadolinia Facility.

What does P.L. 109-401 accomplish?

P.L. 109-401, "The Henry J. Hyde United States-India Peaceful Atomic Energy Cooperation Act of 2006," was signed into law by President Bush on December 18, 2006. It allows the President to waive certain restrictions contained in the Atomic Energy Act, namely that non-nuclear weapon states, as defined by the NPT and U.S. law, must have full scope, or comprehensive safeguards on all nuclear material in their state before the United States can engage in nuclear cooperation with them. P.L. 109-401 sets out seven requirements that the President must determine to have happened before he can exercise his waiver authority. These are 1) provision of a credible separation plan for India's nuclear facilities; 2) approval by the IAEA Board of Governors of India's new nuclear safeguards agreement; 3) substantial progress toward concluding an Additional Protocol; 4) India's active support for the conclusion of a treaty to ban fissile material production for nuclear weapons; 5) India's support for U.S. and international efforts to halt the spread of sensitive nuclear fuel cycle technologies (enrichment and reprocessing); 6) India taking necessary steps to secure nuclear and other sensitive materials and technologies through adherence to multilateral control regimes (like NSG and MTCR); and 7) a consensus decision by the NSG to make an exception for India.

What are the next steps?
1. U.S. and Indian officials must finalize the text of a cooperation agreement (so-called a "123 agreement" after Section 123 of the Atomic Energy Act);
2. Indian and IAEA officials must negotiate a safeguards agreement, and the Board of Governors of the IAEA must approve it;
3. NSG member states must agree by consensus to make an exception for India; and
4. Congress must approve the text of the "123 agreement" in a joint resolution of approval.

REFERENCES

[1]   See CRS Report RL33561, *U.S.-India Nuclear Cooperation: A Side-By-Side Comparison of Current Legislation,* by Sharon Squassoni and Jill Marie Parillo, (hereafter cited as CRS Report RL33561) for more detail on the bills.
[2]   See [http://www.whitehouse.gov/news/releases/2006/12/20061218-12.html].
[3]   For an excellent analysis of the proliferation implications of U.S. nuclear exports to India, see Gary Milhollin, "Stopping the Indian Bomb," *The American Journal of International Law,* July 1987, 81 A.J.I.L. 593. See [http://www.wisconsinproject.org/pubs/ articles/1987/stoppingindianbomb.htm].
[4]   The NNPA, in part, amended the Atomic Energy Act of 1954. See 42 U.S.C. 2151 et seq. Prior to the 1970 NPT, safeguards (inspections, material protection, control and accounting) were applied to specific facilities or materials (known as INFCIRC/66-type agreements). The NPT required safeguards on all nuclear material in all peaceful nuclear activities for non-nuclear-weapon-state parties (those states not having detonated a nuclear explosive device prior to Jan. 1, 1967).
[5]   IAEA Document INFCIRC/254, *Guidelines for Transfers of Nuclear-related Dual-use Equipment, Materials, Software, and Related Technology.* Part 1 covers "trigger list" items: those especially designed or prepared for nuclear use: (i) nuclear material; (ii) nuclear reactors and equipment; (iii) non-nuclear material for reactors; (iv) plant and

equipment for reprocessing, enrichment and conversion of nuclear material and for fuel fabrication and heavy water production; and (v) associated technology. Part 2 covers dual-use items. Additional NSG criteria for dual-use exports include NPT membership and/or full-scope safeguards agreement; appropriate end-use; whether the technology would be used in a reprocessing or enrichment facility; the state's support for nonproliferation; and the risk of potential nuclear terrorism.

[6]   China was not a member of the NSG until 2004. Russia, an NSG member, exported fuel, citing a safety exception, but NSG members objected so strongly that Russia suspended supply in 2004. Russia agreed to resupply Tarapur in late February and informed the NSG on Feb. 27, 2006, reportedly citing the NSG safety exception.

[7]   See also CRS Report RL33072, U.S.-India Bilateral Agreements and "Global Partnership," by K. Alan Kronstadt.

[8]   See fact sheet on the NSSP at [http://www.state.gov/r/pa/prs/ps/2004/36290.htm].

[9]   Joint Statement Between President George W. Bush and Prime Minister Manmohan Singh, White House Press Release, July 18, 2005, Washington, DC (hereafter cited as "July 18 Joint Statement") [http://www.whitehouse.gov/news/ releases/2005/ 07/20050718-6.html].

[10]   July 18 Joint Statement.

[11]   See CRS Report RS22474, *Banning Fissile Material Production for Nuclear Weapons: Prospects for a Treaty (FMCT)*, by Sharon Squassoni, Andrew Demkee, and Jill Marie Parillo, for more detailed information about the issue and negotiations.

[12]   Opening Statement, Chairman Richard G. Lugar, Senate Foreign Relations Committee hearing on "Implications of U.S.-India Nuclear Energy Cooperation," Nov. 2, 2005 (hereafter referred to as Nov. 2, 2005 SFRC India hearing).

[13]   The House International Relations Committee held the following hearings: "The U.S. and India: An Emerging Entente?" (Sept. 8, 2005); "The U.S.-India Global Partnership: The Impact on Nonproliferation"(Oct. 26, 2005); and "U.S.-India Global Partnership: How Significant for American Interests?" (Nov. 16, 2005); "The U.S.-India Global Partnership" (Apr. 5, 2006); "U.S.-India Global Partnership: Legislative Options" (May 11, 2006) See [http://wwwc.house.gov/international_relations/] for testimonies of witnesses. The Senate Foreign Relations Committee held the following hearings: "Implications of U.S.-India Nuclear Energy Cooperation" (Nov. 2, 2005); "U.S.-India Atomic Energy Cooperation: The Indian Separation Plan and the Administration's Legislative Proposal" (Apr. 5, 2006); and "U.S.-India Atomic Energy Cooperation: Strategic and Nonproliferation Implications" (Apr. 26, 2006). See [http://foreign. senate.gov/hearing.html] for testimonies.

[14]   Statement of Under Secretary of State for Political Affairs, R. Nicholas Burns, September 8, 2005, House Committee on International Relations, Hearing on "The U.S. and India: An Emerging Entente?" (hereafter cited as "Sept. 8, 2005, HIRC US-India hearing") p. 1.

[15]   Remarks by Congressman Jim Leach, Sept. 8, 2005, HIRC US-India Hearing.

[16]   Henry Sokolski, "Implementing the Indian Nuclear Deal: What's at Risk, What Congress Should Require," Briefing to Congress, Sept. 2005.

[17]   See "India's Growth Target Unrealistic," *Financial Times*, Jan. 23, 2003, which quotes the Asia Development Bank.

[18]   Brahma Chellaney, "US Deal is a Bad Choice for Power Generation," *International Herald Tribune*, Dec. 27, 2005.

[19]   Statement of Under Secretary of State for Political Affairs, R. Nicholas Burns, November 2, 2005, Senate Foreign Relations Committee Hearing on "Implications of U.S.-India Nuclear Energy Cooperation.

[20]   See Miriam Rajkumar, "Indian Independence," Carnegie Analysis, Sept. 20, 2005, at [http://www.carnegieendowment.org/npp/publications/index.cfm?fa=view   and   id= 17486].

[21]   Dr. Francine Frankel, Statement before the House International Relations Committee, Nov. 16, 2005, "India's Potential Importance for Vital U.S. Geopolitical Objectives in Asia: A Hedge Against a Rising China?"

[22]   "Press Briefing by Foreign Secretary on the events in UN and IAEA," New Delhi, Sept. 26, 2005, available at [http://www.indianembassy.org/press_release/2005/Sept/29.htm].

[23]   Briefing by MEA Official Spokesperson on Draft Resolution on Iran in IAEA, New Delhi, Sept. 24, 2005, available at [http://www.indianembassy.org/ press_release/ 2005/Sept/16.htm].

[24]   See CRS Report RS21592, *Iran's Nuclear Program: Recent Developments*, by Sharon Squassoni.

[25]   "U.S.-India Nuclear Deal Could Die, Envoy Warns," *Washington Post*, Jan. 26, 2006.

[26]   "Ahmadinejad Thanks India for Positive Stands on Iran in IAEA," IRNA, Sept. 23, 2005.

[27]   Sept. 26, 2005 press briefing, op. cit.

[28]   Iran Republic News Agency, "118 countries back Iran's nuclear program" *Iran Times,* Sept. 18, 2006.

[29]   See CRS Report RS22530, *India and Iran: WMD Proliferation Activities,* by Sharon Squassoni, for more information related to sanctions imposed for Indian transfers to Iran.

[30]   See [http://www.nti.org/e_research/profiles/Iran/2867.html].

[31]   "India Denies Nuclear Cooperation with Iran," *Agence France Presse*, Dec. 13, 2003.

[32]   John Larkin and Jay Solomon, "As Ties Between India and Iran Rise, U.S. Grows Edgy," *Wall Street Journal*, March 24, 2005.

[33]   Thionyl chloride is a Schedule 3 chemical under the Chemical Weapons Convention. It has military and civilian uses, and is widely used in the laboratory and in industry.

[34]   See list of sanctions at [http://www.state.gov/t/isn/c15234.htm].

[35]   David Albright and Susan Basu, "India's Gas Centrifuge Program: Stopping Illicit Procurement and the Leakage of Technical Centrifuge Know-How," available at [http://www.isis-online.org/publications/southasia/indianprocurement.pdf].

[36]   "Questions for the Record Submitted to Under Secretaries Nicholas Burns and Robert Joseph by Chairman Richard G. Lugar (#6), Senate Foreign Relations Committee, November 2, 2005."

[37]   Sept. 8, 2005, HIRC US-India hearing.

[38]   See, for example, "Nuclear Nonproliferation System is Challenged," *People's Daily,* Mar. 16, 2006.

[39]   "Concern over Russian Plan to Sell Nuclear Reactor Fuel," *Financial Times*, Mar. 15, 2006.

[40] David S. Jonas, "Variations on Non-nuclear: May the 'Final Four' Join the Nuclear Nonproliferation Treaty as Non-nuclear Weapon States While Retaining Their Nuclear Weapons?" *Michigan State Law Review,* Summer, 2005, p. 417 ff. Mr. Jonas is General Counsel of the National Nuclear Security Agency.

[41] Ambassador Norman Wulf, "Observations from the 2000 NPT Review Conference," *Arms Control Today,* Nov. 2000.

[42] Sept. 8, 2005, HIRC US-India hearing.

[43] Fred McGoldrick, Harold Bengelsdorf, Lawrence Scheinman, "The U.S.-India Nuclear Deal: Taking Stock," *Arms Control Today,* Oct. 2005, pp. 6-12. See [http://www.armscontrol.org/act/2005_10/OCT-Cover.asp].

[44] Statement by Robert J. Einhorn, Center for Strategic and International Studies, "The U.S.-India Global Partnership: The Impact on Nonproliferation" Oct. 26, 2005.

[45] "Backgrounder on India-U.S. Civilian Nuclear Energy Cooperation," Indian Embassy, July 29, 2005. See [http://www.indianembassy.org/press_release/2005/July/29.htm].

[46] Prime Minister Singh, "Excerpts from Prime Minister's Reply to Discussion in Raja Sabha on Civil Nuclear Energy Cooperation with the United States." Remarks are available at the Indian Ministry of External Affairs website, [http://mea.gov.in].

[47] "IAEA Director General Reacts to U.S.-India Cooperation Agreement," See [http://www.iaea.org/NewsCenter/PressReleases/2005/prn200504.html]. Critics of the IAEA point out that it is an organization that measures its success in part by how much nuclear material and how many facilities are under inspection.

[48] On Sept. 29, 2004, the State Department published Public Notice 4845 in the Federal Register imposing sanctions pursuant to the Iran Nonproliferation Act of 2000. Two Indian scientists were named — Dr. Prasad and C. Surendar. The State Department has not revealed what technology or equipment was transferred, but both scientists have worked for the Nuclear Power Corporation of India, Ltd., a government-owned entity that runs India's nuclear power plants. The Indian embassy reported in December 2005 that sanctions on Dr. Surendar had been removed. See [http://www.indianembassy.org/press_release/5.asp]. In the December 30, 2005 Federal Register, Public Notice 5257 stated simply that sanctions on an Indian entity issued in Public Notice 4845 had been rescinded.

[49] Sept 8, 2005, HIRC US-India hearing.

[50] "Backgrounder on India-U.S. Nuclear Energy Cooperation," July 29, 2005.

[51] "Excerpts from Prime Minister's Reply," August 17, 2006, op. cit.

[52] See Zia Mian and M.V. Ramana, "Wrong Ends, Means, and Needs: Behind the U.S. Nuclear Deal with India, *Arms Control Today,* January/February 2006. See also Robert Einhorn, "Limiting the Damage," *The National Interest,* Winter 2005/2006.

[53] Statement of David Albright before the House International Relations Committee on October 26, 2005 (hereafter HIRC Oct 26, 2005 hearing).

[54] Questions for the Record Submitted to Secretary of State Condoleezza Rice by Senator Richard Lugar (#2) Senate Foreign Relations Committee, Apr. 5, 2006.

[55] White House, Office of the Press Secretary, "Press Briefing by Under Secretary of State for Political Affairs Nick Burns," Maurya Sheraton Hotel and Towers, New Delhi, India, March 2, 2006.

[56] Mohamed ElBaradei, "Rethinking Nuclear Safeguards," *Washington Post,* June 14, 2006.

[57] See Henry Sokolski, "Fissile isn't Facile," *Wall Street Journal*, Feb. 21, 2006.

[58] K. Subrahmanyam, former head of the Institute for Defence Studies and Analysis, was appointed Head of the National Security Council Advisory Board (NSCAB) established by the first Vajpayee government to draft the Indian nuclear doctrine. He currently chairs PM Singh's Global Strategic Developments Task Force. See also Dr. A. Gopalakrishnan, "Civilian and Strategic Nuclear Facilities of India," Jan. 5, 2006.

[59] Ashley J. Tellis, "Atoms for War? U.S.-Indian Civilian Nuclear Cooperation and India's Nuclear Arsenal," Carnegie Endowment for International Peace, 2006. Available at [http://www.carnegieendowment.org/files/atomsforwarrevised1.pdf].

[60] Mason Willrich, *Non-proliferation Treaty: Framework for Nuclear Arms Control*, The Michie Company, Charlottesville, VA, 1969, p. 125.

[61] See CRS Report RL33292, *India's Nuclear Separation Plan: Issues and Views*, by Sharon Squassoni, for details on the separation plan.

[62] Prime Minister Singh presented "Implementation of the India-United States Joint Statement of July 18, 2005: India's Separation Plan," to Parliament on March 7, 2006. This is available at [http://indianembassy.org/newsite/ press_release/2006/Mar/ sepplan.pdf]. The plan was updated on May 11, 2006 to include names of reactors and upstream facilities, as well as dates they would be submitted to safeguards.

[63] According to the May 11th update, the 8 indigenous reactors to be safeguarded are: 4 at Rajasthan (RAPS 3, 4, 5 and 6); 2 at Uttar Pradesh (NAPS 1, 2); and 2 at Gujrat (KAPS 1, 2).

[64] Paragraph 16 of INFCIRC/66 states "In the light of Article XII.A.5 of the Statute, it is desirable that safeguards agreements should provide for the continuation of safeguards, subject to the provisions of this document, with respect to produced special fissionable material and to any materials substituted therefor."

[65] Laura Rockwood, "Legal Instruments Related to the Application of the Safeguards," paper for conference, "Safeguards: Verifying Compliance with Nonproliferation Commitments," Kingston, Jamaica, Apr. 25-26, 1996.

[66] Although India maintained a certain ambiguity by calling its 1974 test a "peaceful nuclear explosion," the 1998 tests leave little doubt that the experience gained was put to use in a nuclear weapons program. Plutonium produced in the CIRUS reactor, which the United States supplied with heavy water, was used in the 1974 test. See Victor Gilinsky and Paul Leventhal, "India Cheated," *Washington Post*, June 15, 1998.

[67] The Additional Protocol is a measure to strengthen safeguards by providing for additional information, access and inspection tools. INFCIRC/540, concluded in 1997, is the model upon which states' protocols to their safeguards agreements are based.

[68] There are three basic types of safeguards agreements: INFCIRC/66, INFCIRC/153, and voluntary safeguards agreements made by the five nuclear weapon states. INFCIRC, an abbreviation of "Information Circular," is a designation the IAEA uses to record its agreements with states and organizations. INFCIRC/66 and /153 are model agreements; the actual agreements with states will bear different numbers. INFCIRC/66 agreements predate the NPT and were used in bilateral safeguards arrangements, whereas INFCIRC/153 agreements are "full-scope safeguards" under the NPT.

[69] Statement of Robert G. Joseph, Under Secretary of State for Arms Control and International Security, Nov. 2, 2005, SFRC India hearing.

[70] Statement of Dr. Joseph, Nov. 2, 2005, SFRC India hearing.

[71]   Ibid.

[72]   Condoleezza Rice, "Our Opportunity With India," *Washington Post*, Mar. 13, 2006.

[73]   National Strategy to Combat Weapons of Mass Destruction, Dec. 2002. Available at [http://www.whitehouse.gov/news/releases/2002/12/WMDStrategy.pdf].

[74]   "NSG Begins Mulling Response To U.S.-India Cooperation Deal," *Nuclear Fuel*, Sept. 26, 2005.

[75]   Sept. 12, 2005, Joint Statement by President Chirac and Prime Minister Singh, Paris. "India, France Sign Nuclear Cooperation Declaration," *Financial Express*, Feb. 21, 2006.

[76]   "NSG Begins Mulling Response To U.S.-India Cooperation Deal," *Nuclear Fuel*, Sept. 26, 2005.

[77]   The text of the draft decision was circulated by Daryl Kimball of the Arms Control Association on Mar. 21, 2006.

[78]   Nuclear cooperation includes the distribution of special nuclear material, source material, and byproduct material, to licensing for commercial, medical, and industrial purposes. These terms, "special nuclear material," "source material,"and "byproduct material," as well as other terms used in the statute, are defined in 42 U.S.C. § 2014.

[79]   P.L. 83-703, 42 U.S.C. §§ 2153 et seq.

[80]   In the 1954 Act, the provisions in Section 123 c. covered all agreements for cooperation. Section 123 d. was added in 1958 (P.L. 85-479) to cover military-related agreements. In 1974, P.L. 93-485 amended Section 123 d. to include agreements that covered reactors producing more than 5 MW thermal or special nuclear material connected therewith.

[81]   United States General Accounting Office, "Nuclear Agreement: Cooperation Between the United States and the People's Republic of China," GAO/NSIAD-86-21BR, Nov. 1985, Appendix I-1.

[82]   42 U.S.C. 2153 a.(2). Section 4 (b) of the NNPA specifies that all other terms used in the NNPA not defined in Section 4 "shall have the meanings ascribed to them by the 1954 Act, the Energy Reorganization Act of 1974 and the Treaty [NPT]." S.Rept. 95-467 further clarified that under the NPT, the five nuclear weapon states are the U.S., U.K., China, the Soviet Union, and France. U.S. Code Congressional and Administration News, 95th Cong., 2nd sess., 1978, vol. 3, p. 329.

[83]   This new requirement was added by the Export Administration Amendments Act of 1985, P.L. 99-64, Section 301 (b) (2), 99 Stat. 120.

[84]   The language "fails to disapprove" is an artifact of the 1978 Nuclear Nonproliferation Act, which used legislative vetoes in the form of concurrent resolutions of disapproval. In 1985, following the Supreme Court's *Chadha* decision invalidating the use of legislative vetoes, the Export Administration Amendments Act created a separate approval process for exempted agreements, which this part of Section 123 d. is referring to, that called for a joint resolution of approval. Thus, "fails to disapprove" could be interpreted as "approves" in the form of a joint resolution of approval.

[85]   In light of the *Chadha* decision, passing a concurrent resolution could invite a legal challenge. Although this is not provided for in the AEA, Congress could choose to pass a joint resolution of disapproval or a bill stating in substance it did not approve.

[86]   Section 128 b. (3) refers to a "resolution of disapproval," and this would likely be a joint resolution of disapproval, in light of the *Chadha* decision.

[87] Section 128 b. (2) refers to a "concurrent resolution." In light of the *Chadha* decision, Congress could pass a joint resolution disagreeing with the President's determination, or pass a bill barring nuclear exports for a certain period of time to that country.

[88] Section 129 specifies that the President's determination "shall not become effective if during such sixty-day period the Congress adopts a concurrent resolution stating in substance that it does not favor the determination." Again, in light of *Chadha,* Congress could choose to enact a joint resolution stating it does not favor the determination, or enact a law expressly rejecting the determination.

[89] See CRS Report RL33561, *U.S.-India Nuclear Cooperation: A Side-By-Side Comparison of Current Legislation*, by Sharon Squassoni and Jill Marie Parillo (hereafter cited as CRS Report RL33561) for more detail on the bills.

[90] See H.Rept. 109-590 and for S.Rept. 109-288, dated July 20, 2006, background on the bill.

[91] See [http://www.whitehouse.gov/news/releases/2006/12/20061218-12.html]

In: India on the Move
Editor: Lea M. Surit, pp. 101-128

Chapter 4

U.S.-INDIA NUCLEAR COOPERATION: A SIDE-BY-SIDE COMPARISON OF CURRENT LEGISLATION[*]

Sharon Squassoni and Jill Marie Parillo

ABSTRACT

In March 2006, the Bush Administration proposed legislation to create an exception for India from certain provisions of the Atomic Energy Act to facilitate a future nuclear cooperation agreement. After hearings in April and May, the House International Relations Committee and the Senate Foreign Relations Committee considered bills in late June 2006 to provide an exception for India to certain provisions of the Atomic Energy Act related to a peaceful nuclear cooperation agreement. On July 26, 2006, the House passed its version of the legislation, H.R. 5682, by a vote of 359 to 68. On November 16, 2006, the Senate incorporated the text of S. 3709, as amended, into H.R. 5682 and passed that bill by a vote of 85 to 12. The Senate insisted on its amendment, and a conference committee produced a conference report on December 7, 2006. The House agreed to the conference report (H.Rept. 109-721) on December 8 in a 330-59 vote; the Senate agreed by unanimous consent to the conference report on December 9. The President signed the bill into law (P.L. 109-401) on December 18, 2006.

The Senate and House versions of the India bill contained similar provisions, with four differences. The Senate version contained an additional requirement for the President to execute his waiver authority, an amendment introduced by Senator Harkin and adopted by unanimous consent that the President determine that India is "fully and actively participating in U.S. and international efforts to dissuade, sanction and contain Iran for its nuclear program." This provision was watered down into a reporting requirement in the conference report. The Senate version also had two unique sections related to the cooperation agreement, Sections 106 and 107, both of which appear in the conference report. Section 106 (now Section 104 (d) (4)) prohibits exports of equipment, material or technology related for uranium enrichment, spent fuel reprocessing or heavy water production unless conducted in a multinational facility participating in a project approved by the International Atomic Energy Agency (IAEA) or in a facility

---

[*] Excerpted from CRS Report RL33561, December 22, 2006.

participating in a bilateral or multilateral project to develop a proliferation-resistant fuel cycle. Section 107 (now Section 104 (d) (5)) would establish a program to monitor that U.S. technology is being used appropriately by Indian recipients. Finally, the Senate version also contained the implementing legislation for the U.S. Additional Protocol in Title II, which was retained in the conference bill. Minor differences in reporting requirements and statements of policy are compared in table I of this report.

This article provides a thematic side-by-side comparison of the provisions of the conference report with H.R. 5682 as passed by the House and by the Senate, and compares them with the Administration's initially proposed legislation, H.R. 4974/S. 2429, and the conference report. The report concludes with a list of CRS resources that provide further discussion and more detailed analysis of the issues addressed by the legislation summarized in the table.

OVERVIEW

In July 2005, President Bush announced his intention to conclude a peaceful nuclear cooperation agreement with India. India, which is not a party to the Nuclear Nonproliferation Treaty (NPT), is considered under U.S. law to be a non-nuclear weapon state, yet has tested nuclear weapons and has an ongoing nuclear weapons program. For these reasons, the President would need to make certain waivers and determinations pursuant to the Atomic Energy Act (AEA) before nuclear cooperation with a state such as India could proceed.

The Administration proposed legislation (introduced as H.R. 4974/ S. 2429) in March 2006 that, in addition to providing waivers of relevant provisions of the AEA (Sections 123 a. (2), 128, and 129), would have allowed a nuclear cooperation agreement with India to enter into force without a vote from Congress, as though it conformed to AEA requirements. On July 26, 2006, the House passed H.R. 5682 by a vote of 359 to 68. On November 16, 2006, the Senate passed H.R. 5682 by a vote of 85 to12, substituting the text of S. 3709 as an engrossed amendment; the Senate insisted on its amendment, necessitating a conference to resolve differences between the bills. On December 7, conferrees filed a conference report, and on December 8, the House approved the conference report by a vote of 330 to 59; the Senate approved the conference report by unanimous consent in the early hours of December 9. On December 18, President Bush signed the bill into law, P.L. 109-401. His signing statement is discussed in more detail below.

H.R. 5682 in the House

Committee Actions

The House International Relations Committee met on June 27, 2006 to consider H.R. 5682, "United States and India Nuclear Cooperation Promotion Act of 2006," introduced on June 26 by Representative Hyde.[1] The Committee voted to adopt 6 of 12 amendments (one was withdrawn):

- Representative Royce offered an amendment to ensure that nothing in the act shall be interpreted as permitting any civil nuclear cooperation with India that would in any way assist, encourage, or induce India to manufacture or otherwise acquire nuclear weapons (Section 4 (d) (1));

- Representative Sherman offered an amendment to strengthen one of the determinations the President must make to implement the waivers pertaining to the Nuclear Suppliers Group (NSG), stipulating that the required NSG decision would not permit nuclear commerce with any other non-nuclear weapon state that does not have full-scope International Atomic Energy Act (IAEA) safeguards (Section 4 (b) (7)).
- Representative Schiff offered an amendment with three components: to add a provision to U.S. policy with respect to South Asia (Section 3 (b)(7)) encouraging India not to increase its production of fissile material at military facilities pending a multilateral moratorium on production of such material for nuclear weapons; to add a reporting requirement for the Presidential submission to implement the waivers (Section 4 (c) (2) (I)) on steps taken to ensure the U.S. transfers will not be replicated by India or used in its military facilities and that U.S. nuclear fuel supply does not facilitate military production of high-enriched uranium or plutonium; and to add a reporting requirement for an annual report on the same (Section 4 (o) (2) (C)).
- Representative Crowley offered an amendment to add a requirement (Section 4 (o)(3)) for an annual report on new Indian nuclear facilities.
- Representative Berkley offered two amendments related to India's spent fuel disposal: an annual report describing the disposal of spent nuclear fuel from India's civil nuclear program (Section 4 (o) (4), and a statement of policy that any spent civilian nuclear fuel in India that might be stored in the United States is considered by Congress under existing procedures of the Atomic Energy Act (Section 3 (b) (7)).

An amendment by Ms. Berkley to prohibit any Indian spent fuel from being stored in the United States was rejected by a vote of 15-19. The Committee also voted down four other amendments, including two by Representative Berman designed to place limits on U.S. cooperation until India halts production of fissile material for nuclear weapons. The first Berman amendment, rejected by a vote of 13-32, sought to condition the President's use of waiver authority (by adding a new determination by the President in Section 4 (b) of the bill) on India's adherence to a unilateral or multilateral moratorium or a multilateral treaty prohibiting the production of fissile material for nuclear weapons. The second amendment, rejected by a vote of 12-31, sought to restrict transfers of U.S. nuclear material under a cooperation agreement until such time that India halted fissile material production for weapons, either by adhering to a unilateral or multilateral moratorium, or a multilateral treaty. The Committee also rejected by a vote of 10-32 an amendment by Representative Sherman to condition the President's use of waiver authority on an additional determination, under Section 4 (b) of H.R. 5682, that India's nuclear weapons program was not using more domestic uranium than it had before July 2005.

The amendment would have attached an annual certification that required termination of nuclear cooperation if the certification could not be made. Finally, the Committee rejected, by a vote of 4-37, an amendment by Representative Lee that would have required India to join the Nuclear Nonproliferation Treaty (NPT) before the President could exercise his waiver authority.

The Committee on Rules held a hearing on July 25th to consider amendments to H.R. 5682 and procedures for handling the bill on the floor. H. Res 947 waived all points of order against the bill, specified the allowed amendments and limited floor debate to one hour. The following six amendments were allowed to be offered on the floor:[2]

- Representatives Hyde (IL)/Lantos (CA): Manager's amendment, containing technical and conforming changes to the text, as well as one substantive change: removing an amendment proposed by Representative Sherman and adopted during the full committee markup relating to subsection 4(b)(7).
- Representative Stearns (FL): Reinforces the intent of Congress that the nuclear cooperation into which the governments of the United States and India would enter is for peaceful, productive purposes, not military.
- Representatives Jackson-Lee (TX)/Burton (IN): Sense of Congress declaring the importance of the South Asia region and urging the continuation of the United States' policy of engagement, collaboration, and exchanges with and between India and Pakistan.
- Representative Sherman (CA): Requires that, before any nuclear cooperation with India can go forward, and every year thereafter, the President must certify that during the preceding year India has not increased the level of domestic uranium it sends through its weapons program. Baseline for the determination under the amendment is the 365 day period preceding the July 18, 2005, Bush-Singh declaration on nuclear cooperation.
- Representative Berman (CA): Restricts exports of uranium and other types of nuclear reactor fuel (defined as "source material" and 'special nuclear material' in the Atomic Energy Act of 1954) to India until the President determines that India has halted the production of fissile material (i.e., plutonium and highly enriched uranium) for use in nuclear weapons.
- Representative Fortenberry (NE): Provides Congress with the ability to assess, to the extent possible, whether annual levels of India's nuclear fissile production may imply a possible violation of Article I of the Nuclear Nonproliferation Treaty.

Three amendments were not allowed for consideration on the floor.[3] These were

- an amendment by Representative Woolsey that would have prohibited the export of any nuclear-related item to India until the President has implemented and observed all NPT obligations and commitments of the United States and has revised United States' policies relating to nuclear weapons accordingly;
- an amendment by Representative Barbara Lee that would have required India to place all electricity-producing reactors under safeguards, undertake a binding obligation not to transfer any nuclear-weapon-related information or technology (per Article I of the NPT) and take concrete steps toward disarmament; and
- an amendment by Representatives Markey and Upton that would have prohibited nuclear cooperation with India from commencing until the President has determined that the United States has secured India's full and active support in preventing Iran from acquiring weapons of mass destruction.

Floor Debate and Votes

The House first considered H. Res 947, which, after several objections to limits on time and the exclusion of certain amendments by Representative Markey and others, passed by a vote of 311 to 112. Of the six amendments considered, three passed by voice vote (the Managers' amendment, Representatives Jackson-Lee/Burton's amendment, and Representative Fortenberry's amendment); Representative Stearn's amendment was recorded as 414-0, and the amendments offered by Representatives Sherman and Berman were defeated (the votes, respectively, were 155 to 268, and 184 to 241).

Representative Markey made a motion to recommit the legislation back to the House International Relations Committee with instructions to include language that would require that nuclear cooperation with India could only commence after the president has determined that the United States has secured India's full support in preventing Iran from acquiring weapons of mass destruction. That motion to recommit was defeated in a vote of 192 to 235.

The House passed H.R. 5682, "Henry J. Hyde United States and India Nuclear Cooperation Promotion Act of 2006," as amended, by 359 to 68 on July 26, 2006.

S. 3709/H.R. 5682 in the Senate

Committee Actions

On June 29, 2006, the Senate Foreign Relations Committee considered original legislation, S. 3709, to create an exception for India from relevant provisions of the Atomic Energy Act (See S.Rept. 109-288).[4] The Committee voted to adopt 2 of 3 amendments:

- Senator Chafee offered an amendment making it U.S. policy to ensure that exports of nuclear fuel to India did not encourage India to increase its production of fissile material (Section 103 (9));
- Senator Obama offered an amendment to ensure that the United States did not encourage other states to continue nuclear exports to India, if the United States exports to India terminated under U.S. law (Section 102 (6)).

The Committee rejected an amendment by Senator Feingold requiring an additional presidential determination in Section 105 of the bill by a vote of 5-13. The Feingold amendment would have conditioned the President's use of waiver authority on a determination that U.S. civil nuclear assistance to India would in no way assist, encourage, or induce India to manufacture nuclear weapons or nuclear devices. The amendment was identical in text to the Schiff amendment to H.R. 5682, but sought instead to require a determination rather than a report.

Floor Debate and Votes

An initial attempt to bring S. 3709 to the Senate floor in September failed to gain unanimous consent agreement. Among several issues, two apparently delayed the bill — language in Title II pertaining to implementing legislation for the U.S. Additional Protocol, and potential concern about whether the United States would accept U.S.-origin spent fuel back from Indian reactors. In the first case, concerns appeared to be mostly resolved by incorporating language into a manager's amendment, with the exception of two issues raised by Senator Ensign in two amendments he introduced on the floor on November 16th that did not pass. These are described in more detail below. In the second case, the concern about disposition of Indian spent fuel was dropped prior to the bill's reaching the floor.

On November 15, 2006, the Senate agreed by unanimous consent to consider S. 3709, at a time to be determined by the Majority Leader, in consultation with the Democratic Leader.[5] The unanimous consent agreement specified that a managers' amendment would serve as the original text for the purpose of further amendment; and that the only other amendments to be considered would include the following: Senators Ensign (considered in closed session), Reed, Levin, Obama, Dorgan (two amendments), Feingold, Boxer, Feinstein, Harkin, Bingaman (up to seven amendments), Kennedy, and Dodd. Of these, Senators Reed, Levin, Kennedy, and Dodd did not introduce amendments, and Senator Bingaman introduced three, rather than seven. All but Senator Feingold's amendment were considered to be relevant second-degree amendments and related to the subject matter of the bill. Further, the unanimous consent agreement provided that once the bill was read a third time, the Senate would begin consideration of H.R. 5682, the House-passed companion, striking all text after the enacting clause and inserting the amended text of S. 3709 in its place.

Senator Lugar introduced the bill and offered a section-by-section analysis.[6] The following amendments, in brief, were passed either by unanimous consent or voice vote without debate:

- Senator Lugar introduced a manager's amendment, which contained new language in Title II related to the Additional Protocol (S.Amdt: 5168; unanimous consent);
- Senator Obama introduced an amendment containing a statement of U.S. policy (which became Section 114) that any nuclear power reactor fuel reserve provided to the Government of India for use in safeguarded civilian nuclear facilities should be commensurate with reasonable reactor operating requirements (S.Amdt. 5169; voice vote);[7]
- Senator Harkin introduced an amendment requiring the President to determine, before executing his waiver authority, that India was supporting U.S. and international efforts to dissuade, sanction, and contain Iran's nuclear program (S.Amdt. 5173; unanimous consent);[8]
- Senator Bingaman introduced an amendment to add a reporting requirement to Section 108 (b) on the amount of uranium mined in India during the previous year; the amount of such uranium that has likely been used or allocated for the production of nuclear explosive devices; and the rate of production in India of fissile material for nuclear explosive devices and of nuclear explosive devices as well as an analysis as to whether imported uranium has affected the rate of production in India of nuclear explosive devices (S.Amdt. 5179; unanimous consent);[9]
- Senator Bingaman introduced an amendment to add a new Section in Title I (which became Section 115) requiring the Secretary of Energy to create a Cooperative Threat Reduction Program with India (S.Amdt. 5180; unanimous consent).

Senator Lugar's amendment, S.Amdt. 5168 contained minor changes in Title I of S. 3709 as reported out of Committee. One potentially significant change was the deletion of a Sense of Congress on licensing policy in Section 106. In Title II, however, which contains the implementing legislation for the U.S. Additional Protocol,[10] significant provisions were added. These included Section 202 on findings, Section 251 (3), and Sections 254, 261, 262 and 271-275. In his opening statement, Senator Lugar reported that "a compromise was reached between the Administration, the Senate Foreign Relations Committee, and those Senators who expressed concern about the IAEA Additional Protocol implementing legislation."[11] These additional provisions appear to make explicit existing U.S. rights to exclude inspectors and certain kinds of inspection activities under the Additional Protocol. Several of the modifications address the use of environmental sampling, both for specific locations and for detecting anomalies in a wide-area mode.

Other amendments were introduced, debated, and defeated. These included the following:

- Senator Bingaman introduced an amendment requiring a Presidential determination that the United States and India are taking specific steps to conclude a multilateral treaty on the cessation of fissile material for weapons before U.S. nuclear equipment or technology could be exported under the future agreement for cooperation and that no nuclear materials may be exported to India unless the President has determined that India has stopped producing fissile materials for weapons (S.Amdt. 5174; Vote 26-74);[12]
- Senator Dorgan introduced an amendment to add a declaration of U.S. policy to continue to support implementation of United Nations Security Council Resolution 1172 (S.Amdt. 5178; Vote 27-71);[13]
- Senator Ensign introduced an amendment to Title II of the bill related to the Additional Protocol that would have required any inspection equipment, materials and resources to have been purchased, owned, inspected, and controlled by the United States (S.Amdt. 5181; Vote 27-71);[14]
- Senator Dorgan introduced an amendment that would have required the President to determine, before executing his waiver authority, that India has committed to putting all electricity-producing nuclear reactors under safeguards, has undertaken an obligation not to proliferate nuclear weapons technology, has joined a legally-binding nuclear test moratorium; is verifiably reducing its nuclear weapons stockpile, and has undertaken an obligation to agree to ultimate disarmament (S.Amdt. 5182; voice vote);[15]
- Senator Feingold introduced an amendment that would have required the President to determine, before executing his waiver authority, that the scope and content of the cooperation agreement would not allow India to use U.S. technology, equipment or material in unsafe guarded facilities, would not result in India replicating U.S. technology nuclear fuel and would not facilitate the increased production by India of fissile material in unsafeguarded nuclear facilities (S.Amdt. 5183; Vote 25-71);[16]
- Senator Boxer introduced an amendment that would have required the President to determine, before he could execute his waiver authority, that India had halted military-to-military contacts with Iran (S.Amdt. 5187; Vote 38-59).[17]

Most of these amendments were characterized by Senators Lugar and Biden as "killer amendments." Senator Bingaman described his amendment as implementing a proposal by former Senator Nunn.[18] Senator Dorgan's amendment supporting U.S. implementation of U.N. Security Council 1172 sought to reaffirm U.S. support for the steps endorsed by the U.N. Security Council following the 1998 Indian and Pakistani nuclear tests, including limits

on those nuclear programs such as a ban on deployments, and fissile material production for
weapons, as well as a commitment on all states' parts not to sell nuclear technology to India
and Pakistan. Senator Dorgan's other amendment, S.Amdt. 5182, was similar to
Representative Barbara Lee's amendment to the House bill that was rejected by the House
Rules Committee. That amendment attempted to commit India to undertake the same
obligations as other nuclear weapon states under the NPT. Senator Feingold's amendment
was similar to the one he introduced in Committee that was rejected. Although modified to
address objections voiced in the mark-up, the amendment was described by Senator Lugar on
the floor as requiring a certification that would have been "impossible to make."[19] Senator
Ensign's amendment was debated in closed session, apparently because of the potential need
to discuss classified information relating to the protection of national security information
during IAEA inspections under an Additional Protocol in the United States.

H.R. 5682 Conference Report

On December 7, 2006, conferees on H.R. 5682 filed Conference Report H.Rept. 109-721.
The bill essentially combines many of the provisions of both the House and Senate versions.
Specific differences are highlighted in table 1, below. Of note, the Senate provisions to ban
enrichment, reprocessing, and heavy water production cooperation with India (now Section
104. (d) (4)) and create an end-use monitoring program (now Section 104.(d) (5)) prevailed in
the conference bill, as did Title II, which includes the implementing legislation of the U.S.
Additional Protocol. The so-called Harkin amendment, which added a determination that
India was fully and actively supporting U.S. and international efforts to contain, dissuade, and
sanction Iran for its nuclear weapons program, did not remain as a determination, but became
two reporting requirements: first, as a one-time report when the Section 123 agreement is
submitted to Congress (now Section 104.(c)(2)(H)) and as an annual reporting requirement
(now Section 104.(g)(2)(E)).

P.L. 109-401 Signing Statement

On December 18, 2006, President Bush signed the "Henry J. Hyde United States-India
Peaceful Atomic Energy Cooperation Act of 2006" into law (P.L. 109-401). President Bush
noted that the act "will strengthen the strategic relationship between the United States and
India."[20] In particular, President Bush stated that the executive branch would construe two
sections of the bill as "advisory" only: policy statements in Section 103 and the restriction
contained in Section 104 (d) (2) on transferring items to India that would not meet NSG
guidelines. On the first, the President cited the Constitution's "commitment to the presidency
of the authority to conduct the Nation's foreign affairs;" on the second, the President raised
the question of whether the provision "unconstitutionally delegated legislative power to an
international body." In other words, the President was questioning whether Congress were
ceding authority to approve U.S. exports to the Nuclear Suppliers Group. However, U.S.
officials, including Secretary of State Rice, have formally told Congress multiple times that
the United States government would abide by NSG guidelines. The President's signing

Table 1. Comparison of Current Legislation on Waivers for U.S.-India Nuclear Cooperation

Issue	Description/Purpose	H.R. 4974/S. 2429 as introduced	H.R. 5682 (House version)	H.R. 5682 (Senate version)	H.R. 5682 Conference Report
Waiver authority	Provides authority for President to waive Atomic Energy Act (AEA) requirements.	*Section 1 (a):* President may waive sections of AEA (see below) if he makes a determination.	*Section 4 (a):* Same as H.R. 4974.	*Section 104 (a):* Same as H.R. 4974.	*Section 104 (a):* Same as H.R. 4974.
Section 123 a. (2) of Atomic Energy Act (AEA)	Full-scope safeguards.	*Section 1 (a) (1):* Waived AND the future cooperation agreement enters into force as though it met all Section 123 a. requirements (does not require a Joint Resolution of Approval).	*Section 4 (a) (1):* Waived BUT entry into force requires Joint Resolution of Approval as all other exempted agreements (See also *Section 4 (e)*).	*Section 104 (a) (1):* Equivalent to H.R. 5682. See *Section 104 (b)*.	*Section 104 (a) (1):* Senate version.
Section 128 of AEA	Annual review by Congress of export license for an agreement exempted from fullscope safeguards requirement.	*Section 1 (a) (2):* Application of Section 128 waived without conditions.	*Section 4 (a) (2):* Waiver ends if India engages in any Section 129 actions (see description below for Section 129), except for its ongoing weapons program [129 a. (1) (D)] and future reprocessing transfers to a nonnuclear weapon state [129 a. (2) (C)].	*Section 104 (a) (2):* Section 128 waived without conditions.	*Section 104 (a) (2):* Same as Senate version.

Table 1. Comparison of Current Legislation on Waivers for U.S.-India Nuclear Cooperation

Issue	Description/Purpose	H.R. 4974/S. 2429 as introduced	H.R. 5682 (House version)	H.R. 5682 (Senate version)	H.R. 5682 Conference Report
Section 129 of AEA	a. Terminate U.S. nuclear exports if President determines that a (1) non-nuclear weapon state: (A) Has tested a nuclear device (B) terminates or abrogates IAEA safeguards (C) materially violates IAEA safeguards (D) Has ongoing nuclear weapons program OR if President determines (2) any state (A) materially violates a cooperation agreement (B) assists non-nuclear weapon state in nwrelated activities (C) Has agreement or transfers reprocessing material, technology, or	*Section 1 (a) (3):* "Sanctions" under Section 129 waived.	*Section 4 (a) (3):* Waiver of Section 129 limited to: Indian nuclear tests before 2005 [Section 129 a. (1) (A)] and ongoing nuclear weapons activities [Section 129 a. (1) (D)].	*Section 104 (a) (3):* Equivalent to H.R. 5682 but worded differently. The language specifies waiver for sanctions under Section 129 a. (1) (D), but covers the 1998 Indian nuclear test by waiving any Section 129 sanctions regarding any actions that occurred before July 18, 2005. (There has only been one Presidential determination for India prior to 2005 that is relevant to Section 129 — for the Indian nuclear test in 1998).	*Section 104 (a) (3):* Same as Senate version.

Table 1. Comparison of Current Legislation on Waivers for U.S.-India Nuclear Cooperation

Issue	Description/Purpose	H.R. 4974/S. 2429 as introduced	H.R. 5682 (House version)	H.R. 5682 (Senate version)	H.R. 5682 Conference Report
Determination	Establishes threshold for President to use waiver authority.	*Section 1b* President must make 1 determination that 7 actions have occurred (see below).	*Section 4 (b): Same* requirements with minor changes that strengthen measures. Specifies safeguards in perpetuity.	*Section 105: Same* requirements with minor changes Specifies safeguards in perpetuity. Added determination on India and Iran (Harkin amendment)	*Section 104 (b): Closer to* House-passed version.
Separation plan	Identification of Indian civilian nuclear facilities under to US and IAEA.	(1) India has provided to US and IAEA a credible plan to separate civil and military facilities, materials, and programs, and has filed a declaration regarding its civil facilities with the IAEA.	*Section 4 (b) (1): Same* language as H.R. 4974.	*Section 105 (1)* and *(2)* Same language as H.R. 4974 but separates the declaration provision into *Section 105 (2).*	*Section 104 (b) (1): Closer* to House-passed version.
Safeguards plan	India committed to placing additional civilian nuclear facilities under IAEA safeguards under the July 18, 2005, Joint Statement.	(2) Entry into force of safeguards agreement in accordance with IAEA practices for India's civil nuclear facilities as declared in the plan.	*Section 4 (b) (2):* Specifies safeguards in perpetuity in accordance with IAEA standards, principles and practices. Also mentions safeguards on materials and programs, including materials used in or produced through use of civil nuclear facilities.	*Section 105 (3)* Specifies safeguards in perpetuity in accordance with IAEA standards, principles and practices. Also mentions safeguards on materials and programs.	*Section 104 (b) (2)* Change: Requires concluding "all legal steps prior to signature" (meaning Board of Governors approval of the safeguards agreement). Specifies safeguards in perpetuity with IAEA standards, etc.

Table 1. Comparison of Current Legislation on Waivers for U.S.-India Nuclear Cooperation

Issue	Description/Purpose	H.R. 4974/S. 2429 as introduced	H.R. 5682 (House version)	H.R. 5682 (Senate version)	H.R. 5682 Conference Report
Additional Protocol	An agreement with IAEA to enhance inspections, access, and declarations relevant to safeguards.	(3) Making satisfactory progress toward implementation.	*Section 4 (b) (3)* Specifies "substantial progress" consistent with IAEA principles, practices and policies.	*Section 105 (4)* Specifies "substantial progress."	*Section 104 (b) (3)* "Substantial progress toward concluding and Additional Protocol."
FMCT (Fissile Material Production Cutoff Treaty)	Future negotiations to end production of fissile material for nuclear weapons.	(4) Working with the United States for conclusion of a multilateral FMCT.	*Section 4 (b) (4)* Specifies working "actively" for the "early" conclusion.	*Section 105 (5)* Equivalent to H.R. 4974.	*Section 104 (b) (4)* House version.
Halting enrichment/ reprocessing transfers	July 18, 2005, commitment by India to support U.S. policy to restrict access to enrichment and reprocessing.	(5) Supporting international efforts to prevent the spread of enrichment and reprocessing technology.	*Section 4 (b) (5)* Specifies "working with and supporting US and international efforts."	*Section 105 (6)* Specifies preventing spread "to any state that does not already possess full-scale, functioning enrichment and reprocessing plants."	*Section 104 (b) (5)* Combines both texts.
Export controls	July 18, 2005 commitment by India to strengthen export controls and adhere to international norms, including Missile Technology Control Regime (MTCR) and Nuclear Suppliers Group (NSG) guidelines.	(6) Ensuring that necessary steps are taken to secure nuclear materials and technology through comprehensive export control legislation and regulations; and harmonization and adherence to MTCR and NSG guidelines.	*Section 4 (b) (6)* Specifies enactment and enforcement of export control laws; specifies harmonization of laws, regulations, policies and practices with the policies and practices of MTCR and NSG.	*Section 105 (7)* Specifies effective enforcement actions.	*Section 104 (b) (6)* Closer to House version.

Table 1. Comparison of Current Legislation on Waivers for U.S.-India Nuclear Cooperation

Issue	Description/Purpose	H.R. 4974/S. 2429 as introduced	H.R. 5682 (House version)	H.R. 5682 (Senate version)	H.R. 5682 Conference Report
Nuclear Suppliers Group (NSG)	NSG guidelines currently prohibit nuclear transfers to India; a decision must be taken to allow cooperation. NSG operates by consensus.	(7) Supply to India is consistent with US participation in NSG. This assumes that the NSG will agree to an exception for exports to India.	*Section 4 (b) (7)* Specifies NSG consensus decision.	*Section 105 (9)* Specifies NSG consensus decision that does not permit an exception for another non-nuclear weapon state.	*Section 104 (b) (7)* House version.
Iran	Ensure that India is supporting U.S. and international efforts to dissuade, sanction, and contain Iran's nuclear program	NONE	NONE But see *Section 3 (b) (4)* statement of policy on India's support for U.S. efforts vis-a-vis Iran.	*Section 105 (8)* Requires India's full & active participation in U.S. and international efforts to dissuade, sanction, and contain Iran for its nuclear program consistent with U.N. Security Council resolutions	Senate provision (Harkin amendment) removed and placed in reporting requirements (see Section 104.(c)(2) (H)) and Section 104.(g)(2) (E)).
Report on Determination	Notify Congress that 7 actions have occurred to allow waiver.	*Section 1 c.* Report to HIRC, SFRC that 7 actions have occurred, including basis for determination.	*Section 4 (c) (2):* Provides details about what reports to HIRC, SFRC should contain, specifically on the 7 actions. Also, two other reports are required for the determination: a description of the scope of the 123 agreement with the US and the steps taken to ensure that U.S. assistance will not aid India's nuclear weapons program (Schiff amendment).	*Section 105:* Determination must be made in writing to appropriate Committees. Similar reports are required in *Section 108 (a) (1)*, but are not tied to President's determination.	*Section 104 (c) (1) and (2)* Includes ten requirements in the report to be submitted with the 123 agreement.

Table 1. Comparison of Current Legislation on Waivers for U.S.-India Nuclear Cooperation

Issue	Description/Purpose	H.R. 4974/S. 2429 as introduced	H.R. 5682 (House version)	H.R. 5682 (Senate version)	H.R. 5682 Conference Report
Termination	Establish a threshold for halting U.S. exports to India (now contained in Section 129 of the AEA and in the proposed peaceful nuclear cooperation agreement itself, which is not yet drafted).	*Section 1d.* All waiver authorities (for Section 123 a. (2), Section 128, and Section 129) terminate if India tests a nuclear explosive device.	*Section 4 (a) (3):* All termination provisions of Section 129 of the AEA (except 129 a.(1) (D)) would be in effect (see description of sec.129 waiver above).	*Section 104 (a) (3):* All termination provisions of Section 129 of the AEA (except 129 a.(1) (D)) would be in effect (see description of sec.129 waiver above).	*Section 104 (d) (3):* All termination provisions of Section 129 of the AEA (except 129 a.(1) (D)) would be in effect (see description of sec.129 waiver above).
			ALSO *Section 4 (d) (3):* Exports would terminate if India makes a materially significant transfer of items in violation of NSG guidelines, or of items in violation of MTCR guidelines.	*No equivalent provision* to H.R. 5682 but *Section 108 (b) (3) (A)* contains a reporting reqt if India does not comply with NSG guidelines and *Section 108 (b) (4) (A)* requires an annual certification that India is in full compliance with all July 18, 2005 commitments.	*Section 104 (d) (3):* Incorporated House version Section 4 (d) (3) (Berman amendment).

Table 1. Comparison of Current Legislation on Waivers for U.S.-India Nuclear Cooperation

Issue	Description/Purpose	H.R. 4974/S. 2429 as introduced	H.R. 5682 (House version)	H.R. 5682 (Senate version)	H.R. 5682 Conference Report
Sense of Congress	To describe Congress's policy objectives with respect to nuclear cooperation with India.	NONE	*Section 2* Notes importance of nonproliferation and NPT and focuses on how the United States could strengthen its non-proliferation policy by engaging NPT outliers like India. Sets up criteria (non-proliferation record, democratic government, support for U.S. non-proliferation aims) for engagement and states India meets criteria.	*Section 102* Notes that engaging India is in the national security interest of the United States, but need to minimize proliferation risk. United States should not facilitate trade by other nations if U.S. exports terminated.	*Section 102* Combines both texts.
Statements of Policy (1)* [* President Bush has interpreted as "advisory"]	To describe U.S. policy objectives, with respect to nonproliferation.	NONE	*Section 3 (a)* *General* (1) Oppose nuclear weapons development. (2) Support peaceful uses of nuclear energy, but only with full NPT compliance. (3) Strengthen NSG implementation, including cutoff of exports for violations.	*Section 103* Section 103 (8): maintain support for NPT. *No equivalent* *Similar to Section 103* (6) on support for NSG.	*Section 103* *(a)* *Section 103* *(a)(1)* Combines both. *Section 103* *(a)(2)* House version. *Section 103* *(a)(3) and Section 103(a) (4).*

Table 1. Comparison of Current Legislation on Waivers for U.S.-India Nuclear Cooperation

Issue	Description/Purpose	H.R. 4974/S. 2429 as introduced	H.R. 5682 (House version)	H.R. 5682 (Senate version)	H.R. 5682 Conference Report
Statements of Policy (II)	To describe U.S. policy objectives, with respect to South Asia, U.S.- India bilateral relations, and South Asian proliferation.	NONE	*Section 3 (b) South Asia* (1) Fissile material production moratorium for India, Pakistan, China.	*Section 103 (1),* but moratorium docs not include China.	*Section 103(b)(1)* House version
			(2) FMCT	*No equivalent*	*Section 103(b)(2)* House version
			(3) Other Non-proliferation activities, like PSI, Australia Group, Wassenaar, Convention on Supplementary Compensation.	*Section 103 (2),* but no mention of Convention on Supplementary Compensation	*Section 103(b)(3)* House version
			(4) Support for U.S. policies to prevent Iran from acquiring nuclear weapons.	*No equivalent,* but language similar to *Section 105 (8)* determination	*Section 103(b)(4)* Modified House version
			(5) Cap, roll back and eliminate South Asian nuclear arsenals.	*No equivalent*	*Section 103(b)(5)*
			(6) No spent fuel transfer without Congressional approval.	*No equivalent*	*Section 103(b)(6)*
			(7) Encourage cap on production of fissile material for weapons, pending moratorium.	*No equivalent provision*	*Section 103(b)(7)*

Table 1. Comparison of Current Legislation on Waivers for U.S.-India Nuclear Cooperation

Issue	Description/Purpose	H.R. 4974/S. 2429 as introduced	H.R. 5682 (House version)	H.R. 5682 (Senate version)	H.R. 5682 Conference Report
Statements of Policy (III)		NONE			
			No equivalent provision	*Section 103 (3):* Full compliance with all non-proliferation obligations.	Removed. *Section 103(b)(8)*
			No equivalent provision	*Section 103 (4):* Ensure reliability of safeguards and Additional Protocol.	
			No equivalent provision	*Section 103 (5):* Agreement must meet all other Section 123 a. requirements.	*Section 103(b)(9)*
			No equivalent provision	*Section 103 (6):* Consistency with NSG guidelines.	*Section 103(a)(3)*
			No equivalent provision	*Section 103 (7):* Work with NSG members to restrict transfers of enrichment and reprocessing, also to India.	*Section 103 (a)(5)* Akin to

Table 1. Comparison of Current Legislation on Waivers for U.S.-India Nuclear Cooperation

Issue	Description/Purpose	H.R. 4974/S. 2429 as introduced	H.R. 5682 (House version)	H.R. 5682 (Senate version)	H.R. 5682 Conference Report
			No equivalent provision	*Section 103 (8):* Maintain support for adherence & compliance with NPT.	*Section 102 (2).*
			No equivalent provision	*Section 103 (9):* Exports of nuclear fuel to India should not contribute to or encourage India to increase production of fissile material for military uses.	Removed (see reporting requirements).
			No equivalent provision	*Section 114:* Any nuclear power reactor fuel reserve provided to India should be commensurate with reasonable reactor operating requirements	*Section 103 (b)(10)*

Table 1. Comparison of Current Legislation on Waivers for U.S.-India Nuclear Cooperation

Issue	Description/Purpose	H.R. 4974/S. 2429 as introduced	H.R. 5682 (House version)	H.R. 5682 (Senate version)	H.R. 5682 Conference Report
Expedited procedures	To provide procedures for expedited consideration of Joint Resolution of Approval.	None, except as provided already in Section 130 of AEA.	*Section 4 (f) and (g)*: track with existing law (Section 130 of AEA).	None, except as provided already in Section 130 of AEA.	None, except as provided already in Section 130 of AEA.
End-Use Monitoring	To provide reasonable assurances that the recipient is complying with relevant requirements, terms and conditions of U.S. export licenses.	NONE	NONE	*Section 107* requires following measures: (1) Obtain and implement assurances and conditions regarding end-use monitoring; (2) a detailed system of reporting on technology transfers, including those authorized by Section 57 b of AEA. (3) Fall-back safeguards, should IAEA be unable to implement safeguards in India.	*Section 104 (d)(5)*

Table 1. Comparison of Current Legislation on Waivers for U.S.-India Nuclear Cooperation

Issue	Description/Purpose	H.R. 4974/S. 2429 as introduced	H.R. 5682 (House version)	H.R. 5682 (Senate version)	H.R. 5682 Conference Report
Restrictions on cooperation		NONE	*Section 4 (d)* (1) No assistance that would aid India's nuclear weapons program.	*No equivalent but similar concept behind Section 106.* *Section 103 (9)*	*Section 104 (d)* *Section 104 (d)(1)*
			(2) No transfers if they would violate NSG guidelines.	*Similar to Section 103 (6)*: to act in a manner fully consistent with NSG guidelines (but this is only a Statement of Policy).	*Section 104 (d)(2)** House version. [* President Bush has interpreted as "advisory"]
			(4) President should seek to prevent cooperation by other states with India if United States terminates exports.	*Section 102 (6)*: United States should not seek to facilitate cooperation by other states with India if United States terminates exports.	Similar to *Section 102 (13)*.

Table 1. Comparison of Current Legislation on Waivers for U.S.-India Nuclear Cooperation

Issue	Description/Purpose	H.R. 4974/S. 2429 as introduced	H.R. 5682 (House version)	H.R. 5682 (Senate version)	H.R. 5682 Conference Report
			No equivalent provision	*Section 106* Bans cooperation on enrichment, reprocessing, and heavy water materials, equipment, and technology with exception for multilateral and bilateral fuel cycle cooperation, if President determines that the export will not improve India's ability to produce nuclear weapons. ability to produce fissile material for weapons	*Section 104 (d)(4)* Minor editing changes.
Other reporting		NONE	*Section 4 (j) (1)*: annual report on U.S. policy objectives for South Asia (i.e., steps taken by the United States and India, extent of success, and cooperation by other countries).	*No equivalent provision*	Removed

Table 1. Comparison of Current Legislation on Waivers for U.S.-India Nuclear Cooperation

Issue	Description/Purpose	H.R. 4974/S. 2429 as introduced	H.R. 5682 (House version)	H.R. 5682 (Senate version)	H.R. 5682 Conference Report
			Section 4 (j) (2) Annual report on U.S. nuclear exports to India, including estimates of Indian uranium mining, fissile material and nuclear weapons production rates; as well as impact of imported uranium on such rates. Report also to describe India's use of any U.S. nuclear equipment, material or technology in an uninspected facility; replication of anything transferred and whether imported nuclear fuel has helped to increase fissile material production	*Section 108 (b) (6)* Annual report on estimated amount of uranium mined in India during the previous year(A); amount of such uranium that has likely been used or allocated for the production of nuclear explosive devices (B); and the rate of production in India of fissile material for nuclear explosive devices(C)(I); and of nuclear explosive devices(C)(ii) *Section 108 (b) (7)* Analysis on whether imported uranium has affected the rate of production in India of	*Section 104 (g) (2) (H)* and *Section 104 (g) (2) (J)*

Table 1. Comparison of Current Legislation on Waivers for U.S.-India Nuclear Cooperation

Issue	Description/Purpose	H.R. 4974/S. 2429 as introduced	H.R. 5682 (House version)	H.R. 5682 (Senate version)	H.R. 5682 Conference Report
Other reporting, continued		NONE	Section 4 (i) (3): annual report on new Indian nuclear facilities.	Section 108 (b) (2): list of licenses approved by NRC, DOE, Commerce or any other U.S. authorizations of exports and reexports of nuclear materials and equipment.	Section 104 (g) (2) (B)
			Section 4 (i) (4): annual report on India's spent fuel disposal.	No equivalent provision	Section 104 (g) (2) (L)
			Section 4 (i) (5): annual report on growth in India's military fissile material production, to include information on Indian uranium mining, electricity production, domestic uranium used in civilian electricity production, & military fissile material production, etc.	Section 108 (b) (1): description of additional nuclear facilities/materials India places under IAEA safeguards. Section 108 (a) (3): Implementation & Compliance Report; Information on Nuclear Activities of India; "significant changes in the production by India of nuclear weapons or in the types or amounts of fissile material produced." See also Section 108 (b) (6).	Section 104 (g) (2) (A)

Table 1. Comparison of Current Legislation on Waivers for U.S.-India Nuclear Cooperation

Issue	Description/Purpose	H.R. 4974/S. 2429 as introduced	H.R. 5682 (House version)	H.R. 5682 (Senate version)	H.R. 5682 Conference Report
			No equivalent provision	*Section 108 (b) (3):* Any significant nuclear commerce between India and other countries that does not comply with NSG guidelines, or would not meet standards applied to U.S.-origin material.	*Section 104 (g) (2) (C)*
Other Presidential certifications		NONE	NONE	*Section 108 (b) (4):* That India is in full compliance with following obligations (listed in Section 108 (a) (1)): Joint Statement commitments, separation plan, safeguards agreement, Additional Protocol, 123 agreement, terms and conditions of approved export licenses. If certification is not possible, report on steps, responses and implications.	*Section 104 (g) (2)*

Table 1. Comparison of Current Legislation on Waivers for U.S.-India Nuclear Cooperation

Issue	Description/Purpose	H.R. 4974/S. 2429 as introduced	H.R. 5682 (House version)	H.R. 5682 (Senate version)	H.R. 5682 Conference Report
Consultation with Congress		NONE	*Section 4 (e (2)*: Requires monthly consultations with Congress on progress in 123 agreement negotiations and IAEA safeguards agreement negotiations.	*No equivalent provision*	Removed *Section 104 (g) (1)*
			No equivalent provision	*Section 108 (a)*: keep Congress fully informed on India's: (1) non-compliance (2) nuclear facility construction (3) fissile material production (4) changes in operational status of nuclear facilities.	
Program for cooperative threat reduction	To further common nonproliferation goals, including scientific research and development efforts related to nuclear nonproliferation, with emphasis on nuclear safeguards.	NONE	NONE	*Section 115* Requires Secretary of Energy to establish a United States-India Scientific Cooperative Threat Reduction Program.	*Section 109*

Table 1. Comparison of Current Legislation on Waivers for U.S.-India Nuclear Cooperation

Issue	Description/Purpose	H.R. 4974/S. 2429 as introduced	H.R. 5682 (House version)	H.R. 5682 (Senate version)	H.R. 5682 Conference Report
TITLE II	Implementing Legislation for the U.S. Additional Protocol.	NONE	NONE	*Entire Title II* Sec. S. 2489 for comparison and S. 3709 as reported out of committee for differences between those and the version voted on by the Senate.	*Title II*

statement also noted that the executive branch would construe "provisions of the Act that mandate, regulate, or prohibit submission of information to the Congress, an international organization, or the public, such as sections 104, 109, 261, 271, 272, 273, 274, and 275, in a manner consistent with the President's constitutional authority to protect and control information that could impair foreign relations, national security, the deliberative processes of the Executive, or the performance of the Executive's constitutional duties." This could suggest that the executive branch might limit the scope of reporting required by Congress in those sections.

ADDITIONAL RESOURCES

CRS Report RL33016, U.S. Nuclear Cooperation with India: Issues for Congress, by Sharon Squassoni.

CRS Report RL33292, India's Nuclear Separation Plan: Issues and Views, by Sharon Squassoni.

CRS Report RL33072, U.S.-India Bilateral Agreements and 'Global Partnership,' by K. Alan Kronstadt.

CRS Report RS22474, Banning Fissile Material Production for Nuclear Weapons: Prospects for a Treaty (FMCT), by Sharon Squassoni, Andrew Demkee, and Jill Marie Parillo.

REFERENCES

[1]   The National Journal and Congressional Quarterly wrote reports of the HIRC markup, available at [http://nationaljournal.com/members/markups/ 2006/06/mr_20060627_ 5.htm] and [http://www.cq.com/display.do? dockey=/cqonline/prod/data/ docs/html/ committees/ 109/committees109-2006062700228055.html@committees and metapub= CQ-COMMITTEEMARKUPS and searchIndex=0 and seqNum=1].

[2]   See the description in H.Rept. 109-599, "Providing for Consideration of H.R. 5682, United States and India Nuclear Cooperation Promotion Act of 2006," *Congressional Record*, July 25, 2006, p. H5820.

[3]   A fourth amendment, proposed by Mr. Hyde, would have implemented a Congressional review process for arms sales and exports under the Arms Export Control Act, but this amendment was withdrawn.

[4]   Details on the mark-up are available at *Congressional Quarterly*, [http://www.cq.com/ display.do?dockey=/cqonline/prod/data/docs/html/committees/109/committees109-2006062900228090.html@committees and met apub=CQ-COMMITTEE MARKUPS and searchIndex=0 and seqNum=1] for report of the markup.

[5]   *Congressional Record*, November 15, 2006, p. S. 10941-42, daily edition.

[6]   See Senator Lugar's opening statement in the *Congressional Record*, November 16, 2006, S10982-84, daily edition.

[7]   See *Congressional Record*, November 16, 2006, S11021, daily edition, for the colloquy between Senator Obama and the managers of the bill on the subject of limiting nuclear fuel reserves to provide a disincentive for India to conduct future nuclear tests.

[8]   See *Congressional Record*, November 16, 2006, S10996, daily edition, for Senator Harkin's description of the amendment.

[9]   See *Congressional Record*, November 16, 2006, S. 11003, daily edition for the text of Senator Bingaman's amendments, S.Amdt. 5179 and S.Amdt. 5180.

[10] The Additional Protocol is a protocol to IAEA safeguards agreements under the Nuclear Nonproliferaton Treaty (NPT) which enhances the IAEA's inspection rights, methods, and information. The model agreement is INFCIRC/540. Nuclear weapon states have modified the model to include provisions for national security exclusions, because of their weapons status. The United States signed its additional protocol in 1998, and the Senate gave its consent for ratification in 2004, but the additional protocol requires implementing legislation to enter into force. The Senate Foreign Relations Committee reported out such implementing legislation, S. 2489, in April 2006.

[11] *Congressional Record*, November 16, 2006, S10984, daily edition.

[12] *Congressional Record*, November 16, 2006, S. 10998-11001, daily edition, for Senator Bingaman's explanation of his amendments and responses by Senators Lugar and Biden..

[13] *Congressional Record*, November 16, 2006, S11001, daily edition.

[14] *Congressional Record*, November 16, 2006, S11009, daily edition, for text of Ensign amendment. The debate was held in closed session.

[15] See *Congressional Record*, November 16, 2006, S11006, daily edition, for Senator Dorgan's introduction of the amendment and debate.

[16] See *Congressional Record*, November 16, 2006, S11011-15, daily edition, for Senator Feingold's introduction of the amendment and debate.

[17] See *Congressional Record*, November 16, 2006, S11016-11019, daily edition, for Senator Boxer's introduction of the amendment and debate.

[18] *Congressional Record*, November 16, 2006, S109998-11000, daily edition.

[19] *Congressional Record*, November 16, 2006, S11014, daily edition.

[20] See [http://www.whitehouse.gov/news/releases/2006/12/20061218-12.html].

In: India on the Move
Editor: Lea M. Surit, pp. 129-151

ISBN: 978-1-60021-813-2
© 2007 Nova Science Publishers, Inc.

Chapter 5

INDIA'S NUCLEAR SEPARATION PLAN: ISSUES AND VIEWS[*]

Sharon Squassoni

ABSTRACT

On July 18, 2005, President Bush and Indian Prime Minister Manmohan Singh announced the creation of a "global partnership," which would include "full" civil nuclear cooperation between the United States and India. This is at odds with nearly three decades of U.S. nonproliferation policy and practice. President Bush promised India he would persuade Congress to amend the pertinent laws to approve the agreement, as well as persuade U.S. allies to create an exception to multilateral Nuclear Suppliers Group (NSG) guidelines for India. India committed to, among other things, separating its civilian nuclear facilities from its military nuclear facilities, declaring civilian facilities to the International Atomic Energy Agency (IAEA) and placing them under IAEA safeguards, and signing an Additional Protocol. See CRS Report RL33016, *U.S. Nuclear Cooperation With India: Issues for Congress*, by Sharon Squassoni, for further details on the agreement.

The separation plan announced by Prime Minister Singh and President Bush on March 2, 2006, and further elaborated on May 11, 2006, would place 8 power reactors under inspection, bringing the total up to 14 out of a possible 22 under inspection. Several fuel fabrication and spent fuel storage facilities were declared, as well as 3 heavy water plants that were described as "safeguards-irrelevant." The plan excludes from international inspection 8 indigenous power reactors, enrichment and spent fuel reprocessing facilities (except as currently safeguarded), military production reactors and other military nuclear plants and 3 heavy water plants. Administration officials have defended the separation plan as credible and defensible because it covers more than just a token number of Indian facilities, provides for safeguards in perpetuity, and includes upstream and downstream facilities.

U.S. officials acknowledge the importance of a credible separation plan to ensuring that the United States complies with its Article I obligations under the Nuclear Nonproliferation Treaty (NPT) — to not in any way assist a nuclear weapons program in a non-nuclear weapon state. For almost 30 years, the U.S. legal standard has been that

---

[*] Excerpted from CRS Report RL33292, dated December 22, 2006.

only nuclear safeguards on all nuclear activities in a state provides adequate assurances. The Administration is apparently asking Congress to back a lower level of assurance by proposing that the separation plan take the place of comprehensive safeguards.

Congress is likely to consider this issue as well as others when the Administration eventually submits its cooperation agreement with India for approval by both chambers. P.L. 109-401, signed on December 18, 2006, provides waivers for a nuclear cooperation agreement with India from relevant Atomic Energy Act provisions, and requires detailed information on the separation plan and resultant safeguards. This report, which will be updated as necessary, provides background on India's nuclear fuel cycle, a discussion of various issues involved in separating civilian and military nuclear facilities and potential concerns for Congress as it considers whether the United States has adequate assurances that its nuclear cooperation does not assist, encourage, or induce India's nuclear weapons development, production, or proliferation.

INTRODUCTION

On July 18, 2005, President Bush and Indian Prime Minister Manmohan Singh signed a joint statement that announced the creation of a "global partnership," which would include "full" civil nuclear cooperation between the United States and India. This is at odds with nearly three decades of U.S. nonproliferation policy and practice. President Bush committed to persuading Congress to amend the pertinent laws to approve the agreement, as well as persuading U.S. allies to create an exception to multilateral Nuclear Suppliers Group (NSG) guidelines for India to allow for nuclear cooperation. India committed to separating its civilian from its military nuclear facilities, declaring civilian facilities to the International Atomic Energy Agency (IAEA) and placing them under IAEA safeguards, and signing an Additional Protocol, which provides enhanced access and information for IAEA inspectors.

The United States is obligated under the Nuclear Nonproliferation Treaty (NPT) to ensure that any cooperation it provides to a non-nuclear weapon state does not contribute to that state's capability to produce nuclear weapons. In 1978, Congress passed the Nuclear Nonproliferation Act, which strengthened the restrictions on U.S. nuclear cooperation to include comprehensive (full-scope) safeguards on all nuclear material in non-nuclear weapon states, specifically to help ensure that peaceful cooperation would not be diverted to weapons purposes. The 1978 Act followed India's 1974 peaceful nuclear explosion, which demonstrated to most observers that nuclear technology originally transferred for peaceful purposes could be misused. That test also provided the impetus for creating the Nuclear Suppliers Group (NSG).[1] In 1992, the NSG adopted the full-scope safeguards condition for nuclear exports, and the 1995 NPT Extension Conference and the 2000 NPT Review Conference both endorsed the NSG's new requirement.

India shares a unique status with Pakistan and Israel as de facto nuclear weapon states outside the NPT that have been treated politically, for nonproliferation purposes, as non-nuclear weapon states.[2] The three states do not have comprehensive nuclear safeguards. Instead, they have safeguards agreements that cover only specified facilities and materials.[3] Presently, very few of India's nuclear facilities are subject to international inspections.

The Bush Administration made a "credible" and "defensible" — from a nonproliferation standpoint — separation plan a prerequisite for asking Congress to create an exception to current law for nuclear cooperation with India. P.L. 109-401, the law that provides the executive branch with authority to waive restrictions under the Atomic Energy Act with respect to India, requires the President to determine that the following actions had occurred:

- India has provided the United States and the IAEA with a credible plan to separate civil and military facilities, materials, and programs, and has filed a declaration regarding its civil facilities with the IAEA;
- India and the IAEA have concluded all legal steps required prior to signature by the parties of an agreement requiring the application of safeguards in perpetuity in accordance with IAEA standards, principles, and practices (including IAEA Board of Governors Document GOV/1621 (1973)) to India's civil nuclear facilities, materials and programs as declared in the plan, including materials used in or produced through the use of India's civil nuclear facilities;
- India and the IAEA are making substantial progress toward concluding an Additional Protocol consistent with IAEA principles, practices, and policies that would apply to India's civil nuclear program;
- India is working actively with the United States for the early conclusion of a multilateral treaty on the cessation of the production of fissile materials for use in nuclear weapons;
- India is working with and supporting U.S. and international efforts to prevent the spread of enrichment and reprocessing technology to any state that does not already possess full-scale functioning enrichment or reprocessing plants;
- India is taking the necessary steps to secure nuclear and other sensitive materials and technology through the application of comprehensive export control legislation and regulations, and through harmonization and adherence to Missile Technology Control Regime (MTCR) and Nuclear Suppliers Group (NSG) guidelines; and ! the NSG has decided by consensus to permit supply to India of nuclear items covered by the guidelines of the NSG.

Indian and U.S. officials engaged for several months in discussions on identification of civilian facilities. U.S. officials encouraged India to make a comprehensive declaration of its civilian infrastructure.[4] In various written and oral statements to Congress, State Department officials seem to suggest that more facilities under safeguards would be better than fewer, but critics (on both the U.S. and Indian sides) have suggested that some facilities would be more important to include or exclude. For example, the CIRUS reactor, reportedly the source of plutonium for the 1974 nuclear test, despite India's pledge to use it only for peaceful purposes, is important to some critics to declare as civilian and place under safeguards because of its controversial past. To U.S. officials, facilities associated with the fast breeder reactor program, which could produce plutonium for weapons in the future, reportedly would be key to get under safeguards, particularly if the United States wants to cooperate with India in the Global Nuclear Energy Partnership program.[5] To Indian officials, however, the fast breeder reactor program is key to the future of India's three-stage nuclear fuel cycle and must be kept out of safeguards for maximum flexibility and energy independence.[6]

Several nonproliferation critics of the potential agreement have suggested that no matter how many facilities India places under safeguards, the opening of the international uranium market — forbidden to India since 1992 by the NSG — in effect frees up India's domestic uranium for its nuclear weapons program, and therefore, would assist the Indian nuclear weapons program.[7] Consequently, only India's halt in the production of fissile material for nuclear weapons would ensure that U.S. assistance does not aid India's nuclear programs.[8] Indian officials note that the peaceful nuclear cooperation agreement is not about limiting their strategic program, just about expanding their peaceful nuclear program. Some critics have suggested various options for placing specific facilities under safeguards to diminish the potential "surplus effect" of opening up that uranium market.[9]

One observer, Robert Einhorn, has suggested that in the absence of a fissile material production halt, safeguards on Indian facilities serve primarily a symbolic role in demonstrating India's commitment to nonproliferation.[10] Nonetheless, the safeguards approach, according to Administration officials, is key to assuring that the United States complies with Article I of the NPT — that U.S. cooperation does not in any way assist a nuclear weapons program in a non-nuclear weapon state. U.S. officials have stated that a voluntary safeguards arrangement like those of the other five nuclear weapon states would not meet our NPT Article I obligations. In their view, India must accept some kind of safeguards arrangement that allow safeguards to endure in perpetuity. Indian officials, on the other hand, suggested that having the same responsibilities and practices as other advanced nuclear states translates into a voluntary safeguards arrangement.[11]

This report provides background on India's nuclear fuel cycle, a discussion of various issues involved in separating civilian and military nuclear facilities and potential concerns for Congress as it considers whether the United States has adequate assurances that its nuclear cooperation does not assist, encourage, or induce India's nuclear weapons development, production, or proliferation.

BACKGROUND

India's nuclear program, from its inception in 1948, has been described as inherently dual-purpose.[12] With the establishment of its Atomic Energy Commission in 1948, India pursued both civilian and military applications of nuclear energy. The first indigenous research reactor, Apsara, was developed in the 1950s. Canada provided early assistance under the Colombo Plan, as did the United States under the Atoms for Peace program. A humiliating defeat in a border war with China in 1962, followed by China's first nuclear test in 1964, intensified India's drive for nuclear weapons. India turned to the CIRUS (Canada-India Reactor United States) reactor, as the source for plutonium for its 1974 "peaceful nuclear explosive" test. Foreign assistance dwindled after the 1974 test, but Canada had already transferred the blueprints for heavy water reactors under an agreement for peaceful nuclear cooperation. As a result, India developed a fairly independent nuclear infrastructure that supported both civilian and military purposes. For example, plutonium separated in India's reprocessing plants has been used both for weapons and to make mixed oxide fuel (plutonium mixed with uranium) for nuclear power plants.

India's nuclear fuel cycle development has been driven by an acknowledged lack of uranium reserves. In India's view, energy independence could not be derived from domestic uranium reserves — estimated at 0.8% of world reserves, or 50-60,000 tons — but could be from production of plutonium, recycling of spent fuel, and utilization of thorium (estimated at

32% of world reserves).[13] As a result, India planned 40 years ago to develop a three-stage fuel cycle to reduce its reliance on uranium and use thorium. The first stage would rely on natural uranium-fueled reactors to make plutonium; the second stage would use that plutonium in fast reactors blanketed with thorium to produce U-233 (and more plutonium); and the third stage would use U-233 fuel and thorium fuel in fast reactors blanketed with thorium to produce more U-233 for use for future fuel. India has not advanced beyond the first stage of the fuel cycle, aside from running a fast breeder test reactor (40 MWth Fast Breeder Test Reactor or FBTR) based on a French design and a small research reactor that uses U-233 fuel (Kamini).

The Chairman of the Atomic Energy Commission, Dr. Anil Kakodkar, asserted in a speech in March 2005 that indigenous uranium resources would support 10 GWe of nuclear installed capacity but that breeder reactors, using plutonium bred from indigenous uranium, could support 500 GWe of power generation.[14] The current energy plan is to have 12 GWe installed capacity by 2015 and 20 GWe by 2020. Reportedly, the increase to 20 GWe would be achieved through a mix of pressurized heavy water reactors (PHWRs), light water reactors and fast breeder reactors, including construction of 5 fast breeder reactors of 500 MWe each and the import of 8 light water reactors of 1000 MWe each.[15] India's indigenous, pressurized heavy water reactors (fueled with natural uranium) are planned to provide just half of that 20 GWe capacity (i.e., 10 GWe), but some observers have suggested that indigenous supplies of uranium may not support that many reactors and that India's uranium crisis is already acute.[16] For example, India's Jaduguda uranium mill produces just 220 tons of yellowcake a year, whereas the 13 operating natural-uranium fueled reactors require 300 tons per year, and consequently have reduced their operating capacity from 90% in 2002-2003 to 81% in 2003-2004 and 76% in 2004-2005.[17]

According to two reports, the Department of Atomic Energy has been unable to mine certain uranium deposits because local governments have not yet given clearance.[18]

India's Nuclear Facilities[19]

Figure 1 depicts key sites and facilities of India's nuclear industry; not included are India's heavy water plants and associated research facilities. Apart from two light-water reactors fueled with low-enriched uranium from foreign suppliers (at Tarapur) and two under construction by Russia (VVERs at Kudankulam), India's power reactors rely on natural uranium in reactors that are cooled and moderated by heavy water, known as pressurized heavy water reactors, or alternatively as CANDU-type.[20] Canada built the first two CANDU-type reactors at Rajasthan, and India built the remaining eleven. Most of these produce about 220 MWe, whereas the new Russian reactors at Kudankulam will produce 1000 MWe. The foreign-supplied reactors (Tarapur, Rajasthan and, eventually, Kudankulam) are under IAEA safeguards, but the remaining domestic facilities are, largely, not safeguarded.

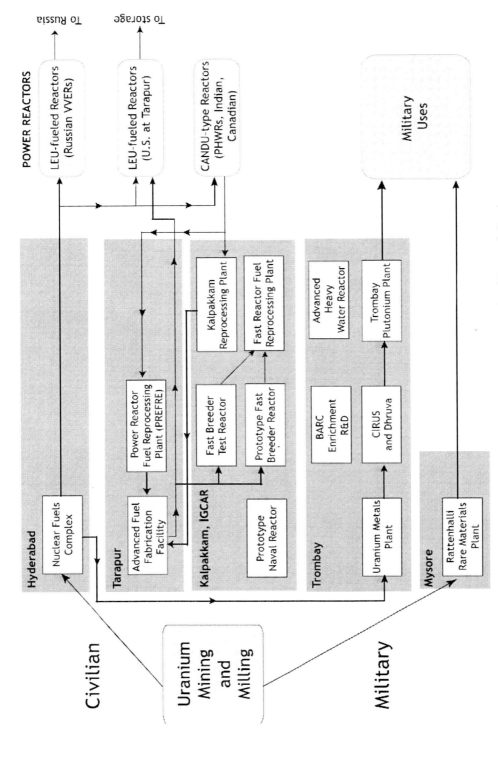

Sources: Dr. Frederick Mackie, Lawrence Livermore National Laboratory, and the Congressional Research Service.

Figure 1. Indian Nuclear Facilities.

At present, India's nuclear facilities include the following:

- research reactors (3);
- power reactors (15 operating, 8 under construction and 3 planned);
- breeder reactors (1 operating, 1 under construction);
- uranium enrichment (1 operating)
- spent fuel reprocessing (3);
- heavy water production plants (6);
- uranium processing (3 mines; 2 copper-mine tailing extraction units, 1 mill (uranium ore concentration) many uranium conversion facilities, 3 or 4 fuel fabrication plants).

Research Reactors

India has three operating research reactors (CIRUS, Dhruva, and Kamini) and four decommissioned reactors.[21] In addition, India's oldest reactor, Apsara, may be considered operational, but is awaiting refurbishment, reportedly to test a new indigenous design of a 5-10 MWt research reactor. It has been used for various experiments, research and production of radioisotopes, and training. CIRUS and Dhruva are located at the Bhabha Atomic Research Center (BARC) in Trombay, while Kamini is located at Kalpakkam.

The CIRUS reactor has been the subject of controversy between the United States and India for much of its life. The United States supplied heavy water, which was not subject to a safeguards agreement, under a 1956 contract in which India pledged to use the material for peaceful purposes only. Yet this reactor reportedly produced the plutonium used in India's 1974 peaceful nuclear explosion. Many nonproliferation experts maintain that India violated its 1956 contract with Canada as well as its contract with the United States. Most recently, according to answers to questions for the record submitted by the Senate Foreign Relations Committee on November 2, 2005, the State Department notes that:

> At the time, the debate on whether India had violated the contract was inconclusive owing to the uncertainty as to whether U.S.-supplied heavy water contributed to the production of the plutonium used for the 1974 device and the lack of a mutual understanding of scope of the 1956 contract language on "peaceful purposes."

Several nonproliferation experts have criticized the Administration for not taking this opportunity to resolve this 30-year-old controversy.[22] The Canadian government in December 2005 encouraged the United States and India to declare the CIRUS reactor as a civilian reactor and place it under IAEA safeguards. Doing so, would "respect the peaceful uses assurance of our original agreement."[23]

The Dhruva reactor is a larger, 100 MWt reactor that began operation in 1985. It is the other reactor that most observers assume is dedicated to India's nuclear weapons program. CIRUS and Dhruva together can produce between 25 and 35 kg of plutonium per year, or enough for 3 to 4 bombs.[24] The Kamini reactor is located at the Indira Gandhi Centre for Atomic Research (IGCAR) in Kalpakkam. It become operational in 1996 and uses U-233 as fuel.

Power Reactors

Table 1 shows India's 22 power reactors (excluding the prototype fast breeder reactor, which is discussed below). Of the total 22, 15 are currently operating, while 7 are under construction. Three more reactors are planned.

Of the 15 operating power reactors, four are under safeguards — the two U.S.-supplied reactors at Tarapur and the two Canadian-supplied reactors at Rajasthan. Two pressurized water reactors under construction by the Russians at Kudankulam will be under IAEA safeguards also. There are 11 remaining reactors operating not under safeguards and five PHWRs under construction. In addition to the reactors under construction, there are five more planned: two at Kaiga (Kaiga 5 and 6); two at Rajasthan (RAPS 7 and 8); and the Advanced Heavy Water Reactor at Trombay.

The 15 operating power reactors have a net capacity of 3602 MWe. Nuclear energy now accounts for about 3% of India's electricity consumption, and India plans to increase the electrical generation capacity from the nuclear sector dramatically over the next few years. Estimates vary from an increase of 8000 MWe additionally by 2015,[25] to a total of 20GWe by 2020.[26] However, India's indigenous pressurized heavy water reactors will likely account for less than half of the total increase.

Breeder Reactors

The breeder reactor program is integral to the second stage of India's three-stage nuclear development plan. "Breeder" reactors have the potential to make more fissile material than they burn up, hence the term "breeder." Stage two envisions plutonium-fueled breeder reactors blanketed with thorium to produce uranium-233. India has run a 40 MWth (13 MWe) Fast Breeder Test Reactor since 1985 at the Indira Gandhi Centre for Atomic Research (IGCAR) and has successfully reprocessed a small amount of the unique fuel irradiated in that reactor. Construction of the 500 MWe prototype breeder reactor has begun, but the initial operating capability is not expected until 2010.

Uranium Enrichment

India began a uranium enrichment program in the 1980s. A gas centrifuge uranium enrichment facility at Mysore (called Rattenhalli) reportedly enriches uranium for naval fuel. There is also a pilot-scale gas centrifuge plant at Trombay for research and development, some laser enrichment-related activities also located at Trombay, and a laser enrichment facility at the Center for Advanced Technology in Indore for research.

Spent Fuel Reprocessing

Plutonium in India is produced for both civilian and military needs. The Trombay Plutonium Plant separates plutonium primarily for weapons purposes, whereas plutonium separation for civilian uses is performed at the Power Reactor Fuel Reprocessing Plant (PREFRE) at Tarapur and at Kalpakkam Reprocessing Plant (KARP). The Fast Reactor Fuel Reprocessing Plant and the Lead Minicell facility, both at Kalpakkam, also perform plutonium separation.

Table 1. India's Power Reactors

Name	Type	Status	Location	Net Capacity (MWe)	Gross Capacity (MWe)	Connected to Grid
Kaiga-1	PHWR	Operational	Karnataka	202	220	2000
Kaiga-2	PHWR	Operational	Karnataka	202	220	1999
Kaiga-3	PHWR	Construction	Karnataka	202	220	2007
Kaiga-4	PHWR	Construction	Karnataka	202	220	2007
Kakrapar-1 (KAPS-1)	PHWR	Operational	Gujrat	202	220	1992
Kakrapar-2 (KAPS-2)	PHWR	Operational	Gujrat	202	220	1995
Kudankulam-1 (KK-1)	VVER	Construction	Tamil Nadu State	917	1000	2007
Kudankulam-2 (KK-2)	VVER	Construction	Tamil Nadu State	917	1000	2008
Madras-1 (MAPS-1)	PHWR	Operational	Tamil Nadu	155	170	1983
Madras-2 (MAPS-2)	PHWR	Operational	Tamil Nadu	202	220	1985
Narora-1 (NAPS-1)	PHWR	Operational	Uttar Pradesh	202	220	1989
Narora-2 (NAPS-2)	PHWR	Operational	Uttar Pradesh	202	220	1992
Rajasthan-1 (RAPS-1)	PHWR	Operational	Rajasthan	90	100	1972
Rajasthan-2 (RAPS-2)	PHWR	Operational	Rajasthan	187	100	1980
Rajasthan-3 (RAPS-3)	PHWR	Operational	Rajasthan	202	220	2000
Rajasthan-4 (RAPS-4)	PHWR	Operational	Rajasthan	202	220	2000
Rajasthan-5 (RAPS-5)	PHWR	Construction	Rajasthan	202	220	2007
Rajasthan-6 (RAPS-6)	PHWR	Construction	Rajasthan	202	220	2007
Tarapur-1 (TAPS-1)	BWR	Operational	Maharastra	150	160	1969
Tarapur-2 (TAPS-2)	BWR	Operational	Maharastra	150	160	1969
Tarapur-3 (TAPS-3)	PHWR	Construction	Maharastra	490	540	2006
Tarapur-4 (TAPS-4)	PHWR	Operational	Maharastra	490	540	2005
			TOTALS	6172	6730	
		Reactors	— construction	2570	2810	
		Reactors	— operating	3602	3920	

Sources: IAEA Power Reactor Information System, Dr. Frederick Mackie of Lawrence Livermore National Laboratory, and the Congressional Research Service.

Notes: Those in italic print are under IAEA safeguards (INFCIRC-66) now or are scheduled to be under safeguards, irrespective of the separation plan. Those reactors in bolded print are the reactors scheduled additionally to be placed under safeguards under the separation plan. The difference between gross capacity and net capacity is the electricity needed to run the reactor. "Connected to Grid" means when the reactor is connected to the electricity grid (versus commercial operation).

Abbreviations: PHWR stands for Pressurized Heavy Water Reactor (CANDU-style); BWR stands for Boiling Water Reactor (use low-enriched uranium fuel).

Heavy Water Production

India has six heavy water production plants in operation, all of which were developed indigenously. Such plants are not required to be safeguarded under comprehensive safeguards agreements, because they do not contain source or special nuclear material, but would be required to be reported under an Additional Protocol. It remains to be seen whether India would report any of these under an Additional Protocol or perhaps just a portion of those that are not required for the military production of plutonium. The extent to which India requires more unsafeguarded plutonium for weapons or as fuel for unsafeguarded breeder reactors would determine how many heavy water plants would remain unreported.

Uranium Recovery and Conversion

India has three uranium mines, two copper-mine tailing extraction units, one mill, many uranium conversion facilities, and three fuel fabrication plants. Under a comprehensive safeguards agreement, the starting point of safeguards is when "any nuclear material of a composition and purity suitable for fuel fabrication or for being isotopically enriched leaves the plant or the process stage in which it has been produced."[27] In other words, the material would be inspected at the end of the uranium conversion process and at the start of the fuel fabrication process. Under an Additional Protocol, a state is required to report on all nuclear fuel cycle activities, including uranium ore, mining, milling, and conversion. It is not clear how or if India will declare some or all of those front end fuel cycle activities.

FACTORS INFLUENCING THE SEPARATION PLAN

U.S. Guidelines: Credible, Defensible, and Transparent

On November 2, 2005, Under Secretary of State Joseph told members of the Senate Foreign Relations Committee that India's separation of facilities must be credible, transparent, meaningful, and defensible from a nonproliferation standpoint. Further, Under Secretary Joseph told Members that a separation plan and resultant safeguards must contribute to U.S. nonproliferation goals, but did not elaborate which particular goals those might be. He noted that the more civil facilities India places under safeguards, the more confident the United States can be that any cooperative arrangements will not further India's military purposes. Specifically, Under Secretary Joseph said that safeguards would have to be applied in perpetuity, and that voluntary safeguards arrangements would not be defensible from a nonproliferation standpoint. The Administration also asserted that "The safeguards must effectively cover India's civil nuclear fuel cycle and provide strong assurances to supplier states and the IAEA that material and technology provided or created through civil cooperation will not be diverted to the military sphere."[28]

One interpretation of those phrases suggests that a credible plan would (1) be perceived to strengthen the nonproliferation regime; (2) be a complete and defensible declaration of its civil nuclear facilities and programs; and (3) mitigate perceptions of nuclear weapons status for India.[29] Such a plan would be guided by the assumption that power reactors, regardless of their potential to produce plutonium for weapons, have a civilian use and should be declared as civilian and safeguarded, as well as their associated fuel fabrication and reprocessing and spent fuel storage facilities.

India's breeder reactors would be safeguarded in this approach because the test reactor has been connected to the electricity grid since 1997, and the prototype fast breeder reactor will have a rating of 500 MWe and thus is meant to be connected to the electrical grid as a source of energy.[30] Since other advanced nuclear states with fast breeder reactors have placed them under safeguards (Japan and France), placing Indian breeder reactors under safeguards would mitigate perceptions of a double standard for India. Given their ability to produce weapons-grade plutonium, fast breeder reactors have been a proliferation concern for many years. Moreover, safeguarding breeder reactors would limit the amount of weapons-usable plutonium worldwide that is not safeguarded, which is clearly an objective of U.S. nonproliferation policy.

Indian Guidelines: Credible and Defensible from a Different View

It can be argued that India also approached creating a separation plan that is credible and defensible from its perspective. Although India had hoped for a safeguards arrangement like those of the nuclear weapon states, where facilities can be put on and taken off a safeguards list at will, the United States has said that such a voluntary safeguards arrangement would not be acceptable. Therefore, in this scheme, placing a facility on the civilian list would eliminate it from any potential use for the weapons program. While Indian officials have said that the July 18th agreement is not about their weapons program, their decisions about the separation plan were fundamentally guided by their future needs in the weapons program. Prime Minister Singh told the Indian Parliament on February 26, 2006 that in deciding on the scope of the separation plan, India took into account its

> current and future strategic needs and programme after careful deliberation of all relevant factors, consistent with our Nuclear Doctrine...[which envisions] a credible minimum nuclear deterrent to inflict unacceptable damage on an adversary indulging in a nuclear first-strike.[31]

From this perspective, a key factor for India is whether there is enough fissile material to meet the requirements of its minimal credible deterrent. If not, India must consider whether to "hedge" its future requirements by keeping some existing facilities out of safeguards so that they can produce plutonium or highly enriched uranium for weapons in the future, or to build new production facilities in the future. The July 18 agreement does not restrict India from doing so, at least until a fissile material production cutoff treaty is in force, but there are obvious costs to such an approach.

Some Indian observers argued to keep a handful (1-2 or preferably 2-4) indigenous pressurized heavy water reactors (PHWRs) out of safeguards for future fissile material production for weapons.[32] Others argued that a phased approach for placing PHWRs under safeguards would be sufficient to give India time to determine if it could meet its minimal credible deterrent.[33] In a controversial interview, AEC Chairman Anil Kakodkar suggested that some of the PHWRs could not be under safeguards because the breeder program, which he recommended not come under safeguards, would require unsafeguarded plutonium for fuel.[34]

Other commentators in India took a different perspective on this point. In a December 13, 2005, discussion at the India International Center, former Defense Research and Development Organization (DRDO) scientist and Institute of Defense Studies and Analysis (IDSA) Director K. Santhanam suggested that India could continue to meet all of its weapons plutonium needs from the CIRUS and Dhruva reactors and that plutonium from power reactors was unsuited for weapons. In a December 12, 2005 article in *The Times of India*, K. Subrahmanyam suggested that "Given India's uranium ore crunch and the need to build up our minimum credible nuclear deterrent arsenal as fast as possible, it is to India's advantage to categorize as many power reactors as possible as civilian ones to be refuelled by imported uranium and conserve our native uranium fuel for weapon-grade plutonium production."[35]

India's need to exclude its breeder reactor program from safeguards appears to be based several factors. Chairman of the Atomic Energy Commission (AEC) Dr. Kakodkar argued that the breeder program could not be put on the civilian list "from the point of maintaining long-term energy security and for maintaining the 'minimum credible deterrent.'"[36] India's Prime Minister Manmohan Singh told the Indian Parliament on February 26, 2006, that

> We will ensure that no impediments are put in the way of our research and development activities. We have made it clear that we cannot accept safeguards on our indigenous fast breeder programme. Our scientists are confident that this technology will mature and that the programme will stabilize and become more robust through the creation of additional capability. This will create greater opportunities.[37]

In general, Indian officials seemed guided by a strong predilection to continue what has been their past approach to safeguards — to place under safeguards only those facilities that have a foreign component (e.g., fuel or technology). AEC Chairman Kakodkar noted in August 2005 that "Anything coming from...external cooperation...will be put under facilities-specific safeguards," and that no research and development will be put under safeguards, including the prototype fast breeder reactor and facilities at the Indira Gandhi Centre for Atomic Research (IGCAR).[38]

Another consideration influencing Indian views are the potential financial and economic costs of separation. In some cases, facilities serve both civilian and military purposes. A. Gopalakrishnan, former chairman of the Atomic Energy Regulatory Board, suggested that certain critical plants at the Nuclear Fuels Complex at Hyderabad were not duplicated and should be kept out of safeguards until they could be replicated.[39]

Finally, assumptions about India's prestige and independence may also have played a role. Some Indian officials have rejected the notion of placing any research and development facilities under safeguards because they equate such safeguards with attempts to constrain India's independence. AEC Chairman Kakodkar told the *Indian Express* in February 2006 that:

> There is a more fundamental question. If I am treated as an advanced country, where is the compulsion for me to do it? I will do R and D in an autonomous manner, finished.[40]

The Separation Plan

On March 2, 2006, during President Bush's visit to India, U.S. and Indian officials agreed upon a final separation plan. According to India's official report, India was guided by the following principles:

- Credible, feasible, and implementable in a transparent manner;
- Consistent with the understandings of the 18 July Statement;
- Consistent with India's national security and R and D requirements as well as not prejudicial to the three-stage nuclear programme in India;
- Must be cost effective in its implementation; and
- Must be acceptable to Parliament and public opinion.[41]

Regarding the application of safeguards, India identified its "overarching criterion" as whether "subjecting a facility to IAEA safeguards would impact adversely on India's national security." Moreover, facilities were excluded from the civilian list if they were located in a larger hub of strategic significance (e.g., BARC), even if they were not normally engaged in activities of strategic significance.[42] This last criterion appears to suggest that the plan did not really seek to separate facilities.

The key elements of India's separation plan are[43]

- eight indigenous Indian power reactors (RAPS 3, 4, 5, 6; KAPS 1, 2; NAPS 1, 2) in addition to 6 already under safeguards;
- future power reactors may also be placed under safeguards, if India declares them as civilian;
- some facilities in the Nuclear Fuel Complex (e.g., fuel fabrication) will be specified as civilian in 2008; and
- nine research facilities and three heavy water plants would be declared as civilian, but are "safeguards-irrelevant."

The following facilities and activities were not on the separation list:

- eight indigenous Indian power reactors (Kaiga 1, 2, 3, 4; MAPS 1, 2; TAPS 3, 4);
- Fast Breeder Test Reactor (FTBR) and Prototype Fast Breeder Reactors (PFBR) under construction;
- enrichment facilities;
- spent fuel reprocessing facilities (except for the existing safeguards on the Power Reactor Fuel Reprocessing (PREFRE) plant);
- research reactors: CIRUS (which will be shut down in 2010), Dhruva, Advanced Heavy Water Reactor;
- three heavy water plants; and
- various military-related plants (e.g., a prototype naval reactor).

The eight additional reactors would be put under safeguards between 2007 and 2014.

The implementation document presented to Parliament stated that "India is not in a position to accept safeguards on the Prototype Fast Breeder Reactor (PFBR) and the Fast Breeder Test Reactor (FTBR), both located at Kalpakkam. The Fast Breeder Programme is at the R and D stage and its technology will take time to mature and reach an advanced stage of development." As for future reactors, the document stated that "India has decided to place under safeguards all future civilian thermal power reactors and civilian breeder reactors, and the Government of India retains the sole right to determine such reactors as civilian."[44] In response to a question about whether it was possible for there to be non-civilian breeder reactors that India would build in the future, Under Secretary of State Nicholas Burns stated that "India could build reactors that would service their nuclear weapons industry...but the great majority of the growth we think will come on the civilian side."[45]

As for research reactors, CIRUS would be shut down in 2010 and not subjected to safeguards. The fuel core of the Apsara reactor would be taken out of BARC and made available to be safeguarded. Some facilities in the Nuclear Fuel Complex would be specified as civilian in 2008, and the Tarapur and Rajasthan spent fuel storage pools would be made available for safeguards (Tarapur 1-2 and Rajasthan 1-2 reactors themselves are already safeguarded.) In addition, India would declare 3 heavy water plants (Thal, Tuticorin and Hazira) as civilian, but these would not be subject to safeguards; 9 research facilities would be declared as civilian also, but these would be considered "safeguards-irrelevant."

India's enrichment facility would not be covered, and India's offering up the Tarapur Power Reactor Fuel Reprocessing Plant (PREFRE) for "campaign" mode safeguards after 2010 is a continuation of its current policy. The Dhruva research reactor is excluded.

Under Secretary of State Burns stated that India "would enter into permanent safeguard arrangements with the International Atomic Energy Agency." However, the Indian statement that an Indian-specific safeguards agreement would "guard against withdrawal of safeguarded nuclear material from civilian use at any time as well as providing for corrective measures that India may take to ensure uninterrupted operation of its civilian nuclear reactors in the event of disruption of foreign fuel supplies"raises questions about exactly what kind of safeguards arrangement is envisioned. Burns noted that the arrangement "achieved a degree of transparency and oversight and impact on the Indian nuclear program that was not possible for three decades."[46]

Figure 2 shows a rough depiction of how the final separation applies to India's civilian and military nuclear facilities.

Assessing the Separation Plan

Congressional views on the separation plan, particularly whether it is credible and defensible from a nonproliferation standpoint, may have an impact on Congress's consideration of the overall peaceful nuclear cooperation agreement.

Quantity vs. Quality

Under Secretary of State Nicholas Burns told reporters on March 2, 2006, that "It's not a perfect deal in the sense that we haven't captured 100 percent of India's nuclear program. That's because India is a nuclear weapons power, and India will preserve part of its nuclear industry to service its nuclear weapons program."[47] Although few observers would have expected to get 100% of India's nuclear program under safeguards, one question that arises is

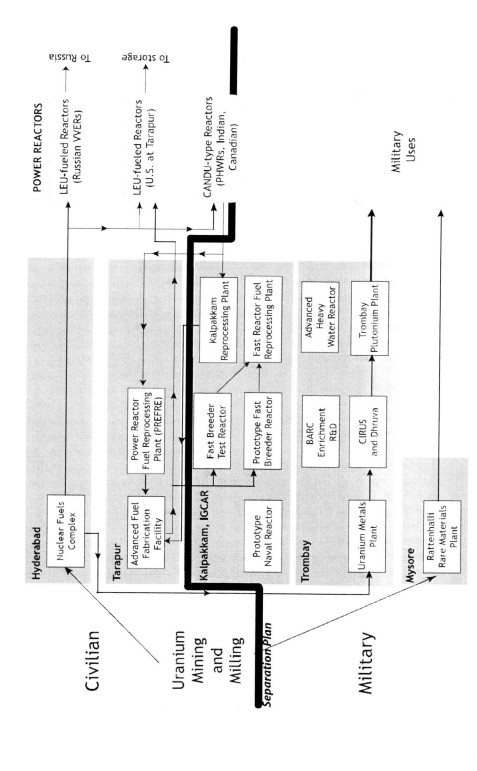

Sources: Dr. Frederick Mackie, Lawrence Livermore National Laboratory, and the Congressional Research Service.

Figure 2. India's Separation Plan.

whether the 65% mark meets the Administration's own standard that "The safeguards must effectively cover India's civil nuclear fuel cycle."[48]

The Administration has defended the separation plan most recently as credible and defensible in this way:

> For [the separation plan] to be credible and defensible from a nonproliferation standpoint, it had to capture more than just a token number of Indian nuclear facilities, which it did by encompassing nearly two-thirds of India's current and planned thermal power reactors as well as all future civil thermal and breeder reactors. Importantly, for the safeguards to be meaningful, India had to commit to apply IAEA safeguards in perpetuity; it did so. Once a reactor is under IAEA safeguards, those safeguards will remain there permanently and on an unconditional basis. Further, in our view, the plan also needed to include upstream and downstream facilities associated with the safeguarded reactors to provide a true separation of civil and military programs.[49]

It should be noted that although declaring 65% of India's reactors as civilian will result in placing almost two-thirds of the current reactors under safeguards, power reactors constitute just one part of the nuclear fuel cycle. Reprocessing capabilities are key to India's three-stage nuclear fuel cycle development plan, and the separation plan provides nothing beyond the intermittent safeguards applied at the Power Reactor Fuel Reprocessing Plant (PREFRE) already.

Some observers could argue that a strictly quantitative approach does not address the question of whether the plan is defensible from a nonproliferation standpoint. Here too, the kinds of facilities included could be key. For example, in terms of preventing terrorist access to fissile material, safeguarding facilities like reprocessing and enrichment plants and breeder reactors would provide a greater nonproliferation benefit because the materials produced by these plants are a few steps closer to potential use in a bomb. In addition, safeguards on enrichment, reprocessing plants, and breeder reactors would support the 2002 U.S. National Strategy to Combat Weapons of Mass Destruction, in which the United States pledged to "continue to discourage the worldwide accumulation of separated plutonium and to minimize the use of highly-enriched uranium."[50]

Breeder Reactors

As noted earlier, breeder reactors, which are key to India's intended second stage of fuel cycle development, have been generally regarded as a proliferation concern because of their production of weapons-grade plutonium.[51] India plans to build at least five commercial-scale breeder reactors and would have the option of dedicating any one or more of those to its military program. Public statements by Indian officials suggest that they have considered the breeder reactor's usefulness in producing plutonium for the strategic arsenal, and some domestic critics have suggested that India should clarify the purpose of the breeder program once and for all. A key obstacle may be the amount of unsafeguarded plutonium available as initial fuel, raising the question of how future civilian breeder reactors would be fueled. Would plutonium from the 10 additional reactors India will be placing under safeguards be used to fuel the reactors, or would India purchase safeguarded plutonium from other states? If the latter case, would this conflict with the Administration's policy of discouraging the worldwide accumulation of separated plutonium?

Other Facilities

Prime Minister Singh told the Indian Parliament on February 26 that "We will offer to place under safeguards only those facilities that can be identified as civilian without damaging our deterrence potential or restricting our R and D effort."[52] Although CIRUS, Dhruva, the Fast Breeder Test Reactor, and the planned Advanced Heavy Water Reactor have been described by Indian facilities as being research facilities, they are not included. The 9 research facilities that will be declared as civilian are considered safeguards-irrelevant, probably because they will have little if any nuclear material in them to be safeguarded.

The absence of research facilities could call into question how far India's separation plan has ventured into the mainstream of nonproliferation. IAEA safeguards for non-nuclear weapon states include all facilities where nuclear material is present, including research and development facilities. The case of precedents in other nuclear weapon states is not applicable, since the IAEA tends not to inspect very many of the sites or facilities on the voluntary safeguards eligible lists. Likewise, the absence of reprocessing and enrichment facilities on the separation plan also could be interpreted by some as falling short of the objective of bringing India into the mainstream of nonproliferation. In particular, the Bush Administration has identified enrichment and reprocessing technologies as sensitive parts of the nuclear fuel cycle that should be limited and has proposed specific arrangements for assured supplies of nuclear fuel that would obviate the need for states to conduct their own enrichment and reprocessing.[53]

India's one operating facility at Rattenhalli is reportedly used to enrich uranium for the prototype naval fuel reactor. Naval fuel occupies a curious place in IAEA safeguards. Full-scope safeguards agreements, the kind that non-nuclear weapon states have, include a provision for the non-application of safeguards to nuclear material to be used in non-peaceful activities — and naval fuel would be one such non-peaceful activity. However, no non-nuclear weapon state has ever implemented this provision for the non-application of safeguards. Under Paragraph 14 of the INFCIRC/153, a state is required to inform the IAEA that

> the use of the nuclear material in a non-proscribed military activity will not be in conflict with an undertaking the State may have given and in respect of which Agency safeguards apply, that the nuclear material will be used only in a peaceful nuclear activity; and that during the period of non-application of safeguards the nuclear material will not be used for the production of nuclear weapons or other nuclear explosive devices.

Brazil has placed its enrichment facilities under safeguards, despite having a naval fuel program, which also raises the question of how far India's separation plan conforms to the standards of the nonproliferation mainstream. The five nuclear weapon states have not encountered this problem thus far, since they have not placed any naval-related facilities on their safeguards-eligible lists. It is not clear which precedent would be less desirable — placing India's naval fuel facilities under safeguards and then going through steps for the nonapplication of safeguards, or simply not safeguarding them at all on the grounds that they are of direct national security significance.

ISSUES FOR CONGRESS

U.S. officials acknowledge the importance of a credible Indian separation plan for ensuring that the United States complies with its Article I obligations under the Nuclear Nonproliferation Treaty (NPT) — to not in any way assist a nuclear weapons program in a non-nuclear weapon state. For almost thirty years, the U.S. legal standard has been that only nuclear safeguards on all nuclear activities in a state provides adequate assurances. The Administration has sought, and Congress has provided, backing for a lower level of assurance by proposing that the separation plan take the place of comprehensive safeguards.

From a broad perspective, Congress may consider whether opening up international cooperation to India after all these years has a net positive effect on India's nuclear weapons program. Under Secretary of State Nicholas Burns told reporters on March 2, 2006, that the agreement will not have an impact on India's strategic program.[54] However, some observers believe that unless India stops production of fissile material for weapons purposes, nuclear safeguards will do little to ensure that assistance is not diverted.

From a narrower perspective, the text of a peaceful nuclear cooperation agreement is necessary for Congress to assess whether or not the United States can comply with its NPT obligations not to assist India's nuclear weapons program. P.L. 109-401, which gives the President authority to waive certain requirements of the Atomic Energy Act, still requires the Administration to send Congress not only the text of a peaceful nuclear cooperation agreement, but also a Nuclear Proliferation Assessment Statement (NPAS), which must address the extent to which U.S. treaty commitments are met.

Under P.L. 109-401, the following sections require reports to Congress related to the separation plan:

- Under the Submission to Congress provision of Section 104 (Section 104. (c) (2) (A)), the Administration will be required to provide "a summary of the plan provided by India to the United States and the IAEA to separate India's civil and military nuclear facilities, materials, and programs, and the declaration made by India to the IAEA identifying India's civil facilities to be placed under IAEA safeguards, including an analysis of the credibility of such plan and declaration, together with copies of the plan and declaration."
- Under the Reporting to Congress provision of Section 104 (Section 104.(g)(1)) the Administration will be required to keep committees informed of

- (A)(ii): material noncompliance with the separation plan;
- (B): "construction of a nuclear facility in India after the date of enactment of this title";
- (C): "significant changes in the production by India of nuclear weapons or in the types or amounts of fissile material produced"; and
- (D): "changes in the purpose or operational status of any unsafeguarded nuclear fuel cycle activities in India."
- Under the Implementation and Compliance Report provision of Section 104 (Section 104.(g)(2)), the Administration is required to report, 180 days after entry into force of the Section 123 agreement and annually thereafter:

- (A): a description of any additional nuclear facilities and nuclear materials that the Government of India has placed or intends to place under IAEA safeguards;
- (F): an analysis of whether U.S. civil nuclear cooperation with India is in any way assisting India's nuclear weapons program;
- (H): an estimate relating to India's production of uranium, fissile material for nuclear explosives;
- (I): an estimate of the amount of electricity produced by India's declared and undeclared reactors; and
- (J): an analysis of whether imported uranium has affected the rate of production in India of nuclear explosive devices.

In the President's signing statement on December 18, 2006, he noted that the executive branch would construe "provisions of the Act that mandate, regulate, or prohibit submission of information to the Congress, an international organization, or the public, such as sections 104, 109, 261, 271, 272, 273, 274, and 275, in a manner consistent with the President's constitutional authority to protect and control information that could impair foreign relations, national security, the deliberative processes of the Executive, or the performance of the Executive's constitutional duties." This could suggest that the executive branch might limit the scope of reporting required by Congress in those sections. Limiting the scope of reporting could have an adverse impact on Congress's ability to assess the nuclear cooperation agreement at three different times: when the agreement is submitted for congressional approval; at random times when there are certain developments in India's nuclear fuel cycle; and on an annual basis when the Administration reports on implementation and compliance.

REFERENCES

[1] The Nuclear Suppliers Group seeks to stem proliferation of nuclear weapons through coordinating nuclear exports and nuclear-related exports. See [http://www.nsg-online.org].

[2] The NPT defines nuclear weapon states as those that have tested nuclear explosive devices before January 1, 1967. This includes the United States, United Kingdom, France, China, and Russia.

[3] These are INFCIRC/66-type agreements. They can cover nuclear material or facilities supplied under project agreements, produced in safeguarded facilities, or unilaterally submitted to safeguards by a state. See CRS Report RL33016, *U.S. Nuclear Cooperation with India: Issues for Congress*, by Sharon Squassoni, for more detail.

[4] Under Secretary of State Robert Joseph, testimony before SFRC Nov. 2, 2005 hearing.

[5] This program, announced in February 2006, seeks to develop, among other things, new reprocessing technologies for future fuel cycles. See [http://www.gnep.energy.gov] for more detail.

[6] "On the Record: Anil Kakodkar, Chairman of the Atomic Energy Commission and Secretary, Department of Atomic Energy," *Indian Express*, Feb. 8, 2006.

[7]   Zia Mian and M.V. Ramana, "Wrong Ends, Means, and Needs: Behind the U.S. Nuclear Deal with India, *Arms Control Today*, January/February 2006. See also Robert Einhorn, "Limiting the Damage," *The National Interest*, Winter 2005/2006.

[8]   Henry Sokolski, in "Fissile isn't Facile," *Wall Street Journal,* Feb. 21, 2006, suggested that "If we want to keep this aid from freeing up India's domestic nuclear resources to make more bombs...we have to get serious about India capping its nuclear weapons program." David Albright made a more direct connection in his testimony before the House International Relations Committee hearing, "The U.S.-India Global Partnership: The Impact on Nonproliferation," on Oct. 26, 2005 (hereafter, HIRC Oct 26, 2005 hearing), stating that "Without India halting production of fissile material for its nuclear weapons programs, nuclear assistance, particularly any in the areas involving the fuel cycle, would likely spill over to India's nuclear weapons program."

[9]   David Albright and Susan Basu, "Separating Indian Military and Civilian Nuclear Facilities," Institute for Science and International Security, Dec. 19, 2005. See also the prepared statement by Leonard Spector before the HIRC Oct. 26, 2005 hearing.

[10] Statement of Robert J. Einhorn before the HIRC Oct. 26, 2005 hearing.

[11] From the July 18, 2005 Joint Statement: "India would reciprocally agree that it would be ready to assume the same responsibilities and practices and acquire the same benefits and advantages as other leading countries with advanced nuclear technology, such as the United States." The Indian Prime Minister's Office issued a background paper on the agreement in July 2005 that said: "IAEA Safeguards shall apply to facilities to be designated by India voluntarily...In this respect there will be no discrimination between India and other Nuclear Weapon States." See [http://pmindia.nic.in/pressrel.htm].

[12] See Perkovich, George, *India's Nuclear Bomb: The Impact on Global Proliferation,* (University of California Press, CA, 1999) for an excellent history of the Indian nuclear program.

[13] See [http://www.npcil.nic.in/nupower_vol11_1-3/chidambaram.htm].

[14] A Gigawatt is one billion watts of energy; a Megawatt is one million watts of energy. Dr. Anil Kakodkar, "Energy in India for the Coming Decades," presentation to IAEA conference on *Nuclear Power for the 21st Century*, Paris, March 2005, available at [http://www.dae.gov.in/iaea/ak-paris0305.doc]. The estimate is 10,000 MWe for 40 years.

[15] M.R. Srinivasan, R.B. Grover, S.A. Bhardwaj, "Nuclear Power in India: Winds of Change," *Economic and Political Weekly*, December 3, 2005. This contrasts with State Department answers to questions for the record from Senator Lugar, dated November 2, 2005, which stated that "India's plan for its nuclear power sector seeks to provide for a 20-fold increase in nuclear-generated electricity by 2020 without reactors from foreign suppliers."

[16] T.S. Subramanian, "Uranium Crisis," *Frontline*, vol. 22, Issue 27, December 31-January 13, 2006.

[17] Ibid. Yellowcake is an impure mixture of uranium oxides obtained during the processing of uranium ore. It must be purified before being fabricated into reactor fuel.

[18] T.S. Subramanian, "Uranium Crisis," *Frontline*, vol. 22, Issue 27, December 31-January 13, 2006 and Dr. A. Gopalakrishnan, "Civilian and Strategic Nuclear Facilities of India," Institute for Defense Studies and Analyses, January 5, 2006.

[19] Many sources were used in collating this data. See [http://www.iaea.org/programmes/a2/ index.html] for a list of India's power reactors and [http://www.iaea.org/worldatom/rrdb/] for a list of research reactors. Other sources include websites maintained by India's Department of Atomic Energy, the Bhabha Atomic Research Center and the Indira Gandhi Centre for Atomic Research. These are, respectively, [http://www.dae.gov.in], [http://www.igcar.ernet.in/], and [http://www.barc.ernet.in/].

[20] These types of reactors constitute about ten percent of all reactors worldwide. Because the reactors can be refueled on-line, they are well-suited for making plutonium for nuclear weapons.

[21] The fast breeder test reactor, although it could technically be considered a research reactor, is discussed below in the breeder reactor section.

[22] An *aide memoire* presented to the Indian Atomic Energy Commission on November 16, 1970 sought to clarify the U.S. view on peaceful uses. The document, declassified in 1980, points out that the U.S. contract stipulated that the heavy water was to be used only in India in connection with research into and use of atomic energy for peaceful purposes, and that "The United States would not consider the use of plutonium produced in CIRUS for peaceful nuclear explosives intended for any purpose to be 'research into and use of atomic energy for peaceful purposes.'" Additionally, the document stated that "the use, for the development of peaceful nuclear explosive devices of plutonium produced therefrom, would be considered by the United States a contravention of the terms under which the American materials were made available." "Aide Memoire Presented to Indian Atomic Energy Commission in Bombay, November 16, 1970," available at [http://www.armscontrol.org/ pdf/ 19701116_US_Aide_Memoire_Indian_AEC.pdf]

[23] Talking points provided by First Secretary of Canada's embassy to the United States, Kelly Anderson, Dec. 20, 2005.

[24] Zia Mian and MV Ramana, "Feeding the Nuclear Fire," *Economic and Political Weekly,* Aug. 27, 2005.

[25] Briefing by Dr. Frederick Mackie, Lawrence Livermore National Laboratory, Dec. 14, 2006.

[26] T.S. Subramanian, "Uranium Crisis," *Frontline*, vol. 22, Issue 27, Dec. 31, 2005-Jan. 13, 2006.

[27] See INFCIRC/153, at [http://www.iaea.org/Publications/Documents/Infcircs/Others/inf153.shtml].

[28] Responses by the State Department to questions for the record submitted by Senator Richard Lugar, November 2, 2005.

[29] Dr. Frederick Mackie, Lawrence Livermore National Laboratory, Briefing, December 14, 2005.

[30] See G. Balachandran, "On separation list," January 2006, and S.B. Bhoje, and S. Govindarajan, "The FBR Programme in India," International Journal of Nuclear Power -Volume 18, No. 2-3, 2004, available on [http://www.dae.gov.in].

[31] "PM Makes a Case for N-tech," PTI. See [http://ia.rediff.com/news/2006/feb/27bush8.htm].

[32] G. Balachandran, "International Nuclear Control Regimes and India's Participation in Civilian Nuclear Trade: Key Issues," *Strategic Analysis*, Vol. 29, No. 4., Oct-Dec. 2005.

[33] Dr. A. Gopalakrishnan, "Civilian and Strategic Nuclear Facilities of India," IDSA strategic comment, January 5, 2006, available at [http://www.idsa.in].

[34] "On the Record: Anil Kakodkar, Chairman of the Atomic Energy Commission and Secretary, Department of Atomic Energy," *Indian Express*, February 8, 2006.

[35] K. Subrahmanyam, former head of the Institute for Defence Studies and Analysis, was appointed Head of the National Security Council Advisory Board (NSCAB) established by the first Vajpayee government to draft the Indian nuclear doctrine. He currently chairs PM Singh's Global Strategic Developments Task Force. See also Dr. A. Gopalakrishnan, "Civilian and Strategic Nuclear Facilities of India," January 5, 2006.

[36] Ibid.

[37] Prime Minister Singh's address to Parliament, February 26, 2006. See "PM Makes a Case for N-tech," PTI. See [http://ia.rediff.com/news/2006/feb/27bush8.htm].

[38] Interview in *The Hindu*, August 12, 2005.

[39] Ibid.

[40] "On the Record: Anil Kakodkar, Chairman of the Atomic Energy Commission and Secretary, Department of Atomic Energy," *Indian Express*, February 8, 2006.

[41] "Implementation of the India-United States Joint Statement of July 18, 2005: India's Separation Plan," tabled in Parliament on March 7, 2006.

[42] Ibid.

[43] Prime Minister Singh presented "Implementation of the India-United States Joint Statement of July 18, 2005: India's Separation Plan," to Parliament on March 7, 2006. This is available at [http://indianembassy.org/newsite/press_release/ 2006/Mar/ sepplan.pdf]. The plan was updated on May 11, 2006, to include names of reactors and upstream facilities, as well as dates they would be submitted to safeguards.

[44] Ibid.

[45] Ibid.

[46] Ibid.

[47] White House, Office of the Press Secretary, "Press Briefing by Under Secretary of State for Political Affairs Nick Burns," Maurya Sheraton Hotel and Towers, New Delhi, India, March 2, 2006.

[48] Responses by the Administration to Questions for The Record Submitted to Under Secretary Robert Joseph by Chairman Richard G. Lugar (#4) Senate Foreign Relations Committee, November 2, 2005.

[49] Questions for the Record Submitted to Secretary of State Condoleezza Rice by Senator Richard Lugar (#2) Senate Foreign Relations Committee, April 5, 2006.

[50] National Strategy to Combat Weapons of Mass Destruction, December 2002. Available at [http://www.whitehouse.gov/news/releases/2002/12/WMDStrategy.pdf].

[51] For many years, the United States discouraged plutonium reprocessing and did not engage in reprocessing in the U.S. civil nuclear fuel cycle. However, with the announcement of the Global Energy Nuclear Partnership (GNEP), the Bush Administration is seeking to develop a recycling method (so-called "proliferation-resistant") that would not result in the separation of plutonium. It is unclear how long it would take for advanced recycling technologies to become commercially available.

Regardless, it is unlikely that India could participate in the GNEP program without a commitment to place its breeder reactors under safeguards. See [http://www.gnep.energy.gov/gnepProliferationResistantRecycling.html].

[52]   "Indian PM Addresses Parliament on Nuclear Pact with US," BBC Monitoring South Asia, February 27, 2006.

[53]   White House, "Fact Sheet: Strengthening International Efforts Against WMD Proliferation," February 11, 2004. Available at [http://www.whitehouse.gov/news/releases/2004/02/20040211-5.html].

[54]   White House, Office of the Press Secretary, "Press Briefing by Under Secretary of State for Political Affairs Nick Burns," Maurya Sheraton Hotel and Towers, New Delhi, India, Mar. 2, 2006.

In: India on the Move
Editor: Lea M. Surit, pp. 153-159

ISBN: 978-1-60021-813-2
© 2007 Nova Science Publishers, Inc.

Chapter 6

INDIA AND IRAN: WMD PROLIFERATION ACTIVITIES[*]

Sharon Squassoni

ABSTRACT

Members of Congress have questioned whether India's cooperation with Iran might affect U.S. and other efforts to prevent Iran from developing nuclear weapons. India's long relationship with Iran and its support of Non-Aligned Movement (NAM) positions on nonproliferation are obstacles to India's taking a hard line on Iran, yet the Bush Administration has asserted that U.S.-India nuclear cooperation would bring India into the "nonproliferation mainstream." India, like most other states, does not support a nuclear weapons option for Iran. However, its views of the Iranian threat and appropriate responses differ significantly from U.S. views. Entities in India and Iran appear to have engaged in very limited nuclear, chemical and missile-related transfers over the years, and some sanctions have been imposed on Indian entities for transfers to Iran, the latest in July 2006. This report will be updated as necessary.

In congressional hearings on the proposed U.S. nuclear cooperation agreement with India, Members questioned how India's cooperation with Iran might affect U.S. efforts to prevent Iran from developing nuclear weapons. India's long relationship with Iran and its support of Non-Aligned Movement (NAM) positions on nonproliferation are obstacles to India's taking a hard line on Iran, yet the Bush Administration has asserted that U.S.-India nuclear cooperation would bring India into the "nonproliferation mainstream." U.S. law requires recipients of U.S. nuclear cooperation to guarantee the nonproliferation of any U.S. material or equipment transferred. If a recipient state assists, encourages or induces a non-nuclear weapon state to engage in nuclear-weapons related activities, exports must cease. India's nonproliferation record continues to be scrutinized, as India continues to take steps to strengthen its own export controls. Additional measures of Indian support *could include* diplomatic support for negotiations with Iran; support for Bush Administration efforts to restrict enrichment and reprocessing; support for multilateral fuel cycle initiatives, and for the Proliferation Security Initiative.

---

[*] Excerpted from CRS Report RS22530, dated November 8, 2006.

INDIA'S RECORD OF SUPPORT

India, like most other states, does not support a nuclear weapons option for Iran. However, Indian views of the threat Iran poses and appropriate responses differ from U.S. views. On September 24, 2005, India voted with 21 other states on International Atomic Energy Agency (IAEA) resolution GOV/2005/77, which found Iran in noncompliance with its safeguards agreement. However, the resolution did not refer the matter immediately to the Security Council, and India apparently was one of several states pressuring the EU-3 to keep the issue at the IAEA. According to Indian Foreign Secretary Shyam Saran, India voted for the resolution and against the majority of NAM states which abstained, because it felt obligated to do so after having pressured the EU-3 to omit reference to immediate referral to the U.N. Security Council.[1] Moreover, the official explanation of India's vote seemed designed to highlight India's differences with the United States:

> In our Explanation of Vote, we have clearly expressed our opposition to Iran being declared as noncompliant with its safeguards agreements. Nor do we agree that the current situation could constitute a threat to international peace and security. Nevertheless, the resolution does not refer the matter to the Security Council and has agreed that outstanding issues be dealt with under the aegis of the IAEA itself. This is in line with our position and therefore, we have extended our support.[2]

Nonetheless, India again voted with the United States on February 4, 2006, when the IAEA Board of Governors voted to refer Iran's noncompliance to the U.N. Security Council.[3] The Ministry of External Affairs responded to questions about its vote in this manner:

> While there will be a report to the Security Council, the Iran nuclear issue remains within the purview of the IAEA. It has been our consistent position that confrontation should be avoided and any outstanding issue ought to be resolved through dialogue.... Our vote in favour of the Resolution should not be interpreted as in any way detracting from the traditionally close and friendly relations we enjoy with Iran. It is our conviction that our active role, along with other friendly countries, enabled the tabling of a resolution that recognizes the right of Iran to peaceful uses of nuclear energy for its development, consistent with its international commitments and obligations, while keeping the door open for further dialogue aimed at resolving the outstanding issues within the purview of the IAEA.[4]

India's Prime Minister told the Indian Parliament on February 17, 2006, that "As a signatory to the NPT, Iran has the legal right to develop peaceful uses of nuclear energy consistent with its international commitments and obligations." Nonetheless, PM Singh also noted that "It is incumbent upon Iran to exercise these rights in the context of safeguards that it has voluntarily accepted upon its nuclear programme under the IAEA."[5]

India has supported the EU-3 negotiations, despite their ostensible objective of halting Iran's pursuit of sensitive nuclear technology (that is, enrichment, reprocessing and heavy water). In part, this may be because the talks offered a second avenue of negotiation that did not necessarily lead to U.N. Security Council sanctions, or because they have offered a viable discussion forum. India welcomed the U.S. decision to join the talks, stating:

India has all along advocated that issues relating to Iran's nuclear programme ought to be resolved through dialogue and that confrontation should be avoided. Against this background, the readiness of the US to join in the dialogue between EU-3 and Iran, which India has all along supported, is to be welcomed.[6]

In September 2006, however, India joined other NAM states in a statement issued at the Havana NAM summit on Iran's nuclear program. The statement "reaffirmed the basic inalienable right of all states, to develop research, production and use of atomic energy for peaceful purposes without any discrimination and in conformity with their respective legal obligations. Therefore, nothing should be interpreted in a way as inhibiting or restricting this right of States to develop atomic energy for peaceful purposes. They furthermore, reaffirmed that States choices and decisions in the field of peaceful uses of nuclear technology and its fuel cycle policies must be respected."[7]

Two other U.S. nonproliferation policies that may help underpin a solution to the Iran crisis are related to restrictions on the nuclear fuel cycle — a ban on transferring enrichment and reprocessing technologies to states that are not already technology holders, and steps toward multilateralizing the nuclear fuel cycle so that sensitive technologies are not as widespread. A key new U.S. initiative in this area is the Global Nuclear Energy Partnership, or GNEP. India, under the July 18, 2005 Joint Statement with the United States, committed to refrain from transferring enrichment and reprocessing technologies to states that do not have them, as well as to support international efforts to limit their spread. India's future support for those policies, however, may be predicated on India being considered one of those technology holders. A recent statement from President Bush on GNEP did not recognize India as such a technology holder:

> My administration has announced a new proposal called the Global Nuclear Energy Partnership. Under this partnership, America will work with nations that have advanced civilian nuclear energy programs — such as Great Britain, France, Japan, and Russia — to share nuclear fuel with nations like India that are developing civilian nuclear energy programs.... The strategy will allow countries like India to produce more electricity from nuclear power, it will enable countries like India to rely less on fossil fuels, it will decrease the amount of nuclear waste that needs to be stored and reduce the risk of nuclear proliferation.[8]

Another tool that may be utilized by those desiring to prevent Iran from developing nuclear weapons is the Proliferation Security Initiative. On November 2, 2005, Under Secretary of State R. Nicholas Burns told the Senate Foreign Relations Committee that "Indian support for the multi-national Proliferation Security Initiative (PSI) would be a boon to the participating nations' goal of tracking and interdicting dangerous terrorist and weapons of mass destruction (WMD) cargoes world-wide. We hope India will choose to join PSI."[9] In April 2006, Secretary of State Rice told the House International Relations Committee that the United States was pressing India to announce its intention to participate in the Proliferation Security Initiative. Both the House (H.R. 5682) and Senate (S. 3709) bills to create an exception for India from relevant provisions of the Atomic Energy Act refer to the desirability of getting India to join PSI, but do not make it a prerequisite for cooperation. Prime Minister Singh told the Parliament in August 2006 that the "Proliferation Security Initiative is an extraneous issue...Therefore, we cannot accept it as a condition for implementing the July Statement. Separately, the Government has examined the PSI. We have certain concerns regarding its legal implications and its linkages with the NPT."

Finally, efforts to prevent Iran from acquiring nuclear weapons rely on coordinated export controls and strong national export control systems. India has agreed to harmonize its export controls with the guidelines of the Nuclear Suppliers Group under the July 18, 2005 Joint Statement. India also passed a new law in May 2005, the Weapons of Mass Destruction and their Delivery Systems (Prohibition of Unlawful Activities) Bill. According to Indian officials, the Act prohibits the "possession, manufacture, transportation, acquisition, development of nuclear weapons, chemical weapons or biological weapons by non-state actors."[10] It would prohibit the export of any good or technology from India "if the exporter knows it is intended to be used in a WMD program." The U.S. Commerce and State Departments have not yet assessed India's export control law and regulations,[11] which were promulgated in response to U.N. Security Council Resolution 1540 requiring all states to take actions to criminalize proliferation, particularly to non-state actors.

Some observers have stated that India does not have the necessary regulations in place to implement the law, and that India's resources for implementation are remarkably limited.[12] A third issue is whether India will follow through in imposing penalties on violators of export control laws and regulations.

INDIA'S NONPROLIFERATION RECORD

In its semi-annual, unclassified report in 2000 to Congress on the acquisition of technology relating to weapons of mass destruction, the CIA identified India, along with Iran and Pakistan, as a "traditional recipient of WMD and missile technology" that could emerge as a new supplier of technology and expertise.[13] The unclassified report also noted that "private companies, scientists, and engineers in Russia, China, and India may be increasing their involvement in WMD- and missile-related assistance, taking advantage of weak or unenforceable national export controls and the growing availability of technology." In 2001, the unclassified CIA report noted that "We are increasingly concerned about the growth of 'secondary proliferation' from maturing state-sponsored programs, such as those in India, Iran, North Korea, and Pakistan."

REPORTED TRANSFERS TO IRAN

Entities in India and Iran appear to have engaged in very limited nuclear, chemical and missile-related transfers over the years. There are no publicly available indications of activities related to biological weapons. In the early 1990s, when Iran actively sought nuclear-related assistance and technology from many foreign sources, India appears to have played only a minor role in contrast to other states. India signed an agreement in November 1991 to provide a 10-megawatt research reactor to Tehran, but cancelled under pressure from the United States. Nonetheless, India reportedly trained Iranian nuclear scientists in the 1990s.[14] More recently, India's Foreign Minister Jaswant Singh stated in December 2003 that India "has and would continue to help Iran in its controversial bid to generate nuclear energy."[15]

From 1998 to 2003, the United States has imposed nonproliferation sanctions on several different Indian entities for chemical and biological-weapons related transfers to Iraq.[16] In 2004, the United States imposed sanctions on two Indian scientists for nuclear-related transfers to Iran: Dr. C. Surendar (sanctions on Dr. Surendar were lifted in December 2005) and Dr. Y.S.R. Prasad. Both scientists were high-ranking officials in the Nuclear Power Corporation of India, Limited (NPCIL). Indian officials protested, stating that cooperation had taken place under the auspices of the IAEA Technical Cooperation program. Other reports suggest that the scientists, who had served as Chairman and Managing Director of the NPCIL, which runs India's power reactors, passed information to Iran on tritium extraction from heavy water reactors.[17] In December 2005, sanctions were imposed on Sabero Organic Chemicals Gujarat Ltd. and Sandhya Organic Chemicals Pvt. Ltd. for transfers of chemical-related items to Iran. In July 2006, sanctions were imposed on two more chemical manufacturers in India for transfers to Iran — Balaji Amines and Prachi Poly Products.

In the chemical area, there is one confirmed transfer of 60 tons of thionyl chloride, a chemical that can be used in the production of mustard gas, from India to Iran in March 1989.[18] Other shipments in that timeframe reportedly were halted under U.S. pressure. India does not appear in the CIA's unclassified nonproliferation report to Congress as a supplier of chemical-weapons-related exports to Iran since the report began publication in 1997. India signed the Chemical Weapons Convention in 1993 and deposited its instrument of ratification until 1996.

OTHER CONSIDERATIONS

One consideration in assessing a country's nonproliferation record is the extent to which its export control and procurement system helps limit or eliminate illicit transfers. David Albright, president of the Institute for Science and International Security, has argued that three factors contribute to a flawed nonproliferation record for India in the nuclear area: a poorly implemented national export control system; an illicit procurement system for its own nuclear weapons program, and a procurement system that may unwittingly transfer sensitive information about uranium enrichment.[19] When asked formally to respond to Albright's allegations, the Administration stated it would be happy to discuss the allegations in a classified session with Members of Congress.[20]

Albright has suggested that the illicit procurement system in India has led entities to mislead suppliers about the ultimate destination of their goods. Such a system could be used to mask onward proliferation. From February 2003 to April 2006, the Department of Commerce opened 63 cases of possible Export Administration Regulations violations by U.S. firms exporting to India; 33 of those cases are still open.[21] In response to Senator Lugar's question for the record on investigations since 1998 into potential violations of U.S. export laws, the State Department reported that in one case, a U.S. firm exported technical information to an entity in India associated with its missile program. In another case, a U.S. firm with a subsidiary in Singapore committed 36 violations of the Export Administration Regulations by exporting various life sciences research products to entities in the Indian

Department of Atomic Energy and Indian Department of Defense. In another case, a U.S. firm attempted the unlicensed export of biotoxins to North Korea via a firm in New Delhi.

REFERENCES

[1]   "Press Briefing by Foreign Secretary on the events in UN and IAEA," New Delhi, Sept. 26, 2005, available at [http://www.indianembassy.org/press_release/2005/Sept/29.htm].

[2]   Briefing by Ministry of External Affairs Official Spokesperson on Draft Resolution on Iran in IAEA, available at [http://www.indianembassy.org/press_release/ 2005/ Sept/16.htm].

[3]   See CRS Report RS21592, *Iran's Nuclear Program: Recent Developments*, by Sharon Squassoni.

[4]   See [http://www.indianembassy.org/newsite/press_release/2006/Feb/2.asp].

[5]   Prime Minister's Suo Motu Statement on Iran, New Delhi, Feb. 17, 2006, available at [http://www.indianembassy.org/newsite/press_release/2006/Feb/7.asp].

[6]   See [http://meaindia.nic.in/pressbriefing/2006/06/01pb01.htm].

[7]   Iran Republic News Agency, "118 countries back Iran's nuclear program," *Iran Times*, Sept. 18, 2006. The article contains the full text of the statement.

[8]   See [http://www.whitehouse.gov/news/releases/2006/02/20060222-2.html]

[9]   R. Nicholas Burns, Under Secretary of State for Political Affairs, "Hearing on U.S.-India Civil Nuclear Cooperation Initiative," Remarks as prepared for the Senate Foreign Relations Committee, November 2, 2005, available at [http://www.state.gov/p/us/ rm/2005/55969.htm].

[10] See [http://www.iaea.org/Publications/Documents/Infcircs/2005/infcirc647.pdf].

[11] Questions for the Record Submitted to Secretary of State Condoleezza Rice by Senator Richard Lugar (#1), Senate Foreign Relations Committee, April 5, 2006.

[12] Conversation with David Albright, Institute for Science and International Security.

[13] Unclassified Report to Congress on the Acquisition of Technology Relating to Weapons of Mass Destruction and Advanced Conventional Munitions, 1 July Through 31 December 2000.

[14] See [http://www.nti.org/e_research/profiles/Iran/2867.html]

[15] "India Denies Nuclear Cooperation with Iran," *Agence France Presse*, December 13, 2003.

[16] This discussion taken from a response to Questions for the Record Submitted to Secretary of State Condoleezza Rice by Senator Richard Lugar (#2), Senate Foreign Relations Committee, April 5, 2006.

[17] John Larkin and Jay Solomon, "As Ties Between India and Iran Rise, U.S. Grows Edgy," *Wall Street Journal*, March 24, 2005.

[18] Thionyl chloride is a Schedule 3 chemical under the Chemical Weapons Convention. It has military and civilian uses, and is widely used in the laboratory and in industry.

[19] David Albright and Susan Basu, "Neither a Determined Proliferation Nor A Responsible State: India's Record Needs Scrutiny," Institute for Science and International Security, April 5, 2006, available at [http://www.isis-online.org/publications/southasia/indiacritique.pdf]. See also Albright and Basu,

"India's Gas Centrifuge Program: Stopping Illicit Procurement and the Leakage of Technical Centrifuge Know-How," March 10, 2006, available at [http://www.isis-online.org/publications/southasia/indianprocurement.pdf].

[20] Questions for the Record Submitted to Secretary of State Condoleezza Rice by Senator Richard Lugar (#3), Senate Foreign Relations Committee, April 5, 2006.

[21] Questions for the Record Submitted to Secretary of State Condoleezza Rice by Senator Richard Lugar (#3), Senate Foreign Relations Committee, April 5, 2006.

In: India on the Move
Editor: Lea M. Surit, pp. 161-166

ISBN: 978-1-60021-813-2
© 2007 Nova Science Publishers, Inc.

Chapter 7

INDIA: CHRONOLOGY OF RECENT EVENTS[*]

K. Alan Kronstadt

ABSTRACT

This report provides a reverse chronology of recent events involving India and India-U.S. relations. Sources include, but are not limited to, major newswires, the U.S. Department of State, and Indian news outlets. For a substantive review, see CRS Report RL33529, *India-U.S. Relations*. This report will be updated regularly.

ACRONYMS

BJP	Bharatiya Janata Party
LOC	Line of Control (Kashmir)
ULFA	United Liberation Front of Assam

10/30/06 — Maharashtra police announced having detained a Muslim man in their first arrest related to the 9/8 bombings in Malegaon.

10/28/06 — Kashmiri separatist leader Yasin Malik reportedly was "severely beaten" in an attack by Indian security forces in Srinagar.

10/27/06 — The Indian Cabinet approved a plan to restore direct cargo shipping links with Pakistan after a 35-year suspension. On the same day, more than 4,000 people fled their homes after gunbattles between two rival militant factions in the northeastern Nagaland state.

10/26/06 — A new law to protect Indian women from domestic abuse came into effect.

10/25/06 — The sixth annual "Malabar" joint U.S.-India naval exercises began in the Arabian Sea and included some 6,500 U.S. Navy personnel. On the same day, U.S. and Indian infantry engaged in joint counterterrorism drills in the Karnataka state.

---

[*] Excerpted from CRS Report RS21589, dated October 30, 2006.

10/24/06 — Pranab Mukherjee was named as India's new foreign minister, a post that had been vacant for nearly one year. A.K. Antony, a three-time chief minister of the southern Kerala state, was named as the new defense minister. On the same day, Prime Minister Singh said India had "credible evidence" of Pakistan's involvement in the 7/11 Bombay train bombings. Also, police in Srinagar, Kashmir, fired tear gas at hundreds of protesters angered by the deaths of a father and son who were killed by a police vehicle. Finally, two civilians and a policeman were killed in separatist-related violence in Kashmir.

10/23/06 — Defense Minister Mukherjee accused Pakistan of trying to "infiltrate and subvert" India's military. On the same day, more than 800 tribal militants reportedly surrendered to government authorities in the northeastern Mizoram state.

10/22/06 — National Security Advisor Narayanan said India had "very good" but not "clinching" evidence that Pakistan's intelligence service colluded in the 7/11 Bombay train bombings. On the same day, suspected Maoist militants shot dead the second-highest ranking police official in the eastern Orissa state. Also, thousands of Kashmiris took to the streets of Srinagar to protest the death of a 19-year-old man while in the custody of the Indian army.

10/21/06 — A new espionage row erupted between India and Pakistan after police in New Delhi arrested an Indian army employee as he allegedly passed classified documents to a Pakistani diplomat. Islamabad formally protested, calling the detention "illegal."

10/20/06 — Prime Minister Singh accepted an invitation to visit Pakistan at an unspecified date. On the same day, seven militants, a civilian, and a child were killed in separatist-related violence in Kashmir. Also, India's Tata Steel agreed to an $8 billion takeover bid for an Anglo-Dutch firm, creating the world's fifth largest steelmaker in India's largest-ever foreign takeover.

10/19/06 — India's Left Front parties demanded extensive curbs on proposed Special Economic Zones favored by the ruling Congress party. On the same day, New Delhi announced a stay of execution for a Kashmiri man for his role in a 2001 militant attack on the Indian Parliament while his wife's mercy petition is considered. Also, four Maoist militants were killed in an explosion in the southern Andhra Pradesh state.

10/17/06 — Indian Army Chief Gen. Singh said levels of violence in Kashmir had decreased by 20% due to more detentions and surrenders of separatist militants.

10/16/06 — Suspected separatist militants shot dead 2 policemen and injured 14 civilians in a series of attacks in Indian Kashmir.

10/14/06 — Former Jammu and Kashmir Chief Minister Farooq Abdullah said India would "go up in flames" if the government executes a Kashmiri man for his role in a 2001 militant attack on the Indian Parliament.

10/13/06 — The benchmark Sensex index of the Bombay Stock Exchange closed at its highest level ever, topping a mark set in May. On the same day, a Defense Ministry statement said the indigenous Trishul naval anti-missile program would be scrapped after more than 20 years in development in favor of co-development of Israel's Barak system. Defense Minister Mukherjee later said the program would be extended through 2007.

10/12/06 — Police in Calcutta seized some 543 anti-personnel mines and other ammunition believed to be for use by Maoist militants. On the same day, two suspected separatist militants were killed and several pounds of high explosive seized in a raid in Indian Kashmir.

10/10/06 — Seven Muslim men who confessed to involvement in the 7/11 Bombay train bombings retracted their confessions, saying they were made under duress after beatings by police. On the same day, a new national law went into effect banning children under 14 from domestic and restaurant work. Also, New Delhi proposed the sale of 10% stakes in four state-owned power companies, possibly signaling a resumption of industrial privatization efforts.

10/09/06 — New Delhi criticized a reported nuclear test by North Korea, saying it "jeopardizes" regional peace and stability.

10/08/06 — Two people were killed and 86 others injured over several days of communal violence between Hindus and Muslims in the southern Kerala state. On the same day, Indian troops shot dead eight suspected separatist militants as they tried to cross the LOC into Indian Kashmir. Two Indian soldiers died in the fighting.

10/06/06 — A press report said India would purchase advanced SpyDer air defense missiles from Israel to address Pakistan's planned purchase of U.S.-built F-16 combat aircraft. On the same day, an attack by tribal militants left 11 people dead in the northeastern Assam state.

10/04/06 — A "bribery index" by Berlin-based Transparency International found India to be the worst offender among the world's top 30 exporting countries. On the same day, separatist militants attacked a security camp in Srinagar, Kashmir, leaving 3 policemen dead and 12 more injured. Also, the chief minister of Pakistan's Baluchistan province accused Indian intelligence services of fueling an armed insurgency there.

10/02/06 — Prime Minster Singh visited Pretoria, where India and South Africa reaffirmed their "strategic partnership."

09/30/06 — Bombay's top police official said the 7/11 train bombings were "planned by Pakistan's [intelligence services] and carried out by Lashkar-e-Taiba and their operatives in India." Islamabad swiftly rejected the allegation as propaganda. India's main opposition BJP later called for severing diplomatic ties with Pakistan.

09/29/06 — New Delhi announced that the Indian economy had expanded by 8.9% during the second quarter of 2006.

09/27/06 — Violent street protests erupted in Srinagar, Kashmir, over the planned execution of a Kashmiri man for his role in a 2001 militant attack on the Indian Parliament. Attacks by suspected separatist militants left one policeman dead and six wounded. On the same day, representatives of the separatist ULFA withdrew from negotiations with the New Delhi government, ending a year-long peace process.

09/26/06 — An Indian army officer and two suspected separatist militants were killed in a gunbattle in Kashmir.

09/25/06 — Defense Minister Mukherjee told an American audience that Pakistan "remains a nursery of global terrorism." On the same day, seven people, including a policewoman, were killed in separatist-related violence in Kashmir.

09/24/06 — New Delhi ended a six-week-long truce with the separatist ULFA after militants shot dead a policeman and a civilian in the northeastern Assam state. ULFA is designated as a terrorist organization under U.S. law. On the same day, Indian troops shot dead four suspected separatist militants in Kashmir.

09/18/06 — A joint U.S.-India army exercise in Hawaii included a contingent of 140 Indian troops.

09/17/06 — Police in the central Chhattisgarh state shot dead at least five suspected Maoist militants in a lengthy gunbattle.

09/16/06 — Meeting on the sidelines of a Nonaligned Movement summit in Cuba, Prime Minister Singh and Pakistani President Musharraf announced a resumption of formal peace negotiations that had been suspended following the 7/11 Bombay bombings and also decided to implement a joint anti-terrorism mechanism.

09/15/06 — The U.S. Department of State's *International Religious Freedom Report 2006* found that, "While the national government took positive steps in key areas to improve religious freedom, the status of religious freedom generally remained the same" and included instances of slow government action to counter societal attacks on religious minorities and attempts by some state and local governments to limit religious freedom.

09/12/06 — An open letter to Congress signed by 16 nonproliferation experts and former U.S. government officials urged redress of "serious flaws that still plague the U.S.-India nuclear trade legislation." On the same day, Prime Minister Singh expressed concern that "the Pakistan government has not done enough to control" terrorist elements on its soil. Also, New York-based Human Rights Watch released a report documenting human rights abuses in Jammu and Kashmir, finding that Indian security forces as well as separatist militants are culpable, and suggesting that the Kashmir insurgency is partly fueled by human rights violations against the citizenry by Indian security forces who remain able to act with impunity.

09/08/06 — Three bombs exploded in and near a mosque in the western, Muslim-majority city of Malegaon, leaving 32 people dead and more than 100 injured. No group claimed responsibility for the attack.

09/07/06 — Police in the southern Andhra Pradesh state seized some 600 rockets and 12 launchers after a raid on an arms depot used by Maoist militants. On the same day, Maoist militants kidnaped two policemen in the central Chhattisgarh state.

08/31/06 — New Delhi announced that Foreign Secretary Saran would become special envoy for negotiations on U.S.-India civil nuclear cooperation following scheduled 9/30 retirement. The current Indian Ambassador to Pakistan, Shiv Shankar Menon, will take over as the new foreign secretary. On the same day, the Defense Ministry announced it would begin allowing private companies to develop high-technology military systems.

08/29/06 — Indian and Bangladeshi border officials met to discuss improved coordination, with New Delhi requesting that Dhaka take action to close some 172 anti-Indian insurgent camps claimed to be in Bangladesh near the shared border.

08/28/06 — Prime Minister Singh said the peace process with Pakistan "cannot go forward if Pakistan does not deal with terrorism firmly."

08/24/06 — New Delhi approved a $44 million plan to purchase the USS Trenton, a decommissioned American amphibious transport dock. On the same day, a senior External Affairs Ministry official told Parliament there were 52 "terrorist training camps" in Pakistan and Pakistani Kashmir, and 172 "Indian insurgent camps" in Bangladesh.

08/23/06 — A meeting of the U.S.-India Financial and Economic Forum was held in Washington, where officials discussed Indian efforts to liberalize its financial sector, among other issues. On the same day, Home Affairs Minister Patil told Parliament there was no evidence Pakistan was acting to dismantle the "infrastructure of terrorism" on its territory.

08/22/06 — A delegation of U.S. officials, including President Bush's top energy and environment advisor, visited New Delhi to meet with top Indian officials and business leaders to discuss energy security and the environment.

08/17/06 — Prime Minister Singh again assured Parliament that proposed civil nuclear cooperation with the United States would be in India's national interest, and he reviewed a number of his government's "concerns" about sections of enabling legislation in the U.S. Congress, including restrictions on reprocessing spent fuel, certification requirements that would "diminish a permanent waiver authority into an annual one," and language pertaining to Iran, among others. Singh indicated that India would have "grave difficulties" accepting the provisions of relevant U.S. legislation in its current form.

08/15/06 — India celebrated its 59th independence day.

08/11/06 — The U.S. State Department issued terror alerts for U.S. citizens in India and Pakistan, warning that foreign terrorists and possibly Al Qaeda members were planning attacks on public facilities in the run-up to those countries' independence day celebrations. On the same day, Assistant Secretary of State Boucher told an Indian television interviewer that the Bush Administration understands and shares some of the "concerns" about certain provisions of U.S. congressional legislation that would enable U.S.-India civil nuclear cooperation, including a legal restriction reprocessing technologies and imposition of end-use certification.

08/07/06 — Assistant Secretary of State Boucher met with top Indian officials in New Delhi.

08/04/06 — The United States formally sanctioned two Indian chemical firms under the Iran Nonproliferation Act for sensitive material transactions with Iran. The firms denied any WMD-related transfers and New Delhi later said the sanctions were "not justified."

08/02/06 — A senior Indian official said that India will bypass Bangladesh in building a proposed pipeline that will bring gas from Burma to India's northeastern states.

07/28/06 — Bombay police said that six suspects detained in connection with the 7/11 Bombay bombings confessed to having received weapons and explosives training in Pakistan.

07/27/06 — Press reports said that the Bush Administration would sanction two Indian firms under the Iran Nonproliferation Act for missile-related transactions with Iran. Some in Congress later criticized the Administration for "deliberately concealing the information" until after the House vote on H.R. 5682. On the same day, Prime Minister Singh told the Parliament that India could withdraw from planned civil nuclear cooperation with the United States if the U.S. legislative process creates a plan inconsistent with the original July 2005 agreement. A State Department official later said the Bush Administration will seek to ensure that nothing is done to "distort, change, and renegotiate" the July 2005 agreement.

07/26/06 — H.R. 5682, the United States and India Nuclear Cooperation Promotion Act of 2006, was passed by the House on a vote of 359-68.

07/25/06 — Indian troops shot dead three suspected separatist militants as they tried to cross the LOC into Indian Kashmir. The fighting injured five civilians.

07/24/06 — The Doha round of global trade negotiations was suspended indefinitely following a failed meeting of the six major participants, including the United States and India. Commerce Minister Nath later blamed the United States for the failure, saying it "brought nothing new to the table." On the same day, senior political figures from four major Indian political parties urged Parliament to pass a resolution rejecting the U.S.-India civil nuclear cooperation deal.

07/23/06 — Iran's foreign minister said "some specific difficulties" must be worked out before India and Iran can move forward with a $22 billion natural gas deal. On the same day, police in the southern Andhra Pradesh state shot dead eight Maoist militants, including a top rebel leader.

07/22/06 — Kenyan police announced the arrest of Abdul Karim "Tunda," said to be a founder of the Lashkar-e-Taiba terrorist group's Indian operation. On the same day, police in Kashmir claimed to have arrested a senior member of the Lashkar-e-Taiba terrorist group. Also, police arrested four more persons in connection with the 7/11 Bombay bombings.

07/21/06 — New Delhi rejected Pakistan's offer to assist in investigating the 7/11 Bombay bombings, saying Islamabad had not taken action in the past when presented with evidence of terrorist networks on its soil. Pakistan denied the allegations. On the same day, Indian troops shot dead five suspected separatist militants in Kashmir.

07/20/06 — Police made their first arrests in connection with the 7/11 Bombay bombings, detaining three Indian Muslims.

07/19/06 — H.Res. 911, condemning "in the strongest possible terms" the 7/11 terrorist attacks in Bombay and expressing condolences to the families of the victims and sympathy to the people of India, was passed by the House. On the same day, the president of the opposition BJP said the stipulations of proposed U.S.-India civil nuclear cooperation would "cap" India's nuclear program and "keep India in perpetual bondage to Washington." Also, Pakistani and Indian security officials met in Lahore for regular talks on cooperative efforts on border security and counternarcotics.

07/18/06 — The Senate Energy Committee held a hearing on U.S.-India Energy Cooperation. On the same day, Pakistani President Musharraf said delaying the India-Pakistan peace process because of the 7/11 Bombay bombings was "playing into the hands of the terrorists."

07/17/06 — President Bush met with Prime Minister Singh on the sidelines of the G-8 Summit in St. Petersburg, Russia, to discuss the 7/11 Bombay bombings and planned U.S.-India civil nuclear cooperation. On the same day, at least 26 villagers were killed, and another 21 injured, in a raid by some 500 Maoist militants in the central Chhattisgarh state.

07/16/06 — India postponed planned foreign secretary-level talks with Pakistan, saying "the environment is not conducive." A Pakistani official called the decision a "negative development" and denied that Pakistani territory was used for terrorism against India. On the same day, Defense Minister Mukherjee said terrorists were entering India from Pakistan. Also, the Dhaka government accused Indian border troops of killing more than 50 innocent Bangladeshis in the past six months. Indian officials said those shot were smugglers or illegal migrants.

07/15/06 — Foreign Secretary Saran said the 7/11 Bombay bombings made it "very difficult to take forward the peace process" with Pakistan.

INDEX

F

G

interest rates, 14

interference, 49, 74

International Atomic Energy Agency (IAEA), ix, x, 71, 72, 88, 90, 92, 102, 131, 132, 156

International Bank for Reconstruction and Development, 25

International Chamber of Commerce, 25

International Confederation of Free Trade Unions, 25

International Monetary Fund, 25, 56

International Olympic Committee, 25

international relations, 36

Internet, 19, 24, 31

intervention, 43

interview, 66, 141

investment, 36, 38, 54, 56, 57

investors, 56

Iran, ix, x, 19, 35, 48, 49, 50, 54, 67, 74, 75, 76, 77, 90, 96, 97, 101, 105, 107, 108, 112, 114, 117, 155, 156, 157, 158, 159, 160, 167, 168

Iraq, 27, 159

Ireland, 86

iron, 7, 13, 16

isolation, 49

Israel, 24, 27, 52, 77, 132, 165

Italy, 15

J

Jamaica, 98

Japan, 15, 16, 34, 76, 83, 141, 157

jobs, viii, 48, 69

journalists, 31

judges, 20

judgment, 89

judicial branch, 20

judiciary, 21, 22

jurisdiction, 21, 85, 93

justice, 20, 62, 63, 64

K

Kashmir, vii, 6, 24, 27, 28, 29, 30, 31, 33, 34, 35, 36, 40, 41, 42, 52, 59, 60, 62, 163, 164, 165, 166, 167, 168

killing, 168

Korea, 27

Kosovo, 27

Kuwait, 27

L

labor, 12, 13, 15, 22

labor force, 13, 15

land, 6, 7, 8, 13

language, 3, 9, 21, 71, 99, 105, 106, 111, 112, 117, 137, 167

Laos, 27

Latin America, 64

laws, viii, ix, 20, 22, 46, 47, 57, 62, 69, 72, 76, 93, 113, 131, 132, 158, 159

leadership, 45

Lebanon, 27

legislation, viii, ix, 15, 34, 38, 44, 47, 48, 49, 50, 54, 69, 70, 73, 87, 90, 101, 102, 105, 107, 108, 113, 129, 133, 166, 167

leprosy, 11

liberalization, 4, 12, 14, 15, 17, 57

Liberia, 27

licenses, 89, 120, 124, 125

life expectancy, 9

life sciences, 160

lifetime, 81

links, 27, 28, 42, 61, 163

liquefied natural gas, 58

livestock, 13

loans, 64

lobbying, 38

local government, 11, 22, 63, 135, 166

locus, 44

M

machinery, 16

major cities, 18

malaria, 11

males, 9, 10

management, 64

manganese, 7

manufacturing, 12, 14, 71, 78

market, viii, 12, 34, 46, 48, 55, 56, 57, 58, 69, 73, 79, 81, 82, 83, 134

market access, 57, 58

market opening, viii, 34

markets, 15, 35, 47, 58

martial law, 4

meanings, 99

measures, xi, 4, 12, 14, 15, 17, 53, 56, 57, 79, 80, 81, 82, 84, 97, 112, 120, 144, 155

media, 23, 31, 67, 68

median, 9

mediation, 60

Q

T